Content Standards Grades 5–8

- ## Science as Inquiry

  Content Standard A: As a result of their activities in grades 5–8, all students should develop

  - Abilities necessary to do scientific inquiry
  - Understandings about scientific inquiry

- ## Physical Science

  Content Standard B: As a result of their activities in grades 5–8, all students should develop an understanding of

  - Properties and changes of properties in matter
  - Motion and forces
  - Transfer of energy

- ## Life Science

  Content Standard C: As a result of their activities in grades 5–8, all students should develop an understanding of

  - Structure and function in living systems
  - Reproduction and heredity
  - Regulation and behavior
  - Population and ecosystems
  - Diversity and adaptations of organisms

- ## Earth and Space Sciences

  Content Standard D: As a result of their activities in grades 5–8, all students should develop an understanding of

  - Structure of the earth system
  - Earth's history
  - Earth in the solar system

- ## Science and Technology

  Content Standard E: As a result of the activities in grades 5–8, all students should develop an understanding of

  - Abilities of technological design
  - Understanding about science and technology

- ## Science in Personal and Social Perspectives

  Content Standard F: As a result of the activities in grades 5–8, all students should develop an understanding of

  - Personal health
  - Populations, resources, and environments
  - Natural hazards
  - Risks and benefits
  - Changes in environments
  - Science and technology in society

- ## History and Nature Of Science

  Content Standard G: As a result of the activities in grades 5–8, all students should develop an understanding of

  - Science as a human endeavor
  - Nature of science
  - History of science

Teaching Children
Science
Discovery Methods for Elementary and Middle Grades

Teaching Children
Science

Discovery Methods for Elementary and Middle Grades

Third edition

Joseph Abruscato

Retired, University of Vermont

Donald A. DeRosa

Boston University

ALLYN & BACON

Boston • New York • San Francisco

Mexico City • Montreal • Toronto • London • Madrid • Munich • Paris

Hong Kong • Singapore • Tokyo • Cape Town • Sydney

Series Editor: Kelly Villella Canton
Series Editorial Assistant: Annalea Manalili
Senior Marketing Manager: Darcy Betts Prybella
Production Editor: Annette Joseph
Editorial Production Service: Dee Josephson/Nesbitt Graphics
Composition Buyer: Linda Cox
Manufacturing Buyer: Megan Cochran
Electronic Composition: Nesbitt Graphics
Interior Design: Denise Hoffman
Photo Researcher: Annie Pickert
Cover Designer: Elena Sidorova

For related titles and support materials, visit our online catalog at www.pearsonhighered.com.

Between the time website information is gathered and then published, it is not unusual for some sites to have closed. Also, the transcription of URLs can result in typographical errors. The publisher would appreciate notification where these errors occur so that they may be corrected in subsequent editions.

Library of Congress Cataloging-in-Publication Data

Abruscato, Joseph.
  Teaching children science : discovery methods for the elementary and middle grades / Joseph Abruscato, Donald A. DeRosa. -- 3rd ed.
    p. cm.
  ISBN 0-13-715453-4 (978-0-13-715453-1)
  1. Science--Study and teaching (Elementary)   2. Science--Study and teaching (Middle school)   I. DeRosa, Donald A. II. Title.

LB1585.A3 2009
372.3'5--dc22

2009002090

Printed in the United States of America
10 9 8 7 6 5 4 3 2 1 B-R 13 12 11 10 09

Credits appear on page 184, which constitutes an extension of the copyright page.

Allyn & Bacon
is an imprint of

www.pearsonhighered.com

ISBN-10: 0-13-715453-4
ISBN-13: 978-0-13-715453-1

For my daughters, Anne Marie and Elizabeth
Like a gentle breeze on a warm summer day, you refresh my spirit and bring me joy! —J. A.

To my children, Claire and Paul, whose childhoods have taught me
so much about how children discover the world. —D. D.

Contents

2 Constructing Knowledge and Discovering Meaning   25

How can I help children learn science?

3 The Inquiry Process Skills   41

How can I help children use the inquiry process skills to make discoveries?

4   Planning and Managing   57

How can I plan and manage inquiry-based, discovery-focused units and lessons?

5 Strategies and QuickChecks   77

*How can I effectively use cooperative learning, questioning
and wait-time strategies, active listening, demonstrations,
and textbooks in my classroom?*

6 Assessment of Understanding and Inquiry   95

A good teacher asks, How am I doing?
A great teacher asks, How are my students doing?

7 Integrating Science   115

How can I integrate inquiry-based science
with other subjects in a child's school day?

8 Using Technology to Enhance Science Learning   131

What comes first, content or technology?

9 Adapting the Science Curriculum   141

How can I adapt the science curriculum for children from diverse cultural backgrounds, children with special needs, and children with special gifts?

Preface

As with previous editions, this edition of *Teaching Children Science: Discovery Methods for the Elementary and Middle Grades* benefits from the wonderful insights and suggestions of readers like you. Education, and especially teaching about teaching, is always a work in progress. Textbooks have always been a two-edged sword. On the one hand, they provide a springboard for ideas; on the other, they can be pedantic and boring to read. Traditionally, *Teaching Children Science: Discovery Methods for the Elementary and Middle Grades* has striven to be conversational, engaging, and practical. We hope it is one of those textbooks that you will keep in your library and refer to for years to come.

Using this lively, streamlined, right-to-the-point book will help you become a great teacher! Its friendly style will deliver information to you that is both practical and immediately useful. Its pages will teach you how to apply all of these skills:

1. Provide children with *inquiry experiences* that lead to *discovery learning*.
2. *Use the National Science Education Standards (NSES)* to provide units and lessons with focus and direction.
3. Design units and lessons that recognize how children *construct knowledge and discover meaning*.
4. Use the *inquiry process skills* as the starting point for children's learning.
5. *Plan and manage* inquiry-based, discovery-focused units and lessons.
6. Plan and use *technology* as a tool to help students extend their ability to discover, deepen their understanding, and seek explanations.
7. *Make effective use of strategies* such as cooperative learning, questioning, wait-time/think-time, and active listening.
8. Use observational tools called *QuickChecks* to assess your own teaching and the teaching you observe during field work or in-class peer teaching.
9. *Assess children's understanding and ability to conduct inquiry* using the National Science Education Standards approach as well as traditional and performance assessment techniques.
10. *Integrate inquiry-based science* with other subjects in a child's school day.
11. *Adapt the science curriculum* for children who come from diverse backgrounds and who have special needs and talents.
12. Use the *Reality Check* feature to reflect on the application of major concepts and themes in authentic situations.

As you read and work with *Discovery Methods*, I hope that you will put all of these skills to work. I also hope that you will keep in mind the overarching ideas within this book that will help you make progress toward the goal of becoming a great teacher. Let me point out some of these "big ideas":

1. Using science to *teach strategies for thinking*. In addition to providing opportunities for children to discover and seek explanations, we also need to model effective thinking strategies. This edition includes useful strategies for seeking explanations across disciplines based on systems analysis that children can use as a foundation for inquiry.

2. *A constructivist approach.* Consider how children construct knowledge and create meaning as you plan and teach. There is little question that we create much of our own reality. One way of looking at how we integrate life experiences into our mental processes is provided by the theory of *constructivism.* When applied in the classroom, this theory guides teachers in thinking about what they are doing to help children get beyond scientific misconceptions and acquire more appropriate knowledge, skills, and values. Constructivism is introduced in Chapter 1, discussed in more detail in Chapter 2, and then used as a guiding principle throughout the rest of the book.

3. *References to standards.* All of us who teach children science need some direction, and the best current direction is provided by the National Science Education Standards (NSES). The NSES for grades K–8 are addressed at relevant points throughout the book, and they are indicated by the icon shown in the margin. The full text of the standards is provided just inside the front cover for handy reference. Another set of guidelines, developed by Project 2061, is also addressed in the text through a series of boxes.

NSES

4. *Productive use of the technology.* Technology in its various forms is now ubiquitous in U.S. classrooms, from kindergartens through the primary grades and on up. However, applying this technology in useful and productive ways remains a challenge for many teachers. In addition to a new chapter entitled Using Technology to Enhance Science Learning, each chapter ends with Internet resources available through links on MyEducationLab, and Internet-related content is identified throughout the text using the icon shown in the margin.

New to This Edition

The third edition of *Teaching Children Science: Discovery Methods for the Elementary and Middle Grades* addresses a practical framework for teaching children thinking strategies for seeking scientific explanations. It strives to present practical classroom applications from the growing body of knowledge on how people learn, which elementary school teachers can incorporate effectively into their teaching methods and strategies.

PEARSON
· **myeducationlab**
The Power of Classroom Practice
www.myeducationlab.com

(www.myeducationlab.com)
This interactive online resource provides research-based learning resources that bring the classroom to life. Throughout the text you will find MyEducationLab icons that indicate where readers can find observation and reflection activities and exercises built around authentic in-class video footage, simulations, examples of authentic teacher and student work, lesson plans, and more. If your instructor did not request access to this resource with your book or you purchased a used book please visit www.myeducationlab.com to purchase online access.

- Chapters 1 and 2 take a deeper look at the meaning of inquiry so we might teach inquiry more effectively. Inquiry is described in the context of a progression of mental modeling: Descriptive models require us to be active observers, integrating prior knowledge and new observations in our explanations. Explanatory models are built on the foundation of good descriptive models, which give rise to hypotheses and predictions. Experimental models provide a systematic method to acquire meaningful data that support or fail to support hypotheses.

- Chapter 3 takes a deeper look at the science-process skills in the context of the progression of inquiry. It also introduces a 5E instructional strategy as a framework for planning inquiry-based units and lessons. The 5E approach is based on engagement, exploration, explanation, elaboration, and evaluation.

- In Chapter 4 you will find a revised outline for planning lessons, highlighting the importance of identifying the content to be taught. Most of us need to review scientific concepts and are often faced with teaching concepts that we have long ago forgotten or never quite learned. This chapter guides you through the process of analyzing the content, identifying what to teach and what not to teach. In-depth examples of lesson plans that can be used as templates are included in this chapter.

- A discussion of science kits and their use in the elementary science classroom has been added to Chapter 5.

- Chapter 6 has been reorganized in terms of formative and summative assessment, and it connects assessment strategies more closely to performance objectives introduced in Chapter 4. Prompts, rubrics, probes, performance, and authentic assessment are addressed in depth with examples of each. Practical guides for designing assessment are provided as well as in-depth discussion about constructing rubrics and scoring guides.

- Whereas Chapter 7 of the previous editions addressed strategies for using art, music, and physical education to teach science, this edition encourages teaching the science of art, music, and physical education.

- Chapter 8, *Using Technology to Enhance Science Learning,* is **new** to this edition. In it you will find strategies for using technology to support inquiry through real-time data collection, authentic science experiences, simulations, WebQuests, information gathering, tutorials and games, ask a scientist, and the use of interactive whiteboards. Sample WebQuests based on the 5E approach introduced in Chapter 4 are introduced in this chapter.

- Chapter 9, Adapting the Science Curriculum, recognizes the growing emphasis on inclusion of all students in the elementary science classroom and the challenges inclusion places on curriculum and instruction. Differentiated learning and universal design for learning (UDL) offer helpful perspectives and strategies for effectively addressing the challenges of inclusion. Consequently, they are two important new topics that have been added to this chapter, and those new topics are accompanied by a discussion of the range of learning disabilities one might encounter in the classroom as well as strategies for teaching gifted learners.

Finally, I hope you take full advantage of the special section at the end of the book called For the Teacher's Desk. The materials in this section are provided as a resource for your use now and in the future. The first part, Your Classroom Enrichment Handbook, includes guidelines for ensuring safety and curriculum planning, among other things. Another section provides position statements from the National Science Teachers Association (NSTA) on these subjects: women in science education; multicultural science education; substance use and abuse; and science competitions. Reviewing these statements should stimulate your thinking about some of the very important issues that teachers face today. The second part, Your Science Source Address Book, provides contact information for a variety of materials, suppliers, and professional organizations. All of this information has been reviewed and updated for this new edition.

Supplements

The Instructor's Manual/Test Bank and PowerPoints for this text are available for download by logging on to the Instructor Resource Center from the Pearson Higher Ed catalog (http://www.pearsonhighered.com/educator) located under the core text *Teaching Children Science: A Discovery Approach,* 7th Edition ISBN 0137156774. Please contact your local Pearson representative if you need assistance downloading this guide.

● **Instructor's Manual/Test Bank** provides concrete suggestions to help instructors fully utilize the text and MyEducationLab. Each chapter contains chapter objectives, key terms and concepts, and discussion and activity suggestions as well as a comprehensive test bank.

● **PowerPoint Presentation** offers slides for each chapter outlining key concepts and including select figures and tables.

(www.myeducationlab.com)
This research-based learning resource brings teaching to life. Through authentic in-class video footage, simulations, examples of authentic teacher and student work, lesson plans and more, MyEducationLab prepares teacher candidates for their careers by affording opportunities for observation and reflection through a series of assignable application activities. Just contact your Pearson sales representative and tell him/her that you'd like to use MyEducationLab with this text next semester. Your representative will work with your bookstore to ensure that your students receive access with their books.

About the New Co-Author

Dr. DeRosa has worked in the field of science education for twenty-four years as a classroom teacher and teacher educator. He is a member of the Department of Curriculum and Teaching at the Boston University School of Education, where he teaches methods in elementary science education. He serves as the director of CityLab, a biotechnology-learning laboratory for teachers and students at the Boston University School of Medicine. His research interests focus on the development of effective methods to teach scientific thinking. He has co-authored several curriculum supplements in biotechnology, frequently conducts workshops on inquiry-based science teaching for in-service teachers, and has consulted in the development of biotechnology programs throughout the United States.

Acknowledgments

Many people have shaped the content of this book, directly and indirectly. We would also like to thank a few of our dearest friends and colleagues for their continued support and encouragement: Lowell J. Bethel at the University of Texas; Jack Hassard at Georgia State University; Russell Agne, Susan Baker, and Joyce Morris at the University of Vermont; Rod Peturson of the Windsor Schools, Ontario, Canada; Marlene Nachbar Hapai at the University of Hawaii, Manoa; William Ritz at California State University, Long Beach; Larry Schaeffer at Syracuse University; Carla Romney, Carl Franzblau, and Peter Bergethon and the Boston University School of Medicine; Carol Jenkins, Lauren Katzman, Douglas Zook, and Peter Garik at the Boston University School of Education; and the public school teachers at Orchard Elementary School, Malletts Bay School, and the F. Lyman Winship Elementary School.

In addition, we would like to thank those individuals who reviewed this edition for Pearson Allyn & Bacon for the valuable suggestions they offered: Anna R. Bergstrom, Texas Lutheran University; Mildred E. Berry, Florida Memorial University; Kim Trask Brown, University of North Carolina–Asheville; Jim Dawson, Rochester College; Dawn Parker, Texas A&M University; Margaret Pope, Mississippi State University; Susan Stratton, SUNY Cortland; and Norma H. Twombley, Johnson State College. And I would like, once again, to thank the reviewers and survey respondents from previous editions: Stan Chu, Bank Street College of Education; Thomas W. Giles, Cumberland College; Steve Gregorich, California State University, Sacramento; Tom Howick, University of Southern Maine; William Hughes, Ashland University; Raymond Jobin, Keene State College; Archibald Sia, California State University, Northridge; Rene Stofflett, University of Illinois; Barbara Kasten, Trinity College; Bonnie Kotvis, Alverno College; Margaret Mason, William Woods College; J. Philip McLaren, Eastern Nazarene College; Lucy J. Orfan, Kean College of New Jersey (now Kean University); and Harold Roberts, Hendrix College.

Finally, we would like to thank Dee Josephson and Michael Goodman for their attention to the details of the book.

D. D.

Teaching Children
Science

Discovery Methods for
Elementary and Middle Grades

Strategies and Techniques

The whoosh and locomotive roar of a powerful tornado, tossing about cars and flattening houses; the careful maneuvering of a brightly colored lady bug, making its way through branches and leaves, touching, smelling, and tasting all in its path; and the first dark, belching breaths of a volcano coming to life after being dormant—all are parts of the natural world in which we live.

Wanting to make sense of that world is a powerful drive that leads us humans to inquire, to discover, and ultimately, to understand. And to empower children to be able to inquire, discover, and understand—not just now but throughout their lives—is the greatest challenge we teachers face. To teach children *science* is to meet that challenge head on.

Part One of this book will help prepare you to meet that challenge. To be sure, there is *much* to know! First of all, you need to know your children. How do children learn, and what can you do to enhance their learning? How can you help them learn the inquiry process skills and construct their own scientific knowledge?

You also need to know what to teach and how to teach it. What are the recommendations of the National Science Education Standards (NSES) and other curriculum guideposts that your school district or state might have? How can you plan meaningful lessons and units and manage an inquiry-based classroom? How can you make good use of the valuable resources of the Internet? How can you integrate science with other subject areas? What specific strategies and techniques will help you foster discovery learning? And what can you do to adapt science activities for children who come from diverse cultural backgrounds and who have special needs and abilities?

Finally, you need to know how and when to assess children's progress in meaningful ways. What are the different approaches to assessment, and how successful are they? Again, what does the NSES recommend? How can children best show what they have learned in terms of both understanding and inquiry?

The chapters in Part One (Chapters 1–9) will answer these questions and more, and, in completing them, you will build a foundation of general knowledge about teaching children science. Once that foundation is firmly in place, you can add the specific knowledge and skills related to the earth/space, life, and physical sciences, which are the subjects of the chapters in Parts Two, Three, and Four, respectively.

Yes, it's a lot to learn! And I encourage you to learn it well, so that you will get off to a good start as a teacher. Mastering this information is essential to developing your own approach to teaching children science.

The truth is, becoming an OK teacher isn't too difficult. But becoming a truly excellent teacher—one who broadens children's horizons, gives them a knowledge base upon which they can build, and raises their hopes and dreams to unexpected heights—takes focus and determination. *That's* what you and I will be working toward throughout this book!

chapter 1

Inquiry: The Path, Discovery: The Destination

Inquiry is not just teaching science, but using science to teach thinking.

▶ **Getting Started**

A man lives on the twelfth floor of an apartment building. Every morning he takes the elevator down to the lobby and leaves the building. In the evening, he gets into the elevator, and, if there is someone else in the elevator—or if it was raining that day—he goes back to his floor directly. Otherwise, he goes to the tenth floor and walks up two flights of stairs to his apartment.[1]

Can you explain why the man sometimes takes the elevator directly to the twelfth floor while at other times he takes it to the tenth floor and walks two flights? You may have seen this puzzle or similar ones, known as lateral thinking puzzles, which challenge us to think creatively outside the box. What does this have to do with science?

Science seeks explanations to our everyday questions and offers us strategies for thinking of what to do when we do not have the answer. Consider how you tried to solve the puzzle. Did your mind go blank? Were you wondering where to begin? Did you know what questions to ask? Science teaching means teaching children how to think and figure out what to do when they do not have the answer. Science thinking skills are the tools of discovery. By teaching your students how to seek explanations, you will lead them onto a path of exploration where they will no longer be restricted by memorizing what others have discovered, but they will use their skills to make their own discoveries and keep pace with an ever-changing world.

As elementary school teachers, you provide the most important link to start the children on the path to discovery. This chapter is about understanding the practical thinking strategies and skills that you can teach your students to embark on this journey. We will revisit the puzzle later in the chapter.

A Chance to Touch Tomorrow

All of the flowers
Of all of the future
Are in the seeds of today
—Source unknown

As you awake and start your new day, I'd like you to think of these three short lines as your gentle alarm. I want them to remind you of the enormous potential that lies in the hearts and minds of children. You are their temporary mindstretcher and caretaker. You are the overseer of the seeds and the creator of the rich soil that will nurture these seeds of new tomorrows to grow. *What* and *how* you teach children will race ahead of you to a time you will never know. The responsibility is enormous. It will take dedication, energy, and the unwavering belief that what you do and how you do it will actually change lives.

What and *how* you teach will touch tomorrow. *You* will touch tomorrow.

Turning Your Teaching Fears into Hope

Now I might be wrong, but my guess is that you are not *that* confident about teaching children science. You may fear that science will be difficult for children to understand and that it will provoke questions that will be hard for you to answer. You may also think that science time will be a period of utter chaos and confusion, as liquids bubble out of beakers and chemicals flash, pop, and bang.

It is my hope that most of you have had wonderful experiences in science and that you will share the challenge of seeking explanations and the thrill of discovery with your students. On the other hand, perhaps your encounters with science have emphasized the memorization of myriad facts and formulas rather than the journey of exploration and discovery that is science. Imagine that children on a Little League team or in a dance troupe are given books to study about the rules, history, and techniques of baseball or dance and practices consist of discussion, reviews, and videos of "real" baseball games or dance recitals. How many of those children do you think will learn to understand and love the game of baseball or the art of the dance? What are the chances that any of them will pursue a career in baseball or ballet? The answer is likely none of them. Most parents expect that the children will take a bat, ball, and glove to the playing field or dance shoes and leotard to the studio and experience the excitement of the game or the movement of the dance.

All too often, science is taught by giving students a textbook, showing them a movie, and telling them the "facts," which they are expected to dutifully recite on tests. In this book, you will learn to help children experience the dynamics and challenges of science through active participation in the processes of science. With your help, elementary school students will enjoy successes as well as failures, but along the way they will acquire new skills, gain confidence, and discover new and deeper understandings of the world and their place in it.

You are embarking on a journey to become not only a coach but also a player on the field of science. The ensuing chapters will explain ways to "show" instead of "tell." You will learn to model sound scientific thinking and strategies for seeking explanations. The most important skill that you teach your students will be the ability to know what to do when they do not have the answer. Scientific thinking is not only good science, it is good thinking. During this journey, you will overcome your fears, expand your hopes, and fulfill your dreams of becoming an elementary science teacher as you experience the thrill of scientific discovery that you can share with your students. Let's begin the journey by considering the children who will be in your classroom.

Your Children: Curious, Aspiring Scientists Who Need Guidance and Direction

Children love to touch! At least, most children do. They also like to look at things, to smell them, to move them about, and to twist and turn them. Children want to know how things work, and, like squirrels, they sometimes horde papers, science materials, and wildlife in their desks for more detailed inspection later.

By providing children with hands-on experiences, you will help them correct faulty knowledge, add new knowledge, and create accurate conceptions about the natural world.

At the heart of science is this natural human desire to explore the world that is directly reachable as well as those worlds that are hard to reach. The children in your classroom are, in this respect, very much like scientists. In fact, some would say that *they* are more like scientists than are teenagers or even college students!

However, do not assume children are adult scientists in small bodies. Curiosity is a wonderful attribute and precursor of scientific thinking, but in order to truly become scientific thinkers, children must develop habits of mind that go beyond their natural curiosity. Scientific inquiry requires careful, active observations of the details and connections of systems and events that we encounter, which often go unnoticed by casual observers. As the famous physicist Richard Feynman once said, "The first principle is that you must not fool yourself and you are the easiest person to fool."[2] Your elementary school children will tend to have boundless energy and curiosity. Your job will be to make sure that you deliver a curriculum that capitalizes on both and encourages them to become active observers and scientific thinkers.

Shaping Young Minds: A Wonderful and Awe-Inspiring Opportunity

As elementary school teachers, you will be entrusted by parents with the responsibility of developing the most important organ in the individual, the brain. The title of a book written by James Zull, *The Art of Changing the Brain*, aptly suggests the magnitude of the career you have chosen. As a teacher, you will be responsible for shaping thousands of young brains. You will actually influence the creation of synapses and neural networks associated with thinking and reasoning. As the gatekeepers of learning, you can start children on the path to a lifetime of discovery by teaching them the thinking skills they need to explore the unknown.

The Developing Brain

The child's brain is not simply a small adult brain. It is undergoing important stages of development. The brain is equipped with an abundance of neurons (specialized brain cells) at birth. As one learns, the connections among neurons (synapses) increase, and the ability of brain cells to transmit signals improves (myelination). The experiences you provide children can stimulate and strengthen connections among brain cells that reinforce learning. Unused synapses are pruned, whereas useful synapses are reinforced and developed. As elementary school teachers, you work with children at a time when their brains are undergoing significant developments that will last a lifetime. Although you do not need to become a cognitive neuroscientist to be a good teacher, you do need to become aware of fundamental ways in which the developing brain processes information.

What Is Scientific Thinking? A Look at Some Masters

Great thinkers such as Einstein, Galileo, and da Vinci had the ability to create detailed mental models. We all create mental models to some extent. When we can "see" or "picture" a situation in our minds, we can often understand and explain it better. Expressions such as, "I see what you mean" or "It is like . . ." suggest this tendency to create mental models. Great thinkers have the extraordinary ability to create and keep complex mental models of a system in their minds and imagine what would happen when different elements in the models interact in novel ways. For example, Einstein could imagine what would happen when someone rode a beam of light, and da Vinci could imagine the miracle of flight. As educators, we need to teach our students the cognitive skills necessary to create mental models and to create a culture of thinking in which these cognitive skills become habits of mind. Habits of mind take years to develop; they cannot be covered in a lesson or two. The habits of good, scientific thinking must become a conscious part of the culture of learning; children need to be made aware of their thinking strategies when they are thinking scientifically.

What Does Scientific Thinking Look Like?

Scientific thinking is a process of asking questions and seeking explanations. In order to teach scientific thinking, it is helpful to identify a framework for scientific thinking that is practical and teachable. One such framework consisting of three primary modeling steps: descriptive modeling, explanatory modeling, and experimental modeling, referred to as the progression of inquiry, provides the foundation for instructional strategies. The three stages will be addressed more fully in Chapter 3.[3]

Descriptive Modeling   Before trying to explain a mystery, we have to be able to describe what we know about the mystery. Most of early elementary school is spent on developing observational skills to make good descriptive models. It is no small accomplishment to be an active observer when one encounters a completely novel phenomenon. Good scientists recognize the distinction between looking and observing. The observational skills that you teach your students will differ only with respect to levels of sophistication and technology from the skills used by experienced scientists. Scientists who use electron microscopes to measure distances in angstroms ask the same descriptive questions as first graders who use rulers to measure distances in centimeters.

Explanatory Modeling   The descriptive model reveals connections and relationships that suggest explanations. Explanations yield hypotheses, or proposed relationships, that may be tested.

Experimental Modeling   Experimental models test predictions that are based on hypotheses. Designing a good experiment requires a prediction that can be tested, the use of independent, dependent, and controlled variables as well as the construction of a controlled experiment. These terms are explained in Chapter 3. The experiment usually leads to new observations, which yield deeper insights that modify the descriptive model, deepen the explanatory model, and lead to more experimentation. Science is a dynamic, ongoing process (Figure 1.1).

Developing Positive Affect   For many teachers, a lesson about a caterpillar becoming a butterfly will only be about a caterpillar and a butterfly. But the same lesson in the hands of a master teacher—a great teacher, an extraordinary teacher, a truly gifted teacher—will be an experience in which the children are thunderstruck with the realization that *one living thing has become a completely different living thing right before their eyes.*

The day of that lesson will be one on which those children's lives will be changed forever. They will leave school filled with a sense of wonder that was sparked by the thrill of discovering brand-new knowledge that is as extraordinary as anything they will see on television. They will want to know more—curious about what may lie around the corner. They will also leave with new attitudes, values, and a confidence in their ability to learn that will shape who they are and who they will become.

This change in attitudes and values signals the development of *positive affect.* The science experiences you deliver to children will do much to create positive affect about science, school, and the wonders of the natural world. It is the classroom environment that will help children grow toward the positive goals presented so beautifully in Dorothy Law Nolte's "Children Learn What They Live" (see Figure 1.2, page 9).

Developing Psychomotor Skills   You might not think of your classroom as a place where children learn to coordinate what their minds *will* with what their bodies *perform*—but it is. Children need to develop gross motor abilities as well as fine motor skills, and well-planned science experiences can help them do so.

Gross motor skills can be developed through inquiry-based activities such as assembling and using simple machines, hoeing and raking a class vegetable garden, and carefully shaping sand on a table to make various land forms. Examples of experiences that develop *fine motor skills* include cutting out leaf shapes with scissors, drawing charts and graphs, and sorting seeds on the basis of physical characteristics. So, in addition to gaining knowledge and understanding and developing positive affect, science time can be a time to improve a child's physical skills.

Figure 1.1

Source: Adapted with permission from P. Bergethon, (1999). *The Path to Science Literacy: From Brain to Mind to Literacy.* Holliston, MA: Symmetry Learning Systems, 16–17.

Developing Responsible Citizens   When your children look at you during science time, they aren't thinking about issues such as raising taxes to pay for a park's underground sprinkler system or what impact the new factory under construction in town may have on worldwide CO_2 emissions and global warming trends. However, at some time in their lives, they will be concerned about societal issues. And to be responsible citizens, they will need to address such issues with wisdom—wisdom based on a foundation of knowledge constructed many years earlier. Perhaps some of that knowledge will be gained in your classroom.

Figure 1.2
A child's environment has a powerful impact on his or her affective development.

Children Learn What They Live

By Dorothy Law Nolte

If children live with criticism, they learn to condemn.

If children live with hostility, they learn to fight.

If children live with fear, they learn to be apprehensive.

If children live with pity, they learn to feel sorry for themselves.

If children live with ridicule, they learn to feel shy.

If children live with jealousy, they learn to feel envy.

If children live with shame, they learn to feel guilty.

If children live with encouragement, they learn to be confident.

If children live with tolerance, they learn patience.

If children live with praise, they learn appreciation.

If children live with acceptance, they learn to love.

If children live with approval, they learn to like themselves.

If children live with recognition, they learn it is good to have a goal.

If children live with sharing, they learn generosity.

If children live with honesty, they learn truthfulness.

If children live with fairness, they learn justice.

If children live with kindness and consideration, they learn respect.

If children live with security, they learn to have faith in themselves and in those about them.

If children live with friendliness, they learn the world is a nice place in which to live.

If you live with serenity, your child will live with peace of mind.

With what is your child living?

With your guidance, children will learn that real inquiry requires gathering evidence before reaching a conclusion. Hopefully, learning to gather knowledge systematically and to reach carefully thought out conclusions will be skills they apply as they confront societal issues in the future. If you do your job, then today's children will make positive contributions to the civic decision-making processes that will lead to a better life for us all.

Scientific Literacy: Your Science Teaching Will Create It

Add *STS* to the list of acronyms you carry in your brain. It stands for *science, technology, and society,* a catchphrase that represents what average citizens should know about two things that affect them and their society constantly: science and technology. In short, STS is related to creating citizens who are scientifically literate.

To create citizens who understand the implications of developments in science and technology is an enormous task. But the task for you, as a teacher, is more specific and reachable: teaching children to become scientifically literate.

To help you in this effort, the National Science Education Standards (NSES) identify what it means to be scientifically literate and suggest what should be taught at various grade levels to reach this goal. The NSES list the following goals for members of a scientifically literate society:

- Experience the richness and excitement of knowing about and understanding the natural world;

- Use appropriate scientific processes and principles in making personal decisions;

- Engage intelligently in public discourse and debate about matters of scientific and technological concern; and

- Increase their economic productivity through the use of the knowledge, understanding, and skills of the scientifically literate person in their careers.*

Note that while the NSES provide a guide to grade-level appropriate content and insights about how the content should be taught, it is ultimately your responsibility as the classroom teacher to make decisions about the teaching strategies that are suitable for your students.

Later in this book (in Chapters 4, 10, 13, and 16), you will learn what content the NSES suggest for your classroom. You will discover that much of the content suggested has, as its focus, the creation of citizens who have a good understanding of new developments in science and technology and what implications those developments have for their lives.

Gender and Equity Issues: Your Science Teaching Will Help Resolve Them

> The scientist is a brain. He spends his days indoors, sitting in a laboratory, pouring things from one test tube into another. . . . He can only eat, breathe, and sleep science. . . . He has no social life, no other intellectual interests, no hobbies or relaxations. . . . He is always reading a book. He brings home work and also brings home creepy things.[4]

Although students made these observations almost 50 years ago, their attitudes reflect, to a large degree, the views of society today. The students' choice of pronoun does not seem to reflect the purposeful use of *he* for *she* but rather the strength of the stereotype of the scientist as male.

One of my favorite classroom activities is to ask each student to draw a picture of a scientist at work (see Figure 1.3). In most cases the scientist is depicted as a bespectacled, old, white male with a slightly mad glint in his eyes, having a very bad hair day. While it may seem amusing, the real harm of this stereotype lies in the fact that it may discourage young females, minorities, and students with disabilities from considering science or science-related careers and foster the notion that they are not expected to succeed in

---

*Reprinted with permission from *National Science Education Standards*© 1996 by the National Academy of Sciences, courtesy of the National Academies Press, Washington, D.C.

Figure 1.3   A sampling of "Draw a Scientist" illustrations by elementary students

science. Hopefully, you will be a classroom leader who is able to create an environment that helps to overcome these stereotypes.

The science classroom can also provide you with a wonderful opportunity to assist children from cultural minorities and for whom English is not their home language. When children are encouraged to explore phenomena that are real to them, to learn and use inquiry skills, and ultimately to make their own discoveries, the power of these experiences will do much to integrate *all* children into the task at hand.

Just think of how fortunate you are to teach children science, a subject whose natural allure for children will draw them into learning experiences irrespective of gender, language, and cultural barriers. By having a classroom that respects cultural and linguistic diversity and addresses gender inequities, you can make a real difference in the lives of children. That's right! *You* can and will make a difference.

Science: What Is It, Really?

Science seeks explanations of the natural world. It consists of the following components:

- A systematic quest for explanations
- The dynamic body of knowledge generated through a systematic quest for explanations

Unfortunately, science is often associated only with the body of knowledge, which is tantamount to skipping the movie and watching only the final scene. The ending does not make sense if you do not know the plot. When science is presented as only facts and answers, it ceases being science. Anyone with access to a computer can find information. Science involves the process of generating information. Science teaches us what to do when we do not have the answer. It is a systematic search with a variety of strategies that results in a dynamic body of scientific knowledge. For example, Pluto is no longer considered a planet, the earth is no longer considered flat, and limitations of Newtonian physics have been accepted. The scientific body of knowledge is not static.

As an elementary school science teacher, you will teach process skills, values, and attitudes associated with seeking scientific explanations as well as the body of knowledge that constitutes current scientific explanations of natural phenomena. (See Table 1.1, page 12.)

Table 1.1   Examples of science as a body of knowledge, as a process, and values associated with science

Body of Knowledge	
• Energy can change form.	• For every action, there is an equal and opposite reaction.
• Matter can change form.	• Like poles of magnets repel each other.
• The total amount of matter and energy in the universe never changes.	• Unlike poles of magnets attract each other.

Inquiry Process Skills		
• Descriptive modeling	• Explanatory modeling	• Experimental modeling
Questioning	Questioning	Questioning
Observing	Hypothesizing	Predicting
Enumerating	Inferring	Identifying variables
Classifying	Interpreting data	Controlling variables
Measuring	Communicating	Controlling experiments
Comparing		Communicating
Communicating		

Values and Attitudes Associated with Scientific Inquiry	
• Skepticism	• Cooperation
• Criticism	• Persistence
Ability to criticize	• Freedom to think originally
Acceptance of criticism	• Organization

The Nature of Science

The American Association for the Advancement of Science (AAAS) suggests that there are particular ways of observing, thinking, experimenting, and validating that reflect how science tends to differ from other modes of knowing. These particular attributes contribute to what is referred to as the nature of science. AAAS suggests the following attributes associated with the nature of science:

- The Scientific World View

    The world is understandable.

    Scientific ideas are subject to change.

    Scientific knowledge is durable (scientists tend to modify rather than reject existing ideas).

    Science cannot provide complete answers to all questions.

- Scientific Inquiry

    Science demands evidence.

    Science is a blend of logic and imagination.

    Science explains and predicts.

    Scientists try to identify and avoid bias.

    Science is not authoritarian.

- The Scientific Enterprise

    Science is a complex social activity.

    Science is organized into content disciplines and is conducted in various institutions.

    There are generally accepted ethical principles in the conduct of science.

    Scientists participate in public affairs both as specialists and as citizens.*

Your Attitude Makes a Difference

If, as a teacher, you emphasize only the facts of science, children will learn that science is an accumulation of factual knowledge. However, if you emphasize the process of science, children will learn that science is a way of seeking explanations. A well-rounded student understands science as both a process and a body of knowledge. Children will enter your classes with their own perceptions of science formed through experiences outside of school, at home, and through the media. Figure 1.4 offers the ideas of some fourth graders about science. As their teacher, you will have a significant impact on their understanding and attitude about what science is and how science is done. It is not only what you teach, but also your attitude toward science that will impact students.

Consider Renee, a third-grade teacher, on bus duty early one spring morning greeting and directing the children as they clamor off the buses. Mary, a curious third grader, can hardly contain her excitement as she runs up to Renee with a plastic container teeming with wriggling worms she and her mother found while planting a garden. Mary grabs a handful of worms to show Renee, who contorts her face into a disgusted grimace exclaiming, "Yuk . . . get those things away from me. Mary, I don't like worms. Please, I hope you are not thinking about bringing them into my classroom." Mary's smile vanishes as

Reality Check

What Would You Do?

During a school committee meeting to discuss the elementary science program, a committee member suggests, "While science is important, it should not be emphasized at the elementary level, since the children need to learn reading, math, and writing during these formative years. Science, after all, requires memorization of a rather extensive amount of factual knowledge, which should be saved for the middle and high school years. It has little to offer developing minds of elementary school students." For this reason, she argues, minimal time should be allotted to elementary science education.

As an elementary school teacher at the meeting, you are asked your opinion on the matter. How would you respond to this school committee member's suggestion?

*American Association for the Advancement of Science (1989). *Science for All Americans.* New York: Oxford University Press. Reprinted with permission

Figure 1.4
A few fourth-grade children offer their definitions of science.

"Science is a class that we go to and learn about important things we have to know. I think science is the funnest class I've ever been to." —*Jennifer*

"Science is . . . I think that science is neat, fun. It is interesting you learn all kinds of neat stuff." —*Renee*

"Science is fun and it can be really hard to do. It is very hard to do some of the worksheets." —*Mark*

"Science is . . . Alot of fun we study Whales. We work in books and get more homework but science is fun learning experiment. We make maps and we blow them up." —*Alan*

"Science is the explanation for the way the things on Earth work." —*Nico*

"Science is important to me. I will be an vet or animal scientist. I love science and when I'm sad or up set I try to be scietific and it cheers me up. It makes me happy when I make a dedution. Once I start trying to think up the answer to a problem and I won't I mean won't stop even for eating and sleeping even reading! So I love science a lot." —*Mary Catherine*

"Science is important to me couse we have alot of pages we have to do. I think it is easy to do." —*Robbie*

"Science is fun. I liked it when we used salt and flour to mold a map. Salt and flour is sticky. I like science." —*Erik*

she walks quietly to the grassy area next to the school and dumps the worms on the soft ground.

Although this scenario may seem somewhat exaggerated, similar scenes have taken place in school yards and classrooms. Mary did not learn anything about worms or their role in the ecosystem of the garden. Much worse, Mary may take home the lesson that adult, educated women should not like worms or be curious about such things one finds in nature. As you may have concluded from the drawings done of scientists on page 11, research using the Draw a Scientist task (DAST) reveals that children in the United States generally think of scientists as white males, most often involved in work in a laboratory.[5] Teachers need to promote images of scientists that reflect a diversity of gender and race, so all students have the opportunity to envision themselves as scientists.

● Science as a Set of Values

Although there are many values you can emphasize as you help children experience science processes and learn content, there are six that you will find particularly useful:

1. Truth
2. Freedom
3. Skepticism
4. Order
5. Originality
6. Communication

Because science seeks to make sense out of our natural world, it has as its most basic value the search for *truth* based on evidence. The scientist seeks to discover not what should be but what *is*. The high value placed on truth applies not only to the discovery of facts, concepts, and principles but also to the recording and reporting of such knowledge.

The search for truth relies on another important value: *freedom*. Real science can only occur when a scientist is able to operate in an environment that provides him or her with the freedom to follow paths wherever they lead. Fortunately, free societies rarely limit the work of scientists. Freedom to follow pathways also means the freedom to risk thinking independently and creatively. As educators, we must provide opportunities for students to think while taking care to think with, not for, students. We must foster the development of foundational thinking strategies so that children can take advantage of the freedom to think afforded them in our open society. A successful free society depends on the ability of its citizens to make informed decisions.

Skepticism—the unwillingness to accept many things at face value—moves scientists to ask difficult questions about the natural world, society, and even each other. Scientists value *skepticism,* and skepticism sometimes causes nonscientists to doubt the results of scientific enterprise. In an article entitled "Uh-Oh, Here Comes the Mailman," James Gleick, a well-known science writer, describes excerpts from some of the letters he has received:

> Here is a lengthy single-spaced essay (painstakingly tied up with what looks like tooth floss) titled "Chaos and Rays." Apparently, one of these rays "impregnates the chaos" and "fructifies the forces."

> A Canadian reader has discovered (he encloses the calculations) that all spheres, including the Earth, are 20 percent larger than geometers have thought—"Perhaps the reason missiles keep crashing short of their course."[6]

While Professor Gleick may smile at these letters, he also makes this observation:

> It's hard to remember, but it's surely true, that the instinct bubbling to the surface in these letters is the same instinct driving real scientists. There is a human curiosity about nature, a desire to peer through the chaos and find the order.[7]

There is, then, an underlying *order* to the processes and content of science. In their search for truth, scientists gather information and then organize it. It is this order that allows scientists to discover patterns in the natural world. Children need to develop this ability to organize information, which is why you will be helping them learn how to organize and keep track of their observations.

For all its order, however, science also values *originality*. Although some may view science as a linear activity—one in which people plod along, acquiring more and more detailed explanations of phenomena—in reality, science is fueled by original ideas and creative thinking. It is this kind of thinking that leads to discoveries.

Children love to talk with each other; so do scientists. The talk of scientists includes reports, articles, speeches, and lectures, as well as casual conversations. The ability to communicate results is vital if knowledge is to grow. Without extensive *communication,* progress would be greatly limited.

As a teacher, you will need to help children understand that science is more than a collection of facts and a group of processes. Science is a human activity that has as its framework a set of values that are important in day-to-day life.

Technology and Engineering: They Are Changing Your Life and Their Lives

Go to **MyEducationLab**, select the topic Technology, watch the video entitled "Technology," and complete the question that accompanies it.

What do these terms have in common: prescription drugs, hip-replacement surgery, instant hair dye, solar panels, fuel cells, soft contact lenses, electric cars, CAT scans, X-ray treatment for cancer, and ramen noodles (noodle-like material that can be reconstituted through the addition of tap water)? The answer, of course, is *technology*. They all are products or procedures that apply science to the solution of human problems—real or imagined.

Today, one of the most immediate technological challenges concerns climate change and the rising costs of fossil fuels, which have created a need to seek alternative methods to generate energy. Green buildings that take advantage of wind, solar, geothermal, and even human energy are emerging at an increasingly rapid pace. These technologies integrate earth science, energy transfer and conversion, simple machines, and biology in meaningful and relevant contexts. In your role as elementary school teachers, you will have a tremendous opportunity to lay the foundation of energy literacy for generations of young people who may become engineers, architects, and designers that make pivotal decisions about life style changes that will affect our planet and its inhabitants for years to come.

NSES

One of your obligations in teaching children science is to pay attention to how technology-based products and procedures work. You will find this goal referred to in any list of curriculum objectives as *technological design*. The NSES point out that children should be able to do these things:

1. Identify a problem.
2. Design a solution.
3. Implement their solution.
4. Critically examine how well their solution worked.
5. Communicate with others about their design and the strengths and weaknesses of their solution.[8]

How might teaching about technological design be translated into your own real-world classroom? Children could design any of the following:

1. A dog-walking machine
2. A machine for removing and sorting garbage and trash from lunch trays
3. A solar oven to cook s'mores
4. A backpack with a self-contained umbrella that automatically opens during a rainstorm

Advances in technology enable us to convert renewable energies such as wind into electricity.

The point is that new and emerging technology impacts virtually every minute of a child's day. In order for children to lead lives in which technology is used intelligently, with minimal negative side effects, they need to understand what technology is, how new products and procedures are designed, what resources are needed, and what deleterious consequences may occur, such as allergic reactions, environmental pollution, and safety hazards. Students need to fully understand the larger impact of new technologies within the context of how those technologies affect their communities—and themselves.

Discovery: Your Destination

"How do we know what we know?"

It certainly seems like a simple question when you look at it. I could even develop a rather complicated answer for it, if I was so disposed—but I won't! I suggest that we know what we know because we have made discoveries, and we have made those discoveries through inquiry. You made discoveries yesterday, you will make discoveries today, and you will make discoveries tomorrow. In fact, you are making discoveries as you read the printed words on these pages.

Discovery, which is part of the subtitle of this book (*A Discovery Approach*), is the journey on which you will lead your students to deeper understanding of the natural world. It is our discoveries that make us what we are. They underlie what we think, feel, and do.

Now the question is, How do you make those discoveries? Although there are many paths to discovery, this book is based on the path called *inquiry*. In fact, the paths of inquiry are different for bakers, accountants, cosmetologists, auto mechanics, and

Make the Case *An Individual or Group Challenge*

● **The Problem**	The children in your classroom may be unaware of the many ways in which science and technology affect their daily lives.

● **Assess Your Prior Knowledge and Beliefs**

To what extent are each of the following aspects of your life affected by science and technology?

Health	very little	little	somewhat	a great deal
Safety	very little	little	somewhat	a great deal
Nutrition	very little	little	somewhat	a great deal
Personal security	very little	little	somewhat	a great deal
Communication	very little	little	somewhat	a great deal
Transportation	very little	little	somewhat	a great deal
Recreation	very little	little	somewhat	a great deal

● **The Challenge**	Your principal has asked you to give a five-minute talk at the next meeting of the Parents/Teachers Organization to encourage parents to cultivate their children's interest in science and technology. Identify five key points you would make in your presentation.

shepherds. We will focus on the way *scientists* inquire because we want children to make their science-related discoveries in the same way that real scientists do. (Shepherds may do it very differently.)

Inquiry: The Path Children Will Take toward Discovery

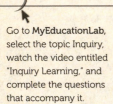

Go to **MyEducationLab**, select the topic Inquiry, watch the video entitled "Inquiry Learning," and complete the questions that accompany it.

"Do chickens have teeth?"

"Why does a light bulb get hot?"

"Why are there holes in cheese?"

"Why can't we send the new baby back?"

Questions, questions, and more questions! Asking questions is what makes we humans what we are. We seem to have a genetic urge to make sense of our surroundings, and this constant questioning is our most powerful tool. When you teach science, that is the tool all children will bring to you—the urge to question their surroundings—and so it will provide the foundation for much of your teaching.

Science seeks explanations, which are sought through a process of inquiry. You are already familiar with the progression of inquiry: descriptive modeling, explanatory modeling, and experimental modeling. These are helpful theoretical categories, but they mean little unless the theory can be translated meaningfully in the classroom.

Inquiry is about asking questions, but the challenge is to know what questions to ask. How often have you been in a new situation and heard, "If you have any questions, just ask," and you do not know where to begin. Peter Bergethon suggests the following set of fundamental questions that provide us with direction when we don't know where to begin:[9]

- What are the elements of the system?
- What are the properties of the elements?
- What is the context or background space of the system?
- What are the rules of interaction (connections) among the elements?
- What are the emergent properties (characteristics) of the system?

These questions guide our initial observations and enable inquirers to be active observers. Often during class, teachers ask students to make observations without teaching them how to observe. They just expect them to look. But looking is not the same as observing. When we look at things we are passive and wait for something to happen; when we observe, we become active participants. The fundamental questions of inquiry guide observation. They provide a starting point to organize our thoughts. Let's use the puzzler at the beginning of the chapter as an example of how to use the fundamental questions of inquiry. Recall the puzzle:

A man lives on the twelfth floor of an apartment building. Every morning he takes the elevator down to the lobby and leaves the building. In the evening, he gets into the elevator, and, if there is someone else in the elevator—or if it was raining that day—he goes back to his floor directly. Otherwise, he goes to the tenth floor and walks up two flights of stairs to his apartment.[10]

The first inclination of most people is to attempt to answer the question right away. Scientific thinking requires us to take a systematic approach, beginning with a descriptive model. In other words, we need to get our minds around the event to understand what we are dealing with before we attempt an explanation. We begin by describing the situation using the fundamental questions of inquiry:

- What are the elements?

    Man, elevator, floors, stairs, apartment, someone else, elevator, rain

- What are the properties of the elements?

    At least 12 floors, 2 flights of stairs

- What is the background space?

    Time (morning, evening), apartment building

- Rules of interaction

    Man goes down 12 floors in the elevator

    Man goes up to the tenth floor in the elevator

    Man walks up two flights of stairs

    Man goes to the twelfth floor directly from the lobby if it is raining outside or if there is someone else in the elevator with him.

- Emergent properties

    Man moves between the lobby and his apartment

At this point, you probably do not have enough information to explain the man's behavior. Much like a detective solving a mystery, your systematic analysis of the situation enables you to ask meaningful questions to deepen your descriptive model. Let's imagine the scene as it unfolds based on our descriptive model and our prior knowledge. Our knowledge of elevators suggests that there must be a panel of buttons on the wall. The rules of interaction between the man and the elevator suggest that the doors open, he steps into the elevator, and pushes the lobby button on the panel. Doing so brings him to the lobby. In the evening, the process is repeated. Except this time we know that he presses the tenth floor button if he is alone, travels to the tenth floor where he exits the elevator, and walks two flights to the twelfth floor. As we continue to run the model in our minds, we imagine the situation with someone else in the elevator. In this situation, someone has to push the twelfth floor button, and the man travels to the twelfth floor where he exits. When it is raining, the man can be alone and press the twelfth floor button to travel directly to the twelfth floor.

Reality Check

To build habits of mind associated with descriptive modeling, begin each class with an entrance activity. Project pictures of familiar scenes and ask students to describe the scene as they enter the classroom. Review the descriptions in terms of the fundamental questions of inquiry. After a few classes, students expect to find a picture and immediately create their descriptive models. As the weeks progress, exchange the familiar pictures with unfamiliar pictures (microscopic images, pond life, ecosystems, molecules), items, or even lateral thinking puzzles and ask students to develop descriptive models. Doing so consistently over a period of time develops habits of mind associated with observation strategies for creating descriptive models as a first step to inquiry.

Do you have an explanation yet? Go to the end of the chapter, p. 24, for the solution. Don't worry if you did not arrive at the correct explanation. Although identifying the best explanation is the desired outcome, it is the process that is important in this example. That is why science inquiry is called re-search, and not simply search; we must seek answers and retry to seek them again. Hopefully you realize that a scientific approach is a strategy that keeps you moving toward a better explanation.

National, State, and Local Standards: They Will Light Your Way

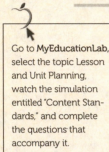

Go to **MyEducationLab**, select the topic Lesson and Unit Planning, watch the simulation entitled "Content Standards," and complete the questions that accompany it.

NSES

Have you ever dreamt that you were lost in a forest and had no idea of how to get out? You may remember such a dream as an overpowering nightmare from which you awoke filled with dread and hopelessness.

The thought of teaching children science may be similarly overwhelming, but it should not leave you feeling hopeless. You should feel uplifted! In the bad dream, you were alone. In the real world of teaching children science, you are not. Many people have spent their entire professional lives developing goals, objectives, procedures, and materials for science teaching. You will have access to the fruits of all of their labor. For now, think about just one aspect of all of this: the goals and objectives of your science teaching.

Again, you will not have to invent them all yourself! A group of scientists and educators have created the *National Science Education Standards (NSES)*, which outline suggested science content by grade level. (You may recall that we discussed the NSES with respect to technology earlier in the chapter.) The NSES are readily available to you in print form and on the Internet, and an important portion of those standards related to the content you should be teaching or at least considering is reprinted inside the front cover of this book.

Project 2061

Implications for Your Inquiry-Based, Discovery-Focused Classroom

To develop an inquiry-based, discovery-focused classroom, you'll need to draw on a wide range of resources. One resource that may prove useful is the curriculum development effort known as *Project 2061*. Developed by scientists and educators, and with the sponsorship of the American Association for the Advancement of Science, this project is intended to help reform K–12 science, mathematics, and technology education. Its basic reference document, *Science for All Americans,* offers recommendations called *benchmarks* in many areas, which will be important to you as you plan and teach.

Project 2061 has twelve benchmarks that you may wish to study in some detail:

- The nature of science
- The nature of mathematics
- The nature of technology
- The physical setting
- The living environment
- The human organism
- Human society
- The designed world
- The mathematical world
- Historical perspectives
- Common themes
- Habits of mind

To find helpful information about any of these benchmarks, visit the Project 2061 website at **www.project2061.org/**.

Although the NSES are like the lighthouse that points to the final destination, they do not set the course. It is up to you and your district or department team to determine how the students will reach the standards. Rest assured that the NSES are only some of many guides available to help determine what to teach. Individual states, provinces, and local communities also have developed standards and curriculum maps. Sometimes called frameworks, they provide varying degrees of guidance in the forms of content, teaching, and sample lessons. Additionally, there is an abundance of resources available through the Internet. In the information age, your biggest challenge will not be to create original science lessons as much as it will be to recognize and choose effective, inquiry-based science lessons. No two classes and teachers are exactly alike; therefore, you will need to adapt and revise each lesson to best fit your teaching style and the needs of the children in your class.

Rest assured that you are not lost and alone in the forest. The path you will take as you lead children to discovery is well marked. You will have many resources as you guide children to explore, inquire, and discover. You are definitely not alone. Sleep well, and then awake and seize the day!

Yes, You Can Do It! Science for All Children, Every Day in Every Way

Go to **MyEducationLab**, select the topic Cross-Curricular Connections, watch the video entitled "Emerging Curriculum Built on Children's Interests" and complete the questions that accompany it.

This book is full of resources that will help you create wonderful classroom experiences for children—experiences in which they explore, inquire, and discover. In Part One of this book (which includes this and the next eight chapters), you will learn basic science-teaching methods that will also help you create that wonderful classroom! And beyond Part One, you will find three very specific parts of the book that deal with teaching the earth/space sciences, the life sciences, and the physical sciences. In the chapters in those parts, you will find unit and lesson "starter ideas," activities and demonstrations, and even basic science content for your reference as you prepare to teach children science.

I am confident that you will be successful if you are motivated to use your talent to its fullest and the available resources to the maximum. If you do, each day in your classroom will be a day when every child has the opportunity to explore, inquire, and discover. So, get started on your journey to discover how children actually learn science.

Summary

You will be teaching children not only science but also strategies for thinking and knowing what to do when they do not have the answer by creating a classroom environment that embraces and directs children's natural curiosity. You will guide children to develop habits of mind necessary to be active and curious observers, to seek explanations based on evidence, and to systematically test explanations through experimentation. In doing so, your students will use and develop inquiry process skills, positive attitudes toward science, and abilities to do science.

Science is both a body of knowledge about the natural world and a systematic way of gathering knowledge. In other words, it is a *product* (an organized set of facts, concepts, and principles) as well as a *process* (a method of obtaining and extending that knowledge). Technology is the application of that knowledge or the systematic ways of getting knowledge to solve human problems.

The general approaches for teaching science that you will use in the classroom will be guided by an understanding of the mental modeling inherent in the progression of inquiry: description, explanation, and experimentation. These three components of the progression of inquiry provide a simple framework that supports instructional strategies. Five fundamental questions of inquiry provide a structure for beginning inquiry:

1. What are the elements of the system being studied?
2. What are the properties of the elements?
3. What is the background space or context of the system?
4. What are the rules of interaction among the elements in the system?
5. What are the emergent properties of the system?

The challenges of teaching children science will require you to use a variety of resources, including units and lessons that you plan yourself, science resource books, and the Internet. Know that you are not alone in your quest for effective science teaching strategies. Organizations such as the National Academy of Sciences (National Science Education Standards) and the American Association for the Advancement of Science (Project 2061) as well as local science standards and frameworks will also be your guide as you plan learning experiences in which children learn to seek explanations through inquiry and discovery.

Going Further

On Your Own

1. Think about when you have observed children in elementary, middle, or high school exploring, doing inquiry, and making discoveries, or recall your own experiences in science. Provide any examples that you can, including examples of students using the inquiry process skills (e.g., observing, interpreting data, etc.).

2. Consider your present feelings about teaching children science, and identify the factors that have influenced your attitudes.

3. If possible, interview an elementary school teacher to find out how he or she would answer such questions as these: How do you feel about teaching children inquiry-based, discovery-focused science?

What do children think science is? What materials for learning science are available in your classroom or school? Do you feel well prepared to teach science? Why or why not?

4. Do some research to determine the role that science and technology have played in shaping present-day society. Consider such questions as these: Would society be better served if science were pursued only for the sake of the technology that results from it? Does the scientist occupy a prestigious position in modern society? What responsibility do scientists have for communicating the results of their work in a way that is understandable to the public?

On Your Own or in a Cooperative Learning Group

5. Discuss the role models that your parents, teachers, textbooks, and the media offered you in elementary school. Can you recall your level of career awareness as an elementary student? What did you want to become?

Why? If you are a woman, what factors tended to turn you toward or away from a scientific career? If you are a man, what stereotypes, if any, did you have about women and careers in science and technology?

Resources for Discovery Learning

Internet Resources

To access these helpful websites, go to **MyEducationLab,** select Resources, and then Web Links. To learn more, click on the following links and you will easily be directed to each website.

- **AAAS Project 2061: Benchmarks for Science Literacy:**
  www.project2061.org/default_flash.htm

- **Inquiry and the National Science Education Standards:**
  http://books.nap.edu/html/inquiry_addendum/

- **Kids Draw a Scientist; Perceptions of Scientists:**
  http://science.easternblotnet/?p=52

- **National Science Education Standards:**
  www.nap.edu/openbook.php?record_id=4962

- **National Science Teachers Association:**
  www.nsta.org/

- **NetLinkd (NSES and AAAS 2061 Relationship):**
  www.sciencenetlinks.org./benchmarks.htm

- **Project 2061 Overview:**
  www.project2061.org/

Print Resources

Suggested Readings

Bodzin, Alec, and Mike Gehringer. "Breaking Science Stereotypes." *Science and Children* 25, no. 5 (January 2001): 36–41.

Coverdale, Gregory. "Science Is for the Birds: Promoting Standards-Based Learning through Backyard Birdwatching." *Science Scope* 26, no. 4 (January 2003): 32–37.

Davis, Elizabeth A., and Fitzpatrick, Doug. "It's All the News: Critiquing Evidence and Claims." *Science Scope* 25, no. 5 (February 2002): 32–37.

Demers, Chris. "Analyzing the Standards." *Science and Children* 37, no. 4 (January 2000): 22–25.

Dillon, Nancy. "Sowing the Seeds of the Standards." *Science and Children* 37, no. 4 (January 2000): 18–21.

Ferrell, Kathy. "Keeping the Joy in Teaching." *Science Scope* 24, no. 6 (March 2001): 50–52.

Fitzner, Kenneth. "Issues-Oriented Science." *Science Scope* 25, no. 6 (March 2002): 16–18.

Goodnough, Karen. "Humble Advice for New Science Teachers." *Science Scope* 23, no.6 (March 2000): 20–24.

Houtz, Lynne E., and Quinn, Thomas H. "Give Me Some Skin: A Hands-On Science Activity Integrating Racial Sensitivity." *Science Scope* 26, no. 5 (February 2003): 18–22.

Jesky-Smith, Romaine. "Me, Teach Science." *Science and Children* 39, no. 6 (March 2002): 26–30.

Kelly, Catherine A. "Reaching the Standards." *Science and Children* 37, no. 4 (January 2000): 30–32.

Koenig, Maureen. "Debating Real-World Issues." *Science Scope* 24, no. 5 (February 2001): 18–24.

Lee, Suzie. "Achieving Gender Equity in Middle School Science Classrooms." *Science Scope* 26, no. 5 (February 2003): 42–43.

Lightbody, Mary. "Countering Gender Bias in the Media." *Science Scope* 25, no. 6 (March 2002): 40–42.

Lowery, Lawrence F. (Ed.). *NSTA Pathways to the Science Standards: Guidelines for Moving the Vision into Practice.* Arlington, VA: National Science Teachers Association, 1997.

Lucking, Robert A., and Christmann, Edwin P. "Tech Trek: Technology in the Classroom." *Science Scope* 26, no. 4 (January 2003): 54–57.

McDuffie, Thomas E., Jr. "Scientists—Geeks and Nerds." *Science and Children* 38, no. 8 (May 2001): 16–19.

National Research Council. *National Science Education Standards.* Washington, DC: National Academy Press, 1996.

Ostlund, Karen, and Mercier, Sheryl. *Rising to the Challenge of the National Science Education Standards: Grades 4–8.* Arlington, VA: National Science Teachers Association, 1996.

Ostlund, Karen, and Mercier, Sheryl. *Rising to the Challenge of the National Science Education Standards: Grades K–6.* Arlington, VA: National Science Teachers Association, 1999.

Timmerman, Barbara. "Keeping Science Current." *Science Scope* 25, no. 6 (March 2002): 12–15.

Notes

1. *Brain Food.* www.rinkworks.com/brainfood/p/latreal1.shtml (accessed 02-10-08).
2. Thinkexist.com. http://thinkexist.com/quotes/richard_feynman/ (Richard Feynman was a theoretical physicist 1918–1988).
3. P. Bergethon, *Introducing Your Students to the Scientific Method* (Holliston, MA: Symmetry Learning Systems, 1999).
4. M. Mead and R. Metraux, "Image of the Scientist among High School Students," *Science* 126, no. 3270 (August 30, 1957): 384–390.
5. C. R. Barman, K. L. Ostlund, C.C. Gatto, M. Halferty, "Fifth Grade Students' Perceptions About Scientists and How They Study and Use Science." 1997 AETS Conference Papers and Summaries of Presentations, 1998.
6. James Gleick, "Uh-Oh, Here Comes the Mailman," *The New York Times Review of Books* 4 (March 1990): 32.
7. Ibid.
8. Based on Lawrence F. Lowery (ed.), *NSTA Pathways to the Science Standards: Guidelines for Moving the Vision into Practice* (Arlington, VA: National Science Teachers Association, 1997), p. 84.
9. P. Bergethon, *Learning the Language of Patterns* (Holliston, MA: Symmetry Learning Systems, 1999).
10. *Brain Food.* www.rinkworks.com/brainfood/p/latreal1.shtml (accessed 02-10-08).

▶ **Answer to Elevator Puzzler:** You may be able to infer (a science process skill) that the man is not capable of pressing the twelfth floor button when he is alone. However, someone else can press it for him when other people are in the elevator. When it is raining, he can push the twelfth floor button with an umbrella. You now have an explanatory model. You can hypothesize that the man is too short to reach the twelfth floor button on the elevator panel.

Note that the hypothesis is a proposed relationship that suggests a rationale behind the explanation. Finally, you would need to observe the man in the elevator to reject or fail to reject your hypothesis. This is an experimental model. If you find out that the man is indeed too short to reach the buttons on the panel, then you fail to reject your explanation and hypothesis. If the evidence does not support your explanation, then you reject your explanation or hypothesis.

chapter 2

Constructing Knowledge and Discovering Meaning

How can I help children learn science?

▶ Getting Started

Suppose one of your fourth-grade students wonders aloud, "Why can't it be summer every day of the year? Summer is such a wonderful time of year!" Before you provide your student with the explanation of why the seasons change, take a moment to think about your response . . .

Consider that graduates were asked to explain the reason for the seasons during commencement at Harvard University in 1987.[1] You may be surprised to learn that twenty-one out of twenty-three graduates got it wrong. The most common answer was that the seasons are caused by the distance of the Earth from the sun, a common misconception. It is possible that several of the students were once taught the correct reason for the seasons at some point in their academic careers, but because it is difficult to let go of explanations, they clung to this common misconception. If so, did they really learn the reason for the seasons the first time around?

So what is learning, really? Learning is the result of deepening or changing our mental models to more accurately describe and explain a phenomenon. It is usable

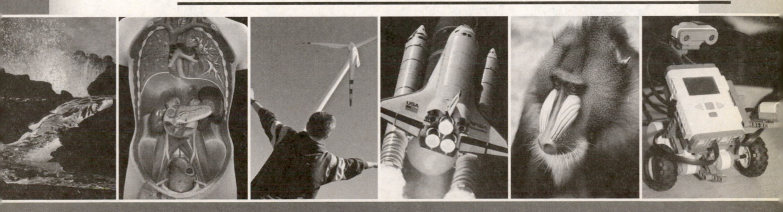

knowledge that can be recognized and applied (transferred) in a novel context. According to the National Research Council, "Experts' knowledge is connected and organized around important concepts (e.g., Newton's second law of motion); it is 'conditionalized' to specify the contexts in which it is applicable; it supports understanding and transfer (to other contexts) rather than only the ability to remember."[2] Understanding change requires us to deepen our understanding by modifying our existing knowledge. To truly understand the reason for the seasons, one first needs to understand the warming effects of indirect light opposed to direct light on a given surface area, and the interaction of sunlight on a planet tilted at approximately 23 degrees as it revolves around the sun. Then one can begin to understand that indirect light warms the earth less in the winter than in the summer.

Learning doesn't happen only for children, and it doesn't happen only in school. Learning is an ongoing process, in which the learner integrates new knowledge with previous knowledge and discovers new ways of thinking, acting, and feeling. We are *always* constructing new meanings in this way. I am always learning, you are always learning, and right now, somewhere a child is learning that it doesn't matter whether a corn seed is planted upside down or rightside up. That child is learning that in the proper environment, new shoots, like young children, grow toward the light.

Traditional Views about How Children Learn Science

There are two traditional and very broad ways of thinking about how children learn. One is known as *behavioral theory,* and the other is known as *cognitive theory.* If you wish to be successful in teaching children science, you will need to use elements of both and integrate these ideas with *constructivism:* a modern view of learning that you will learn about later in this chapter.

Project 2061

Implications for Helping Children Construct Knowledge and Discover Meaning

Project 2061 addresses the thinking skills you may wish to consider as you teach children science. Namely, they are outlined in the benchmark "Habits of mind":

- Values and attitudes
- Computation and estimation
- Manipulation and observation
- Communication skills
- Critical-response skills

Note that the item "Critical-response skills" is intended to help children separate sense from nonsense, which is crucial to helping them become scientifically literate citizens.

You'll find specific benchmarks (or recommendations) for the skills of most interest to you at the Project 2061 website: **www.project2061.org/.**

Behavioral Theory

The behavioral approach suggests that what a child does, and consequently what a child learns, depends on what happens as a result of the child's behavior. From this perspective, your job as a teacher is to create a classroom in which good things happen when children work with science materials, interact with one another in cooperative group work, and complete science projects. If children enjoy these experiences, receive praise from peers and the teacher, and are successful, they will be learning and developing a positive attitude. In order to have more experiences and receive more praise, they will continue to work hard.

From the behavioral perspective, the teacher's job is to create a science-learning environment in which certain behaviors and the acquisition of knowledge, concepts, and skills are increased and reinforced. *Tangible reinforcers* include receiving good grades, winning certificates and prizes in science fairs, earning points for free time, earning the privilege of taking care of the classroom animals for a week, and so forth. *Intangible reinforcers* include recognition of good work and praise from the teacher and the child's peers and parents. Figure 2.1 offers a list of some practical applications of behavioral principles.

Cognitive Theory

Cognitive theorists believe that what children learn depends on their mental processes and what they perceive about the world around them. In other words, learning depends on how children think and how their perceptions and thought patterns interact.

To understand the cognitivist view, try this: Look at the drawing on the left. What does it look like? Now ask other people to look at the drawing. What do they believe it is? If you ask a few people, you will soon discover that people perceive the world differently and that their solutions to questions depend on what they see and how they think.

Figure 2.1 You can find many ways to apply behavioral principles in your science classroom.

Practical Applications

Behavioral Principles for Your Science Classroom

1. *Reinforce positive behavior.*

   EXAMPLES
   - Praise children when they complete projects well.
   - Tell children who do a particularly good job of cleaning up after a messy science activity that you appreciate their efforts.

2. *Reinforce effort.*

   EXAMPLES
   - Thank children for trying to answer questions during class discussions.
   - Praise children whose behavior improves with each field trip.

3. *After a behavior has been established, reinforce the behavior at irregular intervals.*

   EXAMPLES
   - Surprise the class with special visitors or field trips during particularly challenging units.
   - Take individual photographs of children at work on long-term (multiweek) science projects, and present them unannounced at various times during the project.

According to cognitive learning theorists, a teacher should try to understand what a child perceives and how a child thinks and then plan experiences that will capitalize on these.

Many learning theories have evolved from cognitivism. In the sections that follow, you will read about two of the most important of these theories.

Piaget's Theories   Jean Piaget spent his professional life searching for an understanding of how children view the world and make sense of it. His work led him to propose that children progress through stages of cognitive development. The list that follows gives the stages and a few examples of the characteristics of each stage:

1. *Sensorimotor knowledge (0 to 2 years).* Objects and people exist only if the child can see, feel, hear, touch, or taste their presence. Anything outside the child's perceptual field does not exist.

2. *Preoperational (representational) knowledge (2 to 7 years).* The ability to use symbols begins. Although the child is still focused on the "here and now" early in this stage, the child can use language to refer to objects and events that are not in his or her perceptual field. The child has difficulty understanding that objects have multiple properties. For instance, he or she is not completely aware that a block of wood has color, weight, height, and depth all at once. Concepts of space and time are difficult to grasp. The child does not *conserve* attributes such as mass, weight, and number. For example, the child views a drink placed in a tall, narrow glass as more than the same amount of drink placed in a short, wide glass.

3. *Concrete operations (7 to 11 years).* The child can group objects into classes and arrange the objects in a class into some appropriate order. The child understands that mass, weight, volume, area, and length are conserved. The child has some difficulty isolating the variables in a situation and determining their relationships. The concepts of space and time become clearer.

4. *Formal operations (12 years through adulthood).* The child is able to think in abstract terms, is able to isolate the variables in a situation, and is able to understand their relationship to one another. The child's ability to solve complex verbal and mathematical problems emerges as a consequence of being able to manipulate the meanings represented by symbols.

Giving students opportunities to deepen their understanding through discovery is essential to constructing new knowledge.

Bruner's Theories   Jerome Bruner's research reveals that teachers need to provide children with experiences to help them discover underlying ideas, concepts, and patterns. Bruner is a proponent of *inductive* thinking, or going from the specific to the general. You are using inductive thinking when you get an idea from one experience that you use in another situation. Bruner believes that children are able to grasp any concept, provided it is approached in a manner appropriate for their particular grade level. Therefore, teachers should encourage children to handle increasingly complex challenges.

Constructivism: A Modern View of How Children Learn Science

What Is Constructivism?

Constructivism is a theory of human learning that is rooted in cognitive psychology and, to a lesser extent, behavioral psychology. It provides modern science teachers invaluable guidance. In fact, if you grasp the essential principles of constructivism, you will find it much easier to answer the two questions that will always be running through your mind as you approach a topic: *What should I teach?* and *How should I teach?*

Three Constructivist Principles to Guide Your Planning and Teaching

Go to **MyEducationLab**, select the topic Teaching Strategies, watch the video entitled "Constructivist Classrooms," and complete the question that accompanies it.

Three fundamental principles underlie the theory of constructivism:

1. *Naive conceptions.* A person never really knows the world as it is. Each person constructs beliefs about what is real.
2. *Assimilation.* Students try to reconcile new experiences and data with their present understanding so that the new data support and deepen but do not change their fundamental mental model.
3. *Accommodation.* Students cannot reconcile new experiences and data with their present understanding and they have to change their mental model to logically explain the experience.

Naive Conceptions   The first of these three principles is very important to teachers. Your experience with children probably has already taught you that not everything a child believes or knows is true. For example, Tom may believe that sweaters keep him warm because sweaters are warm. Uncle Harry, who lives with Tom's family, has told him many times to wear a warm sweater on a cool day. The belief that a sweater is warm is an example of a *naive conception:* an idea that does not fit reality when its validity is checked. Children and adults have many naive conceptions, and it is extremely difficult for a teacher to help a child construct new understandings if the child's naive conceptions filter out new experiences.

Assimilating and Accommodating New Learnings   Much of teaching is really re-teaching and challenging mental models with discrepant events, which leads to assimilation or accommodation. Different, but complementary to one another, these last two principles both address ways in which a child tries to fit new ideas into those already in place. Suppose, for example, that Eddie enters class believing Earth is flat, based on his daily encounters with a seemingly flat world, and is taught that Earth is round. In order to reconcile his prior belief that Earth is flat with the new information that Earth is round, he creates a mental model of a pancake shaped Earth that fits both with his prior understanding of a flat Earth and with the new information that Earth is round. Cognitive psychologists use a term to describe this situation: *assimilation.*

Inquiry requires children to be active observers of the world around them.

Suppose, however, that Eddie learns that ships sailing over the horizon do not fall off the edge of Earth or that if one sails far enough west, he ends up back in the east! When challenged to explain this phenomenon, he cannot reconcile it with his current mental model of a flat Earth. He is faced with the choice of either having to reject the evidence, or *accommodate* his mental model to one of a spherical Earth. Assimilation and accommodation are not mutually exclusive. They often complement each other in the learning process.

Constructivism focuses on the interplay between what the child already knows and the experiences the teacher provides. The conceptions and naive conceptions that the child has before an experiment make a very real difference in what the child will learn. Figure 2.2 identifies some practical applications of constructivism.

Figure 2.2   Practical strategies for identifying prior knowledge

Constructivism for Your Science Classroom

1. Prior to a lesson or unit, ask your students what they think and believe about a topic, and organize their input with a simple graphic organizer on a piece of newsprint that can be kept in the class for the duration of the unit. Label one column, "What we know" (to assess prior knowledge), and the other column, "What we want to learn" (to initiate the inquiry process). Enter the children's initial thoughts, and then add a third column labeled, "What we learned" to be completed by the class over the course of the unit.

2. Develop some true/false questions about the topic. Children's responses will give you a sense of their prior knowledge. Example:

   a. Water can move rocks. T/F

   b. Rocks never change. T/F

   c. All rocks are the same. T/F

   d. Some rocks can float. T/F

3. The Internet is also another way to get an idea of children's common prior knowledge or misconceptions before you prepare a lesson. There are several sites available through most search engines or go to MyEducationLab for more links.

4. Probe prior knowledge with an authentic experience. For example, if the unit topic was weathering and erosion, you might want to show them a rock with evidence of weathering or take them out on the school grounds where there is a good example of weathering and erosion. Point out evidence that you know is the result of weathering and erosion (i.e., rock outcropping with cracks and splits and smaller rocks at the base). Wonder out loud how the smaller rocks got there, and ask the students for their explanations.

• Contributions of Neuroscience

Developments in the technology of cognitive neuroscience provide windows into the workings of the human brain like never before. Teachers in the twenty-first century will need to become increasingly familiar with ways in which the brain processes information to understand the implications for learning. Educators need to know how to interpret, critically assess, and appropriately implement the emerging research on the neuroscience of thinking and learning.

Ways to Support Your Constructivist Teaching

NSES   • The NSE Standards

Here is a question for you: Do you know what *rebar* is? Oh, you don't. Before I reveal its meaning, you must answer another question: Have you ever thought of becoming a construction worker instead of a science teacher? Perhaps you haven't.

Surprisingly, teaching children science has elements of the construction industry in it. For one thing, you want to build a foundation that will give your children the knowledge, skills, and attitudes to keep them interested and constantly learning about science and technology. Without that foundation, children will find it difficult, if not impossible, to add new layers of learning.

That's where rebar comes in. It is a thick strand of steel that runs within the concrete slabs of a foundation. You probably have seen rebar sticking out from chunks of broken concrete. The rebar strengthens the concrete so that the foundation is durable and can stand the test of time.

The specific science content identified in the National Science Education Standards (NSES) is our teaching "rebar." Content from the standards must cross and recross the plans you create and the lessons you teach. That content will strengthen the foundation on which children will construct knowledge and discover meaning.

Let's be more specific about how the NSES will support and reinforce your constructivist teaching. I'll discuss this support within the three guiding principles of constructivism presented earlier in this section:

1. **Naive conceptions.** *A person never really knows the world as it is. Each person constructs beliefs about what is real.*

   The most basic support for this principle comes from the existence of the NSES themselves. Since we finally have science standards, you, as a teacher, have something against which to compare students' prior knowledge and beliefs. If you listen carefully to children, you'll hear some amazing things about how they think the world works. Unfortunately, some of those beliefs are simply wrong!

   What you need to do is first carefully study the standards to ascertain within which standard children's inaccurate knowledge and misconceptions lie. Then, you can take guidance from the chapters of this book and other resources to properly address the deficiencies.

   Here are two examples:

   A child says: "I think that the moon followed us when my mom walked me to Janet's house for a sleepover."

   This misconception can be dealt with by providing content and experiences related to Earth and Space Sciences Standards ESS 2 and ESS 3—"Objects in the sky" and "Changes in earth and sky."

   A child says: "My dad said Becky caught a cold because she played outside without her jacket on."

   This misconception can be dealt with by providing content and experiences related to Science in Personal and Social Perspectives Standard SPSP 1—"Personal health."

Make the Case *An Individual or Group Challenge*

● **The Problem**

Providing a rich learning environment for children may require the teacher to take them out of the traditional classroom occasionally and into the real world. Sometimes, it is difficult for new teachers to identify real-world experiences that will really improve children's achievement in science.

● **Assess Your Prior Knowledge and Beliefs**

What do you presently believe about the way in which children learn both in and out of the classroom?

1. Children learn best from direct experience with natural objects and phenomena.

   _____ agree   _____ disagree

   Your evidence: _____

2. Hands-on science experiences automatically reinforce children's learning.

   _____ agree   _____ disagree

   Your evidence: _____

3. A child's prior knowledge and beliefs should be assessed before new experiences are introduced to ensure that the experiences will be meaningful.

   _____ agree   _____ disagree

   Your evidence: _____

4. Children have few misconceptions about the natural world.

   _____ agree   _____ disagree

   Your evidence: _____

5. For highly able children, it probably makes little difference whether direct or hands-on instruction is used in the classroom.

   _____ agree   _____ disagree

   Your evidence: _____

6. Because children progress through identifiable stages of development, teachers should provide experiences that fit only the stage of development indicated by the children's age.

   _____ agree   _____ disagree

   Your reasoning: _____

● **The Challenge**

Integrate your knowledge of how children learn into one paragraph that will provide a rationale for taking the children to locations beyond the school grounds. Your intention is to use this paragraph in a letter you will send (with your principal's permission) to community leaders who may be willing to donate funds for this curriculum enrichment project.

2. **Assimilation.** *Students try to reconcile new experiences and data with their present understanding so that the new data support and deepen, but do not change their fundamental mental model.*

The NSES clearly state that children should have the ability both to do scientific inquiry and to understand scientific inquiry (see Content Standard A). By creating science unit and lesson plans for children that are consistent with the methods advocated in this book, you will be infusing the curriculum with discovery experiences and activities that are based on careful inquiry. Children will learn to confront the differences between what they believe and what they discover with their own senses. Your challenge is to teach them that firsthand, personally gathered knowledge must override incorrect beliefs.

Here are two examples:

A young child might say: "Magnets pull on everything."

This misconception can be countered and replaced by having children actually do magnet activities in which they make discoveries to the contrary.

An older child might say: "It's starting to get hot. Earth must be getting closer to the sun."

This misconception can be countered by doing an activity in which children use models to discover that the inclination of Earth as it proceeds in orbit varies the surface area upon which a given amount of sunlight falls. In other words, when Earth is in a position in orbit in which the Northern Hemisphere is inclined away from the sun, a given amount of sunlight is spread over a larger surface area and people in the Northern Hemisphere have winter. The warming of Earth doesn't have much to do with how close Earth is to the sun.

3. **Accommodation.** *Students cannot reconcile new experiences and data with their present understanding, and they have to change their mental model to logically explain the experience.*

By helping children learn about *and* practice the scientific methods of inquiry—as expressed in the Science and Technology Standards S&T 2 and S&T 5, "Understanding about science and technology," and in History and Nature of Science Standards HNS 1 and HNS 2, "Science as a human endeavor"—children will learn that some ways of getting knowledge are better than others.

Children's lives and future success will be greatly enhanced if they learn to appreciate the importance of stating hypotheses, gathering information systematically, and withholding the drawing of conclusions until all the facts are in. If you emphasize the nature of careful scientific inquiry as children make discoveries, they will construct new and more complete understandings about the world in which they live.

Reality Check

As you begin a unit on light, you place an apple on the table and ask the children to write down whether they think that they would still be able to see the apple if the room was completely dark, (with no light present at all) and to explain their answer. After reading some of the answers, you realize that some children believe that they could see the apple because the light goes from their eyes to the apple. Explain how the children might use assimilation, accommodation, or a combination of both to change their mental model.

Gardner's Multiple Intelligences

If you intend to create a discovery-focused, inquiry-based classroom, in which children construct knowledge and discover meaning, you will need to consider a "raw material" that is more important than any aquarium, ant colony, or microscope in the room. That raw material is the intelligence of children.

Introductory psychology books tell us that intelligence is measured by IQ tests, which is a less than satisfying answer. At the very minimum, *intelligence* relates to a capacity to learn as well as an ability to apply that learning. It is usually reported as a number called an *intelligence quotient,* or *IQ.* Someone of normal or average intelligence has an IQ of 100.

How will knowing that number for each of your students help you create a classroom in which all children can construct knowledge and discover meaning? For instance, would knowing that Maria has an IQ of 135 and Ricky has an IQ of 110 change how you teach Maria and Ricky? Probably not. In fact, this traditional way of measuring and reporting a child's theoretical capacity to learn will be of little help as you plan science experiences that are responsive to individual differences.

Gardner's Original Theory   Howard Gardner has suggested a radically new way of thinking about intelligence. Early in his work, he discovered seven different intelligences that he believes each of us has to various degrees:

1. Logical-mathematical
2. Linguistic
3. Musical
4. Spatial
5. Bodily-kinesthetic
6. Interpersonal
7. Intrapersonal[3]

According to Gardner's theory, each child can be viewed as having a greater or lesser capacity to learn in each specific area. This means, in turn, that you as a teacher can focus on particular intelligences as you create science-learning experiences. You can teach to each child's strengths and find appropriate ways to help him or her grow in weak areas.

Gardner's Addition: Naturalist Intelligence   In more recent years, Gardner's work has led to what he describes as *naturalist intelligence:* the ability to discern subtle characteristics and patterns and then easily group objects or events in appropriate categories.[4]

As a science teacher, the possibility that this intelligence exists could be very important, since you might be able to identify how much individuals are "science prone" based on their measured naturalist intelligence. Knowing this could help you adjust your teaching to build on the abilities of children who have strong naturalist intelligence and to develop ways to be more responsive to children who have a more modest level of naturalist intelligence. Adjustments might include providing some children with more sophisticated observation and classification challenges and others with more time to complete work that requires high levels of naturalist intelligence. Making adjustments like these is at the heart of constructivist teaching, as doing so helps you capitalize on the wide range of intelligences a child might have.

See Figure 2.3 for a few real-world examples of how you can help children grow in all eight of Gardner's multiple intelligences.

Figure 2.3 Gardner's theory of multiple intelligences has implications and many practical applications for providing a variety of learning experiences in the classroom.

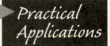

Practical Applications

Gardner's Theory of Multiple Intelligences for Your Science Classroom

1. *Logical-mathematical*

    EXAMPLES
    - Emphasize the underlying patterns children observe in science activities.
    - Have children list the steps they undertook in an activity and what they thought at each step.

2. *Linguistic*

    EXAMPLES
    - Emphasize writing down predictions, observations, and so on in science journals and the importance of using appropriate descriptive words and new terminology.
    - Encourage children to maintain their own science dictionaries, which will include new science terms and drawings to illustrate word meanings.

3. *Musical*

    EXAMPLES
    - Whenever possible, use vocal and instrumental music selections to accompany the introduction of new concepts. For example, use songs related to the seasons when carrying out a unit on climate.
    - When teaching a unit on sound, emphasize the connections to music, such as the effect of changing the thickness of a string or the length of the air column of an instrument.

4. *Spatial*

    EXAMPLE
    - Have children express what they have learned through drawings and models.

5. *Bodily-kinesthetic*

    EXAMPLES
    - Encourage children to use equipment that builds upon coordination skills, such as the microscope, balance, and hand lens.
    - Wherever possible, have children demonstrate new learnings through movement and dance. For example, children might create a dance to illustrate the expansion of a balloon resulting from increasing the energy of motion of the molecules contained within it.

6. *Interpersonal*

    EXAMPLES
    - Have children create simulated television advertising on issues investigated in class, such as the environment or proper nutrition.
    - When doing cooperative group work, provide time for children to process how well their group has worked on a science project.

7. *Intrapersonal*

    EXAMPLE
    - Provide opportunities for children to informally assess their interest in science, how well they are learning, and how they feel about matters related to science and technology.

8. *Naturalist*

    EXAMPLE
    - Early in the school year, give children sets of natural objects or pictures of natural objects or events they have not previously seen (e.g., rocks, leaves, pictures of various cloud types). Then ask them to observe and group members of each set.

Be careful not to interpret Gardner's intelligences as exclusive domains. Most students will possess each intelligence to a degree. Some students may be more adept at processing information in a particular domain.

Alternative Learning Styles

Go to **MyEducationLab**, select the topic Diverse Learners, watch the simulation entitled "Providing Instructional Supports: Facilitating Mastery of New Skills," and complete the questions that accompany it.

Think about what's the best way for you to learn. Is it enough to read the material and perhaps highlight key points here and there? Do you take notes, as well? Or does your best learning come from discussing the ideas with others or from doing a project or activity? And what about the person sitting next to you in a class? Does he or she learn in the same way that you do?

Constructivism is based on the idea that we are unique as a result of our different life experiences and that these experiences result in our individual knowledge and beliefs. It is these differences in knowledge and beliefs that make us different from one another. And because we are all fundamentally different in this sense, we will all learn differently, too. We have individual *learning styles*. And for you, as a science teacher, the implications of this are enormous.

One of your greatest challenges will be creating a classroom atmosphere and learning experiences that optimize learning for children with a diversity of learning abilities. It is not unusual for classrooms to have students with emotional, physical, and cognitive disabilities, gifted talents, or English language barriers. Differentiated learning and Universal Design for Learning (UDL) provide important teaching strategies that address the range of learning styles often encountered in a classroom.

Differentiated instruction acknowledges that all children do not learn alike and that instruction should provide several options for learning. Teachers need to create flexible, yet focused learning experiences that recognize the diversity of learning approaches.

UDL is an approach to teaching that facilitates differentiated instruction. It is similar in its approach to universal design in architecture by integrating structures everyone can use. Curb cuts and ramps that benefit wheelchair users are equally accessible by ambulatory people. Likewise, graphic organizers, visual displays, and vocabulary lists benefit all students, not just those with reading challenges. UDL is based on the following three general strategies:

Multiple means of representation: provide learners various ways of acquiring information and knowledge

Multiple means of expression: provide learners alternatives for demonstrating what they know and learn

Multiple means of engagement: pique learners' interests, challenge them appropriately, and motivate them to learn

Differentiated learning and UDL will play an integral role in lesson plans and strategies developed in Chapter 9.

If you are an experienced teacher who has attended many in-service workshops or courses or you are a preservice teacher who has had a variety of courses concerning how to teach, you may have heard and learned about learning styles. This is an interesting area of study because so many experts have their own ideas about the learning styles that people may have. Some expound about convergent and divergent thinkers; some emphasize the idea that some people prefer concrete experiences and others prefer abstract discussions of ideas and principles; some suggest that people can be grouped on the basis of whether they respond quickly (impulsive) or think first and talk or act later (reflective). See Figure 2.4 for some practical applications of this theory.

Figure 2.4   An understanding of individual learning styles can help you prepare science experiences that all children can learn from and enjoy.

Learning Styles for Your Science Classroom

1. *It is likely that children prefer to learn in different ways.*

   EXAMPLE • Study curriculum materials to ascertain whether they will accommodate differences in learning styles, and then develop some alternative teaching techniques. For example, if children are expected to name and describe the functions of the organs of the digestive system, study the unit carefully and try to come up with two or three different ways for children to learn this information.

2. *You can tell a great deal about how children learn by observing how they deal with new learning experiences.*

   EXAMPLE • Early in the year, provide activities that include studying a section in a reference book, doing hands-on activities, doing library research, and working with a computer program. Observe how various children approach each task and their relative success with each.

3. *Provide a range of experiences in the classroom so that all children have opportunities to put their preferred learning styles to use as often as possible.*

   EXAMPLE • Think about the extent to which the activities for each unit are the same or different in terms of what children actually do, and consider how you could build in variations in approach. For example, suppose you realize that all the activities for a unit on sound require the children to do the activity first, observe phenomena, and then report results. To accommodate children who have trouble with this approach, adapt a few of the activities early in the unit, so that children have the option of reading and talking about a concept before beginning an activity.

4. *Familiarize yourself with the needs of your students.*

   EXAMPLE • Review Individualized Education Plans and speak with guidance counselors or previous teachers. Are there students in your class for whom English is a second language? Do any of the students have physical disabilities such as hearing or visual impairments? Are there children with learning disabilities among your students?

5. *Study the curriculum materials to ascertain whether they will accommodate a variety of learning options. Look for ways that you can incorporate multiple means of representation, expression, and engagement.*

   EXAMPLE • As an engagement exercise, you plan to have students distinguish the sounds of mystery objects in a drop box, but this will be difficult for the hearing impaired students. Therefore, you could place the drop box on an improvised drum made out of a box with a balloon stretched across the top. All students can put their fingertips on the drumhead and feel the vibrations of different objects when they are dropped. This tactile experience not only benefits the hearing impaired students but also introduces all students to the role of vibrations in sound and sets the foundation for inquiries about frequency and pitch.

Summary

Constructivism, a useful theory about how children learn, has evolved from classical learning theories such as behaviorism and cognitivism. Constructivism recognizes that individuals enter a learning situation with prior knowledge and that individuals modify or change their view of the world (mental models) through assimilation and/or accommodation. Learning is the acquisition of usable knowledge that can be recognized and applied (transferred) in a novel context. The challenge for you as a teacher is to help children replace naive conceptions or lack of knowledge about the natural world by constructing more accurate and complete understandings.

Additional interesting insights about teaching and learning come from the NSES and from the idea that each of us has a preferred style of learning. Children come to our classrooms with a wide range of abilities. The more options available for learning experiences that challenge and deepen mental models the more likely children will encounter rich learning experiences that connect with their learning styles. Differentiated instruction and UDL are two approaches that help us optimize learning for children with a diversity of learning styles.

Going Further

On Your Own

1. Informally assess the extent to which you can apply your knowledge of the NSES, UDL, and learning styles to support constructivist teaching in an actual science classroom. Do this by interviewing a primary-, elementary-, or middle-grade teacher to determine what factors he or she believes affect how well a child learns science and what types of science experiences happen in the classroom. Gather as much information as you can without guiding the interview toward any of the ideas from this chapter. After the interview, make a list that summarizes the key points made by the teacher. Categorize the items with respect to their relevance to constructivism, the standards, multiple intelligences, and learning styles. (Be mindful of preserving the confidentiality of your interviewee in any summary report you prepare.)

2. Interview a school principal to determine what he or she believes are the key factors that affect the quality of science instruction in the school. After the interview, prepare a chart that relates key phrases from the interview to the major ideas of this chapter.

3. Based on your personal experiences as a student or teacher, to what extent are behavioral principles applied when children have science experiences? Provide as many firsthand examples as you can.

4. Based on your personal experiences as a student or teacher, to what extent are cognitivist principles applied when children have science experiences? Provide as many firsthand examples as you can.

5. Based on your personal experiences as a student in science classrooms, would you say that you have a preferred style of learning that leads to success in such environments? If you would, identify the factors that contribute to your preference.

On Your Own or in a Cooperative Learning Group

6. Have each member of the group interview at least one child to find out about his or her knowledge or beliefs about a key concept from the life, earth/space, or physical sciences and technology. In the course of each interview, be sure to encourage the child to respond to questions that might reveal some naive conceptions. Use questions such as these: Why doesn't the moon fall to the earth? Are whales fish? Does the sun move across the sky? Is a sweater warm?

7. As a group, reflect on the difference between *assimilation* and *accommodation*. Have group members identify one or two naive conceptions that they once had about the life, earth/space, or physical sciences and technology. Have individuals indicate whether it was difficult or easy for them to revise these conceptions when they learned facts to the contrary or had direct experiences that produced results in conflict with their conceptions. Based on this group work, prepare a list of implications for teachers who wish to create science classroom environments in which children have experiences that reveal naive conceptions and lead to new learnings.

Resources for Discovery Learning

Internet Resources

To access these helpful websites, go to **MyEducationLab,** select Resources, and then Web Links. To learn more, click on the following link and you will easily be directed to the website.

- **North Central Regional Educational Laboratory:** www.ncrel.org/sdrs/areas/issues/content/cntareas/science/sc500.htm

- **Science Myths** www.amasci.com/miscon/miscon.html

Print Resources

Suggested Readings

Aram, Roberta J., and Bradshaw, Brenda. "How Do Children Know What They Know?" *Science and Children* 39, no. 2 (October 2001): 28–33.

Association for Supervision and Curriculum Development. "The Science of Learning [special section]." *Educational Leadership* 58, no. 3 (November 2000): 8–78.

Avraamidou, L., et. al. "Giving Priority to Evidence in Science Teaching: A First-Year Elementary Teacher's Specialized Practices and Knowledge." *Journal of Research in Science Teaching* 42 (November 2005): 965–986.

Bransford, Jon, Cocking, Rodney, and Brown, Ann. *How People Learn: Brain, Mind, Experience, and School.* Washington, DC: National Academy Press, 2000.

Buck, Gloria A., and Meduna, Patricia. "Exploring Alternative Conceptions." *Science Scope* 25, no. 1 (September 2001): 41–45.

Burris, S., et. al. "The Language of Learning Styles." *Techniques* (Association for Career and Technical Education) 83, no. 2 (February 2008): 44–48.

Farenga, Stephen J., et al. "Balancing the Equity Equation: The Importance of Experience and Culture in Science Learning." *Science Scope* 26, no. 5 (February 2003): 12–15.

Fetters, Marcia, et al. "Making Science Accessible: Strategies to Meet the Needs of a Diverse Student Population." *Science Scope* 26, no. 5 (February 2003): 26–29.

Flores, M. M. "Universal Design in Elementary and Middle School." *Childhood Education* 84, no. 4 (Summer 2008).

Frazier, Richard. "Rethinking Models." *Science Scope* 26, no. 4 (January 2003): 29–33.

Kang, N. H. "Elementary Teachers' Epistemological and Ontological Understanding of Teaching for Conceptual Learning." *Journal of Research in Science Teaching* 44, no. 9 (November 2007): 1292–1317.

Levy, H. M. "Meeting the Needs of All Students through Differentiated Instruction: Helping Every Child Reach and Exceed Standards." *The Clearing House* 81, no. 4 (March/April 2008): 161–164.

Otero, V. K., et al. "Preservice Elementary Teachers' Views of Their Students' Prior Knowledge of Science." *Journal of Research in Science Teaching* 45, no. 4 (April 2008): 497–523.

Pusey, Douglas. "Accessible Reading Assignments." *Science Scope* 26, no. 5 (February 2003): 44–46.

Science Scope 26, no. 4 (January 2003). (Entire issue emphasizes how to address misconceptions about science.)

Searson, Robert, and Dunn, Rita. "The Learning-Style Teaching Model." *Science and Children* 38, no. 5 (February 2001): 22–26.

Van Klaveren, Karen, et al. "How Do Your Students Learn?" *Science Scope* 25 no. 7 (April 2002): 24–29.

Yilmaz, K. "Constructivism: Its Theoretical Underpinnings, Variations, and Implications for Classroom Instruction." *Educational Horizons* 86, no. 3 (Spring 2008): 161–172.

Notes

1. M. H. Schneps and P. M. Sadler, *A Private Universe* (Harvard-Smithsonian Center for Astrophysics: Pyramid Films, 1988).

2. John D. Bransford, Ann L. Brown, and Rodney R. Cocking, editors. *How People Learn: Brain, Mind, Experience.* (Washington, D.C.: National Academy Press, 1999).

3. Thomas Armstrong, *Multiple Intelligences in the Classroom* (Washington, DC: Association for Supervision and Curriculum Development, 1994), pp. 2–3.

4. Kathy Checkley, "The first seven . . . and the eighth: A conversation with Howard Gardner," *Educational Leadership* 55, no. 1 (September 1997): 8, 9.

chapter 3

The Inquiry Process Skills

How can I help children use the inquiry process skills to make discoveries?

▶ **Getting Started**

Her lips are starting to swell and crack under the broiling desert sun. Hot dry air has been relentlessly attacking since daybreak. She stops for a moment, lifts the bandana covering her mouth and nose, and shakes out her stringy hair. Incredibly, with that headshake, something catches her attention. To her left, a tiny, gray fossil bone fragment sticks out from the soil. The last gust of wind must have revealed it. Now she doesn't feel the sun or the heat or the dust at all! Her full attention is focused on the fragment.

A series of images flashes through her mind as she compares what she can tell about this fragment to what she already knows. Her mental pictures are of dinosaur skeletons, and none has the anatomical structure into which this tiny bone would fit. It is a toe bone, for sure—but one she has never seen before. Her heart starts to race at the thought of this.

From her grimy tool pack, she carefully pulls several tiny dental picks and small brushes and gently works away the material around the bone. With each gentle poke and sweep of the brush, she grasps more clearly what has just been revealed to her eyes

alone: A brand-new dinosaur has stuck its toe into her world and ours. Her careful observation has led to an extraordinary discovery.

She will draw the fossil, photograph it, plot its location, and then ever so slowly search the surrounding area for more fragments. Eventually, she will pull from the reluctant earth a creature that so far has only been imagined. A wonderful discovery has been made—and she made it!

Discovery: The Destination

When we discover, we find or gain knowledge, usually for the first time. And while the act of discovery may only take an instant, getting there can take a long, long time.

When we teach science with the focus on discovery, we prepare children to make their personal discoveries with our strong guidance. We give them their very own "tool packs." And with any luck at all, they will use those tools in a variety of contexts all through their lives. Only a few children will find brand-new dinosaurs, but all of them will use the tools of scientific inquiry to unearth the facts and develop the concepts, principles, attitudes, and values that will help them lead full and productive lives.

It's now time to focus on how you can make discovery learning a central feature of every class you teach. First, we'll look at a formal definition of *discovery learning* that will give direction to the science units and lessons you plan and teach.

● What Is Discovery?

"Discovery simply means coming to know something you didn't know before."

Discovery learning happens when a child uncovers new information or gleans new insight about how to approach a problem or task and then completes the task or solves the problem on her or his own. It is an individual and personal experience. *Classrooms don't discover; individual children do.*

More important than uncovering new information, discovery learning is obtaining new ways to find answers. Discovery seeks explanations based primarily on observation and description. Discovery and inquiry are closely related; however, Leslie Trowbridge and Roger Bybee make an important distinction between discovery and inquiry. "Discovery occurs when an individual is mainly involved in using his mental processes to mediate (or discover) some concept or principle."[1] True inquiry goes beyond discovery to seek verification through identifying questions and designing thoughtful investigations based on hypotheses, predictions, experimentation, data collection, and analysis.[2] As an elementary school teacher, you will emphasize discovery skills as a foundation for inquiry.

● How Do I Teach So Discovery Learning Happens?

To teach for discovery learning, you must, wherever possible, provide hands-on, mind-stretching experiences that will enable children to use their knowledge and skills to make discoveries. Your challenge is to provide the physical and intellectual context that ensures that these new discoveries are related to what learning has come before and to what learning will follow. Discovery learning does not happen in a vacuum. It is connected to the past and to the future. It is your job to be sure that these connections are made.

Your role as teacher goes beyond providing students with the opportunity to discover; you must also teach them how to discover. Your charge is to craft interactive learning experiences that guide students to develop the intellectual and physical tools necessary to seek explanations.

● Is Discovery Time Really "Circus Time"?

OK, it's true: Some science classrooms *do* become accidental "circuses." It happens from time to time when teachers make the naive assumption that if they just provide a super-rich context of science "stuff," then good things will automatically happen. Well, sometimes they do, and sometimes they don't.

There is nothing accidental about good teaching. Teaching discovery does not happen by simply providing an engaging activity and hoping children will learn something of value. Avoid the temptation to let the activity drive the learning. It is not productive to build a model of a volcano as a fun activity without carefully building it around a lesson about convection and pressure. Select activities carefully and use them as experiences to develop the targeted learning objectives.

Inquiry: The Path

By now, you should understand that the point of your science experiences with children is to foster discovery learning. Remember to think of discovery learning as a *destination*.

You must also be firm in your conviction that discovery learning does not happen by accident. It must be clearly guided—by you. In fact, some educators use the term *guided discovery* to describe learning experiences for children.

The obvious question at this point (which I really hope is running through your mind) is, How do I guide children so they really get on the path of discovery and then actually make their own discoveries? Recall from earlier chapters that that path is *inquiry*.

● What Is Inquiry?

Within the current educational scene, the term *inquiry* has far too many definitions, and that's unfortunate. I will explain it as clearly as I can, beginning with this straightforward definition:

> *Inquiry is the careful and systematic method of asking questions and seeking explanations.*

To further enhance your understanding of the term, let me share this detailed definition proposed by the National Science Education Standards (NSES):

> Scientific inquiry refers to the diverse ways in which scientists study the natural world and propose explanations based on the evidence derived from their work. Inquiry also refers to the activities of students in which they develop knowledge and understanding of scientific ideas, as well as an understanding of how scientists study the natural world.[3]

As a teacher, you will use inquiry to teach science as well as teach students to inquire. You should have a fairly clear understanding of what discoveries will be made and how to guide children's inquiry in fruitful ways. The information in the following section will help you with that.

● Examples of Inquiry Methods

In describing *inquiry* in further detail, the NSES give examples of activities that children or scientists would do if they were engaged in inquiry:

1. Making observations
2. Posing questions
3. Examining books and other sources of information to see what is already known

4. Planning investigations

5. Reviewing what is already known based on experimental evidence

6. Using tools to gather, analyze, and interpret data

7. Proposing answers, explanations, and predictions and communicating the results

8. Identifying assumptions, using critical and logical thinking, and considering alternative explanations[4]

This is an overwhelming range of activities! Fortunately, over the years, these ideas have been transformed into much more useful forms. Educators have identified the specific classroom skills that children need in order to actively participate in the activities listed above. They are commonly called the *inquiry process skills* or *skills of inquiry*.

A little later in this chapter, we will learn what these skills are. (See the section titled "The Inquiry Process Skills," on pages 46–53.) But for now, I want to turn your attention to a topic that will help you grasp how to incorporate discovery-focused, inquiry-based science in your classroom. Educators have devised a way for you to think about this "big picture" in a simple and effective way. It's called the *learning cycle*.

The Learning Cycle

A Framework for Teaching Inquiry: The 5E Instructional Strategy

Go to **MyEducationLab**, select the topic Inquiry, watch the video entitled "The Learning Cycle," and complete the question that accompanies it.

Learning cycles are models of how people encounter and acquire new knowledge. They provide a framework for the educator to design effective learning experiences. Over the years, there have been several variations on the learning cycle. We will use one in this book that is commonly used among science educators to frame the inquiry-based, discovery learning that is characteristic of science education. It consists of five phases commonly referred to as the 5E's: Engagement, Exploration, Explanation, Elaboration, and Evaluation.[5,6] See Table 3.1.

Go to **MyEducationLab**, select the topic Earth and Space Science, and read the lesson plan entitled "How Can You Measure How Fast the Wind Blows?" "How Does the Wind Speed Vary with Location and Time?" for an example of Engage, Explore, and Explain.

Engagement   Engagement piques children's interest, solicits prior knowledge, and establishes focus usually in the form of an essential question. The essential question will anchor the lesson as it progresses. Often the engagement presents children with a discrepant event that challenges their perception of the world and encourages them to raise questions, which are the foundations of inquiry. It is during the engagement that children construct their initial descriptive model.

Exploration   Exploration provides opportunities for children to encounter new information necessary to answer the essential question. The new information should challenge the children's mental models and lead to assimilation or accommodation resulting in a deeper mental model that more accurately explains the phenomenon. Exploration activities are student centered. They may be in the form of information gathering, experimentation, or how-to activities. Stations, interactive demonstrations, and experimentation are just some of the methods that may be used during the exploration. It is not unusual for children to experience some cognitive dissonance during the exploration as their prior knowledge is challenged.

Explanation   Explanation is an opportunity for the children to express what they have discovered during the exploration. You may be tempted to explain what the children should have learned rather than listening to what the children learned. However, if the exploration is effective, children should make connections that answer the essential

Go to **MyEducationLab**, select the topic Inquiry, watch the video entitled "Explanation," and complete the question that accompanies it.

question. If the children express misconceptions, you must correct them by challenging the children's incorrect mental model in light of new data. This is the phase at which an explanatory model is constructed.

Elaboration   Elaboration is a time for children to apply, exercise, and transfer their newly acquired knowledge. Often the elaboration challenges children to recognize the application of their new understanding in a different context, reinforcing and deepening their understanding of the new information.

Evaluation   Evaluation is both formative and summative. Formative evaluation occurs throughout the learning experience to inform teachers and children about their progress. The teacher receives feedback through a variety of message checks about

Table 3.1   Summary of the 5E instructional model as it relates to the progression of inquiry

Phase	Instructional Goals	Learning Goals
Engagement	Create discrepant events Encourage children to express prior knowledge Prompt Question Process children's responses Listen	Develop a descriptive model Express prior knowledge Generate questions
Exploration	Orchestrate learning experiences for students to encounter new knowledge and deepen descriptive models Question Coach	Deepen descriptive model Employ experimental model Encounter new knowledge through observation, experimentation, manipulation Make connections Generate, collect, record data
Explanation	Restate essential question Process student responses Reinforce correct responses Correct misconceptions	Create an explanatory model Articulate response to essential question Correct misconceptions
Elaboration	Create challenges for students to apply and transfer newly acquired knowledge	Reinforce explanatory model Apply new knowledge in a novel context
Evaluation	Collect student feedback through message checks Identify specific benchmarks to gauge student progress toward concept attainment Modify lesson in response to student feedback Create summative assessments to evaluate individual student learning	Demonstrate mastery of new knowledge at the nominal, descriptive, and explanatory levels of understanding (see Chapter 6)

Go to **My EducationLab**, select the topic Inquiry, watch the video entitled "Evaluation," and complete the question that accompanies it.

whether children are making progress toward the learning objectives, while children receive feedback to reinforce or redirect them on the right track. Summative assessment usually occurs at the end of a unit to inform the teacher that the children are learning what the teacher intended to teach. See Chapter 6 for a more in depth look at evaluation and assessment.

It is not necessary to use all the phases of the 5E instructional model in each lesson. For example, the first lesson in a unit may be engagement, while the following three unit lessons may be explorations, and the fifth lesson an explanation. The 5E instructional strategy will be used as a framework for creating lessons and units throughout this text.

The Inquiry Process Skills

Recall that science is about the process of seeking explanations through a progression of inquiry: descriptive modeling, explanatory modeling, and experimental modeling. The 5E instructional strategy is a framework for designing lessons during which children experience this progression to deepen their understanding of science content and process. In doing so, they will develop and reinforce a range of important process skills associated with the progression of inquiry listed in Table 3.1. In the following section, I discuss specific inquiry process skills in the context of the progression of inquiry.

Inquiry Process Skills Used to Create Descriptive Models

Go to **MyEducationLab**, select the topic Inquiry, and read the lesson plan entitled "How Can You Improve Your Inquiry Skills?"

Process skills can be closely associated with the phases of the progression of inquiry. We begin with the inquiry skills commonly associated with descriptive modeling.

- Observing
- Using space/time relationships
- Using numbers
- Questioning

Project 2061

Implications for Including the Inquiry Process Skills in Your Teaching

Project 2061 has a very strong emphasis on teaching inquiry process skills to students. It suggests that teachers should help students look at the world in a more scientific or objective manner, that students should be actively involved in exploration, and that everyone should be aware that scientific exploration is an important enterprise of modern society. Project 2061 addresses these three areas within the benchmark "The nature of science":

- The scientific world view
- Scientific inquiry
- The scientific enterprise

To find specific recommendations for each area, visit the Project 2061 website at **www.project2061.org/.**

- Classifying
- Measuring
- Communicating

Observing

▶ *What Does It Mean?*

Observing means using the senses to obtain information, or *data*, about objects and events. It is the most basic process of science. Casual observations spark almost every inquiry we make about our environment. Organized observations form the basis for more structured investigations. Acquiring the ability to make careful observations will create a foundation for making inferences or hypotheses that can be tested by further observations.

Careful, organized observations require the observer to take an active role. It is easy to confuse active observation with passive looking. The active observer uses five fundamental questions of inquiry proposed by Peter Bergethon:[7]

- What are the elements of the system?
- What are the properties of the elements?
- What is the context or background space of the system?
- What are the rules of interaction among the elements?
- What are the emergent properties of the system?

Sample Activity

Children can observe that different animals have very different solutions to the problem of getting from place to place. By directly observing animals outdoors or displayed in the classroom, children can describe whether each animal walks, swims, or flies. You may wish to challenge children to identify animals that can do all three—for example, ducks.

Observing is the most basic of all the inquiry process skills.

Using the Inquiry Process Skills to Create a Descriptive Model of a Butterfly

Practical Application

Table 3.2 illustrates how the fundamental questions of inquiry may be used to generate a simple descriptive model of a butterfly. Note how the descriptive model facilitates other inquiry process skills such as **enumeration** (number of legs) and **ordination** (head is above the thorax). **Questioning** is inherent in the fundamental questions of inquiry. Although these are general questions that apply to any system, construction of the descriptive model inevitably leads to more system-specific questions: "Why do some butterflies have brightly colored wings while others have very plainly colored wings?" "How do butterflies eat?" and so on. These questions can be selected and used by the teacher to address learning objectives. In fact, as the teacher, you will deliberately craft the engagement experience to pique curiosity around the questions that you want to address. **Measuring** is simply an application of technology to deepen the accuracy of the descriptive model. Children can measure the length of the head, thorax, and abdomen, the height of the wings, or the overall length and height of the butterfly. When several descriptive models of butterflies are collected, children can compare and **classify** the butterflies according to elements and properties. Children may use **space/time relationships,** noting that the butterflies move among similar types of flowers and are most active at certain times of day. Lastly, children need to **communicate** their models, which can be achieved through a variety of modalities such as writing, drawing, verbalizing, or simulating. Note the dependency of a good descriptive model on the implementation of inquiry process skills.

Using Space/Time Relationships

▶ *What Does It Mean?*

All objects occupy a place in space. The inquiry skill *using space/time relationships* involves the ability to discern and describe directions, spatial arrangements, motion and speed, symmetry, and rate of change.

Sample Activity

Provide each child or group of children with a small metal mirror (metal instead of glass as a safety precaution) and half an apple or a pear made by a lengthwise cut through the fruit. Ask children to discover if the right and left sides of the half are symmetrical. They can put the mirror lengthwise down the middle of the fruit section to see if they can observe the image of a complete fruit.

Using Numbers

▶ *What Does It Mean?*

We need numbers to manipulate measurements, order objects, and classify objects. The amount of time spent on the activities devoted to *using numbers* should depend largely on the school's mathematics program. It is important for children to realize that the ability to use numbers is also a fundamental process of science.

Sample Activity

Help young children learn to compare sets with the use of natural objects such as rocks. Place a collection of rocks on a table. Pick out a set of six rocks, and ask various children to come to the collection and make a set containing one more element

Table 3.2   Description of a butterfly—based on the fundamental questions of inquiry

Elements	Properties	Background space	Rules of interaction	Emergent properties
• Legs ⟶	• 4 long, 2 short, black	• Light (sunlight?) seemingly outside, on a plant	• Legs and wings attached to thorax	• Colorful
• Antennae ⟶	• Black 2, long		• Head in front of thorax	• Still
• Wings ⟶	• Yellow, black, blue, curved, 2 wings			• Fragile
• Head ⟶	• Black, round, round proboscis		• Abdomen behind thorax	
• Thorax ⟶	• Red, black, larger than head		• Butterfly on leaf	
• Abdomen ⟶	• Yellow, black dots, 8 segments			

than your set. Encourage children to use language such as the following to describe their set: "My set has seven, which is more than your set of six rocks." Do this with other sets of rocks.

Classifying

▶ What Does It Mean?

Classifying is the process scientists use to impose order on collections of objects or events. Classification schemes are used in science and other disciplines to identify objects or events and to show similarities, differences, and interrelationships.

Sample Activity

Ask children to bring pictures of plants and animals to school. Use the pictures from all the children to develop entries for a classification system.

Measuring

▶ What Does It Mean?

Measuring is the way observations are quantified. Skill in measuring requires, not only the ability to use measuring instruments properly, but also the ability to carry out calculations with these instruments. The process involves judgment about which instrument to use and when approximate rather than precise measurements are acceptable. Children can learn to measure length, area, volume, mass, temperature, force, and speed as they work on this process skill.

Sample Activity

Have children estimate the linear dimensions of classroom objects using centimeters, decimeters, or meters, and then use metersticks to measure the objects.

Communicating

▶ What Does It Mean?

Clear, precise communication is essential to all human endeavors and fundamental to all scientific work, which makes *communicating* skills valuable. Scientists communicate orally, with written words, and through the use of diagrams, maps, graphs, mathematical equations, and other visual demonstrations.

Sample Activity

Display a small animal such as a gerbil, hamster, or water snail. Ask children to write descriptions of the organism, emphasizing the need to include details such as size, shape, color, texture, and method of locomotion.

● Inquiry Process Skills Used to Create an Explanatory Model

- Inferring
- Hypothesizing

Inferring

▶ What Does It Mean?

Inferring is using logic to make assumptions from what we observe and question. The ability to distinguish between an observation and an inference is fundamental to clear thinking. An observation is an experience that is obtained through the senses. An inference is an assumption based on an observation. Consider the observation that butterflies are often found on flowering plants. One might infer that butterflies use the flowers as a source of food.

Sample Activity

Take children on a mini–field trip to a tree on school property, and have them prepare a list of observations about the ground at the base of the tree, the tree bark, and the leaves. Ask children to make inferences from their observations about the animals that may live in or near the tree (e.g., birds, insects, squirrels).

Hypotheses and Predictions

▶ What Do They Mean?

Hypotheses are often confused with predictions. A hypothesis, which begins with an explanatory model, is a proposed relationship put forth to explain a phenomenon. One might hypothesize that butterflies prefer yellow flowers. The *prediction* is the basis for an experiment. A prediction based on our hypothesis would be that if butterflies are presented with yellow flowers and white flowers, then the butterflies will land on the yellow flowers.

Sample Activity

Fill one plastic bag with cold air and one with hot air. (Use a hair dryer on low heat, being careful not to touch the bag with the hair dryer.) Ask your students to explain why the bag with hot air floated to the ceiling. They could hypothesize that hot air is lighter (less dense) than cold air. Ask them to make a testable prediction based on the hypothesis. For example, if we fill two equal size bags with hot air and cold air, the bag with hot air will weigh less.

Inquiry Process Skills Used to Create an Experimental Model

Experiments test predictions. A good experiment should test one variable and keep all other conditions the same. Failure to do so results in confusion about what variable caused the results.

Good experiments employ the following inquiry process skills:

- Predicting
- Identifying variables
  - Independent
  - Dependent
  - Controlled
- Designing experimental controls

Predicting

▶ *What Does It Mean?*

A *prediction* is a specific forecast of a future observation or event. Predictions are based on observations, measurements, and inferences about relationships between observed variables. A prediction that is not based on observation is only a guess. Accurate predictions result from careful observations and precise measurements.

Sample Activity

Have children construct a questionnaire about breakfast cereal preference and gather data from all the classrooms in the school except one. Have students analyze their data and make a prediction about the outcome of the survey of the children in the last room before polling those children.

Identifying Variables   Variables are factors that can make a difference in an investigation. Experimental design consists of one independent variable, one dependent variable, and several controlled variables.

1. **Independent variable**

   The *independent variable* is the variable being tested. It is the variable that the experimenter manipulates or changes. For example, if one were to follow through with an experiment to test the hypothesis that butterflies prefer yellow flowers, the independent variable is the color of the flowers.

2. **Dependent variable**

   The *dependent variable* is the change that is measured. It changes in response to the independent variable. In our example, the dependent variable would be the number of butterflies that are attracted to the yellow flower.

3. **Controlled variables**

   For an experiment to be informative it must measure the effects of just one variable. Therefore, the only variables that change are the independent and dependent variables. All the other factors that could change must be kept the same or *controlled*. Referring to the sample experiment, the same butterflies and types of flowers should be used under the same conditions such as location, lighting, time of day, and temperature.

4. Experimental control

The *experimental control* is a parallel experiment that is usually done to determine whether the independent variable is responsible for the observed effect. In the control, the factor being tested is not applied. In this case, one would replace the yellow flowers with white flowers to determine whether the butterflies display a preference for the substituted flowers.

Experimenting encompasses all of the basic and integrated inquiry process skills.

Sample Activity

Ask children whether bread will last longer (not become moldy) if it is kept at 4°C rather than at room temperature. Design an experiment by leaving one piece of bread in a plastic bag on a counter and one piece of bread in a plastic bag in a refrigerator at 4°C. Record the room temperature. Count the number of days until each piece of bread becomes moldy. The independent variable is temperature. The dependent variable is the time for the bread to become moldy. The controlled variables are bread from the same loaf, same size of bread pieces, same size and type of plastic bag, and the same handling procedures. The controlled experiment is bread stored at room temperature.

Interpreting Data

▶ *What Does It Mean?*

The process of *interpreting data* involves making predictions, inferences, and hypotheses from the data collected in an investigation. We are constantly interpreting data when we read weather maps, watch the news on television, and look at photographs in newspapers and magazines. Students should have had previous experience in observing, classifying, and measuring before the process of interpreting data is approached.

Sample Activity

Ask the students to interpret the data in the graph below, of the distance from the starting point a person on a bike is over a time period of 15 seconds.

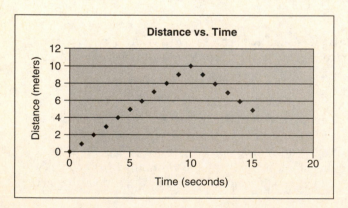

How far away from the starting point was the bike after 5 seconds? 10 seconds? 15 seconds?

How fast was the bike traveling expressed as meters per second during the first 10 seconds?

Describe what took place after 10 seconds.

Defining Operationally

▶ *What Does It Mean?*

When students use the *defining operationally* process, they define terms in the context of their own experiences. That is, they work with a definition instead of memorizing it. A definition that limits the number of things to be considered and is experiential is more useful than one that encompasses all possible variations that might be encountered. In the physical sciences, an operational definition is based on what is done and what is observed. In the biological sciences, an operational definition is often descriptive.

Sample Activity

Have students invent operational definitions for plant parts based on the functions of the parts they observe. For example, part of an operational definition for a *stem* is that "water moves up it." This definition might be derived by observing that a carnation stem placed in colored water serves to conduct the coloring to the petals. Part of the operational definition for a *bud* might include a reference to it as a site where students have observed a flower or a leaf emerge.

Make the Case *An Individual or Group Challenge*

● **The Problem**

Children in discovery-focused, inquiry-based classrooms may become so involved in their explorations that they spend too much time *doing* and too little time *thinking*.

● **Assess Your Prior Knowledge and Beliefs**

What are your present beliefs about each of the following?

1. Before engaging in an activity, children should establish a hypothesis.

   _____ agree   _____ disagree

   Your reasoning: _____

2. Even if there is an official recorder, all the children in a group should record their personal observations.

   _____ agree   _____ disagree

   Your reasoning: _____

3. As long as children have hands-on, inquiry-based experiences, they will learn the inquiry process skills.

   _____ agree   _____ disagree

   Your reasoning: _____

● **The Challenge**

Your state or province has awarded you a $500 grant for a single discovery-focused science project that involves a simulation of life in a space colony on Mars. At the end of the year, you must write a report describing what the children have learned. Describe how you would incorporate the children's mastery of the basic inquiry process skills as central elements of your report.

Summary

The science knowledge, concepts, skills, attitudes, and values that are the fabric of your curriculum are all the result of discoveries made over many years of scientific inquiry. One important approach to teaching children science is to create a classroom environment in which they make their own discoveries through careful inquiry about various aspects of the natural world.

Although there are many ways to foster discovery-focused, inquiry-based learning in the science classroom, one important strategy involves the five stage learning cycle, called the 5E's, that consists of engaging, exploring, explaining, elaborating, and evaluating. These stages can be the framework for both units and lesson plans to foster the discovery and construction of new knowledge. As children progress through these stages,

Reality Check

Watch the teaching video "Animal Behavior" on MyEducationLab. Use the chart below to identify the use of the inquiry process skills by students. To access the video, go to MyEducationLab, select the topic Life and Environmental Science, and watch the video entitled "Animal Behavior."

Inquiry process skills	Frequency count as ⊮	Comments
Observing		
Using space/time relationships		
Using numbers		
Questioning		
Classifying		
Measuring		
Communicating		
Predicting		
Identifying variables		
Independent		
Dependent		
Controlled		
Designing experimental controls		
Inferring		
Hypothesizing		

Watch the same video to identify evidence for each of the stages of the 5E instructional strategy.

they become actively involved in the progression of inquiry and a variety of science processes skills used in developing descriptive, explanatory, and experimental models. Use the 5E's as a guide to plan your science inquiry units and lessons. Look for the application of the inquiry process skills as evidence that children are inquiring in your science classroom.

Going Further

On Your Own

1. This chapter described a five-stage learning cycle that can be useful as you think about fostering discovery learning in the classroom. Pick a science topic that you might teach a group of children, and provide examples of specific things you might do to involve students in each stage of the cycle.

2. Some of the inquiry process skills discussed in this chapter are also used in the nonscience portions of the elementary/middle school curriculum (e.g., social studies, language arts, and so on). Select three inquiry process skills, and discuss how each might be used to integrate at least one other subject with science.

3. This chapter discussed the importance of using the inquiry process skills in doing hands-on science. What potential is there for an elementary- or middle-grade teacher to teach some of these skills through classroom demonstrations? Explain your response.

4. Some resistance to including the inquiry process skills comes from teachers who have not had much personal experience with science activities or experiments in college. To what extent did your college-level experience include opportunities to utilize the inquiry process skills?

On Your Own or in a Cooperative Learning Group

5. How might a week of classroom time (30 minutes per day) early in the school year be used to teach children in primary, elementary, or middle school that science is a way of doing things as well as an organizational collection of facts, concepts, and principles? Illustrate your idea with specific examples.

Resources for Discovery Learning

Internet Resources

To access these helpful websites, go to **MyEducationLab,** select Resources, and then Web Links. To learn more, click on the following links and you will easily be directed to each website.

*   **Constructivism and the Five E's:**
    www.miamisci.org/ph/lpintro5e.html

*   **Eisenhower National Clearinghouse: The Ohio State University:**
    www.enc.org/

*   **Exploratorium Institute for Inquiry:**
    www.exploratorium.edu/IFI/resources/websites.html

*   **Science Education Projects Funded by the National Science Foundation:**
    http://watt.enc.org/nsf.html

*   **The Science Learning Network:**
    www.sln.org/

*   **Professional Development Summer Opportunities for Teachers: NSF-Funded Projects:**
    www.ehr.nsf.gov/her/esie/teso/

*   **Project 2061: American Association for the Advancement of Science:**
    www.project2061.org/

Print Resources

Suggested Readings

Barman, Charles. *A Procedure for Helping Prospective Elementary Teachers Integrate the Learning Cycle into Science Textbooks.* Monograph 4. Arlington, VA: Council for Elementary Science International, an affiliate of the National Science Teachers Association, n.d.

Bybee, R. W., Taylor, J. A., Gardner, A., Van Scotter, P., Powell, J. C., Westbrook, A, and Landes, N. *The BSCS 5E Instructional Model: Origins, Effectiveness, and Applications Executive Summary.* Colorado Springs, CO: BSCS, 2006.

Colburn, Alan. "An Inquiry Primer." *Science Scope* 23, no. 6 (March 2000): 42–44.

Delisle, Robert. *How to Use Problem Based Learning in the Classroom.* Alexandria, VA: Association for Supervision and Curriculum Development, 1997.

Denniston, Erin. "What a Puzzle!" *Science and Children* 39, no. 8 (May 2002): 14–18.

Hall, Sue, and Hall, Dori. "Packing Peanut Properties." *Science and Children* 39, no. 5 (February 2002): 31–35.

Hammrich, Penny L., and Fadigan, Kathleen. "Investigations in the Science of Sports." *Science Scope* 26, no. 5 (February 2003): 30–35.

Hanuscin, D. L., et al. "Learning to Observe and Infer." *Science and Children* 45, no. 6 (February 2008): 56–57.

Inquiry and the National Science Education Standards: A Guide for Teaching and Learning. Center for Science, Mathematics, and Engineering Education (CSMEE), National Research Council. Washington, D.C.: National Academy Press, 2000.

Koschmann, Mark, and Shepardson, Dan. "A Pond Investigation." *Science and Children* 39, no. 8 (May 2002): 20–23.

McWilliams, Susan. "Journey into the Five Senses." *Science and Children* 40, no. 5 (February 2003): 38–43.

Morrison, J. A. "Individual **Inquiry** Investigations in an **Elementary Science** Methods Course." *Journal of Science Teacher Education* 19, no. 2 (April 2008): 117–134.

Pathways to the Science Standards: Elementary School Edition. Arlington VA: NSTA Press, 2000.

Pine, J., et al. "Students' Learning of Inquiry in 'Inquiry' Curricula." *Phi Delta Kappan* 88, no. 4 (December 2006): 308–313.

Shaw, Mike. "A Dastardly Density Deed." *Science Scope* 26, no. 4 (January 2003): 18–21.

Sitzman, Daniel. "Bread Making: Classic Biotechnology and Experimental Design." *Science Scope* 26, no. 4 (January 2003): 27–31.

Thompson, R., et al. "Investigating Minerals: Promoting Integrated Inquiry." *Science Activities* 44, no. 2 (Summer 2007): 56–60.

Thompson, S. L. "Inquiry in the Life Sciences: The Plant-in-a-Jar as a Catalyst for Learning." *Science Activities* 43, no. 4 (Winter 2007): 27–33.

Waffler, Elizabeth Sumner. "Inspired Inquiry." *Science and Children* 38, no. 4 (January 2001): 28–31.

Wittrock, Cathy A., and Barrow, Lloyd H. "Blow-by-Blow Inquiry." *Science and Children* 37, no. 5 (February 2000): 34–38.

Notes

1. L. W. Trowbridge and R. W. Bybee, *Becoming a Secondary School Science Teacher* 4th ed. (Columbus, OH: Merrill Publishing Co., 1986), p. 182.
2. Ibid., pp. 182–183.
3. National Research Council, *National Science Education Standards* (Washington, DC: National Academy Press, 1996), p. 23.
4. Ibid.
5. R. W. Bybee, et al. (2006). *The BSCS 5E Instructional Model: Origins, Effectiveness, and Applications.* (BSCS: Colorado Springs, CO).
6. You may encounter variations on the 5E model, such as the 6E model, which adds "e-search" representing explicit technology integration.
7. P. Bergethon, *Learning the Language of Patterns* (Holliston, MA: Symmetry Learning Systems, 1999).

chapter 4

Planning and Managing

How can I plan and manage inquiry-based, discovery-focused units and lessons?

 Getting Started

Children are beginning to gather in the school yard. Family and parents of the youngest children give a final hug and wave good-bye, pausing just out of sight only to peek back around the corner for one last look at their children as they begin the first day of school. Friendly teachers greet the younger children, who make their way tentatively into the school yard. The older children run without hesitation onto the playground, greeting classmates and immediately starting a spirited game of tag.

Suddenly, I am standing all alone in the classroom, the walls are bare and my plan book is empty. A wave of panic slowly begins to creep over me. In an instant the children are somehow sitting at their desks. Twenty-four little faces look up at me with great expectations. I have nothing to offer them.

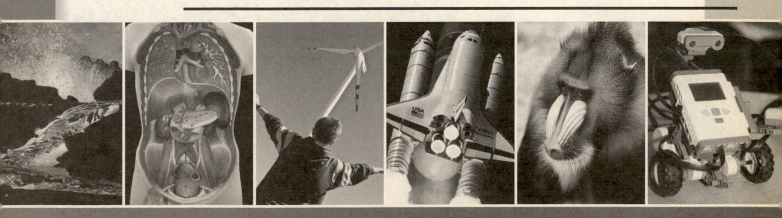

Several teachers have had similar dreams just before the start of a new school year. Although this chapter may not prevent such dreams, it will help you plan inquiry-based science lessons in advance so waking will be much more pleasant.

Curriculum, Unit Planning, and Lesson Planning—How Are They Different?

Sometimes the terms "curriculum," "unit," and "lesson" are used interchangeably, but they differ primarily in scope. Curricula are made up of a sequence of units and lessons that address a primary subject. Third-grade science or fourth-grade social studies are two examples of curricula. Units address subtopics within a curriculum, such as a unit on life cycles or the forces that shape the earth. Lessons address topics within a unit and target specific learning objectives. Describing the four stages of the butterfly life cycle or discovering how simple machines work are examples of lesson topics. As you read on, you will gain a deeper understanding of each term.

The Scope of the Science Curriculum

Imagine observing a tiny gnat walking across a pebble as lightning flashes in the sky. How does each component of this scene fit into the area of knowledge we call *science*? The gnat is understood through biology, the science of living things. The origin and characteristics of the pebble are understood through the earth/space sciences. The energy of the lightning flash and the atoms and molecules that make up the gnat and the pebble are understood

Good planning will result in dynamic and effective learning adventures for your students.

through the physical sciences. Each component of the scene represents one part of the *scope,* or breadth of content, of science.

The scope of the curriculum refers to the range and depth of content while the sequence of the curriculum refers to the order in which the content will be addressed. The scope of science illustrated in the brief example of the gnat, pebble, and lightning reminds us that science is an integration of earth/space, life, and physical sciences.

The *earth/space sciences* represent our knowledge of the origins of the universe and of our Earth in particular. They include astronomy, geology, meteorology, and other areas of study. The earth/space science topics commonly taught in elementary school include the following:

1. The stars, sun, and planets

2. The soil, rocks, and mountains

3. The weather

The *life sciences* include botany, zoology, and ecology. These disciplines are usually represented in the elementary science curriculum as the following topics:

1. The study of plants

2. The study of animals

3. The study of the relationship between plants and animals

4. The study of the relationship between living things and the environment

The *physical sciences* include physics and chemistry. Physics is concerned with the relationship between matter and energy. Chemistry is concerned with the manner through which various types of matter combine and change. In the elementary school, the following topics would be considered part of the physical sciences component of a science curriculum:

1. The study of matter and energy

2. The study of the chemical changes that matter undergoes

Technology and engineering represent the application of scientific principles by humans to solve problems. Content Standard E of the National Science Education Standards (NSES) suggests that elementary students develop:

• Abilities of technological design

• Understanding about science and technology

• Abilities to distinguish between natural objects and objects made by humans[1]

Children should learn how to use principles of science to design solutions to problems and make useful things. This may involve modeling, such as building a bridge out of toothpicks, or the actual design and construction of a solar oven. Just as inquiry is fundamental to the discovery in science, the engineering design process is fundamental to problem solving and creativity in technology.

● The National Science Education Standards: Implications for Appropriate Scope

The NSES were developed by the National Academy of Sciences in 1996 to guide state and local school communities toward the appropriate content, professional development, and general teaching strategies for science education. As such, they provide a wonderful reference to the "big picture" of effective science education and lend credibility to decisions based on the principles and guidelines. Most often states will interpret the NSES to create science standards relevant to the needs of the region. In turn, local school districts will further refine state standards to address the needs and resources of the community. It is up to you, the teacher, to ultimately translate the district's vision into positive and effective learning experiences for your students. This chapter will help you plan such a learning experience. The area of the standards that will probably be of most interest to you will be that dealing with what you should be teaching. If you wish to teach content that is sensitive to the NSES recommendations, then its scope should at least range across the following eight topics, or *standards:*

1. Unifying concepts and processes in science
2. Science as inquiry
3. Physical science
4. Life science
5. Earth and space sciences
6. Science and technology
7. Science in personal and social perspectives
8. History and nature of science[2]

The first standard—"Unifying concepts and processes in science"—identifies broad science concepts that are needed to tie the other content areas together:

1. Systems, order, and organization
2. Evidence, models, and explanation
3. Change, constancy, and measurement
4. Evolution and equilibrium
5. Form and function[3]

If you presently lack a strong science content background, you will need to study the explanations and examples of these unifying concepts presented in the full NSES report.

The second standard—"Science as inquiry"—essentially states that children should be expected to ask questions about objects, organisms, and events; plan and carry out investigations; gather data; explain what they have learned; and communicate what they have learned. Teachers are expected to help children understand that scientists continually engage in these aspects of inquiry themselves.[4]

Standards 3 through 8 are more straightforward than the first two. Study Figure 4.1 (pages 61–63) to get a clear picture of the intended scope for units and lessons based on the NSES. Also use this figure as a reference as you consider the appropriate sequence of topics for children. As you use these lists, however, please bear in mind that they are *recommendations* and should be treated as such.

Figure 4.1   The National Science Education Standards,
Grades K—8

Unifying Concepts and Processes

Standard: As a result of activities in grades K–12, all students should develop understandings and abilities aligned with the following concepts and processes.

Systems, order, and organization

Evidence, models, and explanation

Constancy, change, and measurement

Evolution and equilibrium

Form and function

Content Standards Grades K–4

SCIENCE AS INQUIRY*

Content Standard A: As a result of activities in grades K–4, all students should develop

- Abilities necessary to do scientific inquiry
- Understanding about scientific inquiry

PHYSICAL SCIENCE [PS]**

Content Standard B: As a result of the activities in grades K–4, all students should develop an understanding of

- Properties of objects and materials [PS 1]
- Position and motion of objects [PS 2]
- Light, heat, electricity, and magnetism [PS 3]

LIFE SCIENCE [LS]

Content Standard C: As a result of the activities in grades K–4, all students should develop an understanding of

- The characteristics of organisms [LS 1]
- Life cycles of organisms [LS 2]
- Organisms and environments [LS 3]

EARTH AND SPACE SCIENCES [ESS]

Content Standard D: As a result of the activities in grades K–4, all students should develop an understanding of
- Properties of earth materials [ESS 1]
- Objects in the sky [ESS 2]
- Changes in earth and sky [ESS 3]

SCIENCE AND TECHNOLOGY [S&T]

Content Standard E: As a result of the activities in grades K–4, all students should develop an understanding of
- Abilities of technological design [S&T 1]
- Understanding about science and technology [S&T 2]
- Ability to distinguish between natural objects and objects made by humans [S&T 3]

*This general standard is the foundation of all the NSES. Since it is emphasized in all *Teaching Children Science* activities, it is not identified for each experience.

**All the bracketed symbols to the right of the standards were prepared for this book by this author.

(continued)

Figure 4.1   The National Science Education Standards,
Grades K—8 (continued)

SCIENCE IN PERSONAL AND SOCIAL PERSPECTIVES [SPSP]

Content Standard F: As a result of the activities in grades K–4, all students should develop an understanding of

- Personal health [SPSP 1]
- Characteristics and changes in populations [SPSP 2]
- Types of resources [SPSP 3]
- Changes in environments [SPSP 4]
- Science and technology in local challenges [SPSP 5]

HISTORY AND NATURE OF SCIENCE [HNS]

Content Standard G: As a result of the activities in grades K–4, all students should develop an understanding of

- Science as a human endeavor [HNS 1]

Content Standards Grades 5–8

SCIENCE AS INQUIRY

Content Standard A: As a result of their activities in grades 5–8, all students should develop

- Abilities necessary to do scientific inquiry
- Understandings about scientific inquiry

PHYSICAL SCIENCE [PS]

Content Standard B: As a result of their activities in grades 5–8, all students should develop an understanding of

- Properties and changes of properties in matter [PS 4]
- Motion and forces [PS 5]
- Transfer of energy [PS 6]

LIFE SCIENCE [LS]

Content Standard C: As a result of their activities in grades 5–8, all students should develop an understanding of

- Structure and function in living systems [LS 4]
- Reproduction and heredity [LS 5]
- Regulation and behavior [LS 6]
- Population and ecosystems [LS 7]
- Diversity and adaptations of organisms [LS 8]

EARTH AND SPACE SCIENCES [ESS]

Content Standard D: As a result of their activities in grades 5–8, all students should develop an understanding of

- Structure of the earth system [ESS 4]
- Earth's history [ESS 5]
- Earth in the solar system [ESS 6]

Figure 4.1   The National Science Education Standards,
Grades K—8 (continued)

SCIENCE AND TECHNOLOGY [S&T]

Content Standard E: As a result of the activities in grades 5–8, all students should develop an understanding of

- Abilities of technological design [S&T 4]
- Understanding about science and technology [S&T 5]

SCIENCE IN PERSONAL AND SOCIAL PERSPECTIVES [SPSP]

Content Standard F: As a result of the activities in grades 5–8, all students should develop an understanding of

- Personal health [SPSP 6]
- Populations, resources, and environments [SPSP 7]
- Natural hazards [SPSP 8]
- Risks and benefits [SPSP 9]
- Changes in environments [SPSP 10]
- Science and technology in society [SPSP 11]

HISTORY AND NATURE OF SCIENCE [HNS]

Content Standard G: As a result of the activities in grades 5–8, all students should develop an understanding of

- Science as a human endeavor [HNS 2]
- Nature of science [HNS 3]
- History of science [HNS 4]

The Sequence of the Science Curriculum

A knowledge of the scope of science will help you decide what topics can be reasonably included within the body of science experiences you present to children. However, one important question still remains: In what order should these topics be presented? For example, should children learn about the earth they live on before they learn about the structure and function of their bodies, or should the sequence be reversed?

The NSES: Implications for Appropriate Sequence

One of the very best ways of starting a spirited discussion in a teachers' meeting is to say something like, "The butterfly life cycle is too complicated for second-graders." If you are silly enough to make such a statement, you should be prepared to immediately weave your own protective chrysalis!

Too often, interested parties tell us that first-graders should learn X, second-graders should learn Y, and so on. That approach is much too specific and assumes that children in certain grades are homogeneous in terms of their present knowledge of science as well as their interest and ability to pursue science concepts. They are not. What children are able to do at a given grade level largely depends on the particular children, the teacher, and the resources available.

The NSES take a more sensible and flexible approach to recommending the sequence in which science topics should be introduced. They identify the recommended content for grades K–4 and 5–8, as shown in Figure 4.1.

Determining the Sequence of Your Curriculum

There is no definitive answer to the question of sequence. However, these four guidelines may help you consider the place of science in a child's school experience:

1. Research suggests that learning is optimized when the content is relevant and meaningful for the learner.[5] Any decision you make should favor those topics that will generate the most learner involvement and interest.

2. As a general rule, organize learning experiences from the child outward. That is, select experiences that relate first to the child and then to the science content. In teaching electricity, for example, have children consider how they use electricity before they study its source.

3. In general, when deciding to expose children to a concept that can be considered concretely or abstractly, use the concrete approach first.

4. The sequence of topics should be logically connected. There are many possible connections among topics. For example, when teaching a unit about the water cycle, one might choose to begin the unit with principles of evaporation and condensation. Alternatively, the big idea of the water cycle could be introduced first and explained more deeply in subsequent lessons about evaporation and condensation. However you choose to sequence the content, the connections among topics should make sense.

Unit Planning

What Makes a Good Unit Plan?

When full-time teachers lack a sense of the "big picture," their students have, in effect, a substitute teacher every day of the school year. Each school day that children have learning experiences that are not part of any larger context is a day that relates neither to the past nor to the future.

Children need appropriate learning experiences in school—activities that will reflect their teacher's concern with goals and that will involve them cognitively, affectively, and

---

Project 2061

Implications for Your Planning and Managing

Clearly, Project 2061 tells you much about what you *should* teach, but it also provides some direction about *how* you should go about it. It draws on research about how children learn as well as what methods effective teachers tend to use with children. This latter area is referred to as *craft knowledge.*

Project 2061 presents its recommendations for what you should actually do in the classroom in the benchmark "Effective learning and teaching." There are two key ideas within this benchmark:

- Principles of learning
- Teaching science, mathematics, and technology

You'll find specific recommendations for these ideas at the Project 2061 website: **www.project2061.org/.**

Figure 4.2
A science unit may have many components, but each component has a specific purpose.

Component	Purpose
• Rationale	• Helps you think through the reasons for doing a unit on a particular topic
• Performance objectives	• Help you focus on the intended outcomes of the unit
• Content to be taught*	• Clearly identifies and specifies the content children are intended to learn in the unit
• Content outline (for teachers)	• Helps you review the content that will provide the foundation for the learning experience
• Daily lesson plans*	• Help you think through learning activities and their relationship to engagement, exploration, and concept explanation
• Materials list	• Helps you make certain that you have all the materials needed for science activities that occur in daily lessons
• Audiovisual materials and list	• Help you make certain that you have such tools as computer hardware and software, videotapes, and other required equipment
• Accommodations	• Identifies accommodations and modifications necessary to provide the least restrictive and most accessible learning experience for the children in your class
• Assessment strategies	• Help you consider informal and formal ways to assess the extent to which children have achieved cognitive, psychomotor, and affective growth during the unit

*Considered in greater detail later in this chapter

physically. To accomplish this, teachers must plan their science units. Unit plans can take a variety of forms. The list of possible components in Figure 4.2 may prove useful when you develop your own unit plans.

The Role of Textbooks in Unit Planning

Many schools use textbooks or curriculum guides as organizing elements for the curriculum. With some creative planning on your part, such materials can offer a starting point for the development of meaningful science experiences for children. After diagnosing student needs and interests, you can use a portion of a textbook or curriculum guide as a basis for a unit plan. Indeed, the teacher's editions of many recent science textbooks can be important planning resources. Many contain lists of concepts to show scope and sequence; lists of emphasized inquiry process skills; ideas for beginning units and lessons; lesson plans; lists of science materials needed; science content for the teacher; lesson enrichment ideas; bulletin board and field trip ideas; lists of related children's books and websites; and computer software and audiovisual aids.

Although a teacher's edition can be an important resource, it is not a recipe book and should not be used in place of your own planning. After all, you are the one who best knows the needs of the children in your class.

Lesson Planning

"Be very, very careful what you put into that head, because you will never, ever get it out."

—Cardinal Wolsey (1475 ?-1530)

● What Makes a Good Lesson Plan?

If you were to lock three teachers in a room and ask them (under pain of losing their parking spaces) to reach a consensus about the best format for a lesson plan, you would probably end up with four formats (and three teachers walking to school). The fact is, there are many approaches to lesson planning, and it is difficult to know in advance which one will work best for you.

● Developing a Good Lesson Plan Using Six Elements

Go to **MyEducationLab**, select the topic Earth and Space Science, watch the video entitled "Properties of Air: Pressure," and complete the questions that accompany it.

The lesson plan outline discussed here includes major elements to be considered in your lesson planning. Your department or district will likely have variations that you should incorporate as well. Hopefully this discussion will help you develop effective and engaging lessons.

Although developing lesson plans can be daunting at first, the payoffs are well worth the effort. Good lesson plans result in focused, dynamic learning experiences wherein children are thoughtful and engaged. Well-thought-out lesson plans also facilitate good classroom management, which maximizes student time on learning and minimizes disorder and discipline issues. Be that as it may, you need a starting point for lesson planning. The following six key elements—enhanced with additional components suggested by veteran teachers, school administrators, and others—will serve you well. Creating a targeted learning experience is similar to writing a play with a thought-provoking engagement to set the plot, development of the plot, and a culminating scene that ties the story together. To better visualize each element of a lesson plan, we will walk through a sample lesson plan, "Sinking and Floating," in Figure 4.3.

Element 1: Content to be Taught: Identify What You Intend to Teach

Although identifying the content to be taught may be an obvious first step of lesson planning, it is often taken for granted. Be very clear about what you intend to teach. If you are unclear about what you want the children to learn at the start, then your lesson will become increasingly more difficult to plan. It is like trying to button your shirt. If you miss the first button, then all the buttons are off.

Most likely you will be developing lessons from a unit based on a topic in the science standards. Let's use an example from the NSES Earth and Space Sciences for grades K–4, Content Standard B: As a result of the activities in grades K–4, all students should develop an understanding of properties of objects and materials.[6]

Let's try to outline the content for the sinking and floating example. Information is easily accessible through the Internet, making it relatively easy to create a content outline. If you use Internet sites, be sure to use reputable sources for your content outline such as university or nationally recognized sources. Cross-check references if in doubt. An example of a content outline is given in Figure 4.4. Note that the content outline is for you, the teacher. You will need to decide the depth of content to teach depending on the children's abilities. The underlying concept for this lesson is buoyancy, quite a difficult concept for students to get their minds around, let alone third-graders. Although you may not teach the complete story of buoyancy to third-graders, you can provide an encounter with the idea that lays a foundation so that they are prepared to develop a deeper understanding of buoyancy in later years.

Figure 4.3 Sample Lesson Plan:
Sinking and Floating

Lesson Plan

Content to Be Taught:

Children will learn that the shape of a material affects whether it will sink or float. The greater the area covered by the material, the more likely it is to float, because it can rest on a larger area of water that holds the material up by exerting a force that pushes back on it.

Children's Prior Knowledge and Misconceptions:

The children have learned in a prior lesson that certain materials float or sink. A common misconception is that for an object to float, it must be made from a material that itself will not sink when placed in water.

Performance Objective:

Given two equal amounts of clay (condition), children will form the clay into shapes that will float or sink and explain in writing (performance) that the greater the area covered by the material, the more likely it is to float, because it can rest on a larger area of water that holds the clay up by exerting a force that pushes back on it (criteria).

Concept Development:

ENGAGEMENT

Materials: 3 balls of clay, gallon container of water

Safety: The floor may become wet and slippery. Place a tray to collect overflow under the container of water. Provide paper towels or newspaper to absorb spills.

Ask the children to predict whether they think the clay will float or sink when you drop it into the water. You are likely to get mixed responses. Either way, record the children's thoughts on the board. Drop the ball of clay into the water. When the clay sinks it will be a discrepant event for those children who thought it would float. Even for the children who thought it would sink, they are at least invested in the question. Now challenge the children by asking, "How can you make the clay float?" This becomes your essential question.

EXPLORATION

Materials per groups of three: 3 equal size balls of clay, gallon container, red and green cups taped together (These will be used to indicate that the group is finished, red cup on top, or that the group has questions, green cup on top.)

Procedure: Each child should have a science notebook.[7]

Part I: Ask each child to record in their science notebooks what they need to do to the clay to make it float.

Part II: Arrange children in groups of three. Instruct the children to discuss among the members of their group how they could make the clay float. Tell the children to record any questions or wonderments (use the thought stem, "I wonder . . .) in their science notebook. When they finish, tell them to turn the red/green cups so red is on top, indicating that the group is finished and ready for Part III. The teacher will bring instructions for Part III to each group.

Part III: Tell the children to use the clay and container of water to test their ideas. Let each person take a turn doing a test. Instruct the children to draw a picture of their design and explain in writing why they think the clay did or did not float. All entries are to be written in their science notebooks.

(continued)

Figure 4.3   Sample Lesson Plan:
Sinking and Floating (continued)

Lesson
Plan

EXPLANATION

Ask the children, "Did anyone succeed in making the clay float?"

Process responses: Create two spaces on a table in the front of the room, label one *floaters* and one *sinkers.* Have children bring the clay models that they made to the table and group them according to floaters or sinkers. If they all have floaters, be prepared with a few shapes that will sink and place them along with the original ball of clay in the sinker group.

Individual reflection: Ask each child to create a descriptive model of floaters and sinkers; be sure they include the observed interactions of the clay with the water. Then have them write an explanation in their science notebook describing why they think the floaters floated, and the sinkers sank.

Pairing and sharing: Have the children share their ideas with a partner.

Then lead a discussion of the children's ideas in class. Prompts might include:

What do the floaters have in common?

How are the floaters different from the ball of clay that sank?

Why do you think the shape makes a difference?

What advice would you give to someone who wanted to make a ship out of steel?

Summarize: Demonstrate and reinforce the concepts that the greater the area covered by the material, the more likely it is to float, because it can rest on a larger area of water that holds the clay up by exerting a force that pushes back on it.

ELABORATION

Ask the children to explain how a ship made of steel can float.

EVALUATION

Instructions:
1. *You will be given two bricks of clay that are the same size.*
2. *Form one brick of clay into a shape that you think will sink.*
3. *Form the other ball of clay into a shape that you think will float.*
4. *Draw a picture of each design in the space below.*
5. *Write an explanation that describes why your designs sink or float.*

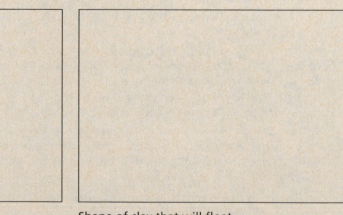

Shape of clay that will sink   Shape of clay that will float

Figure 4.3 Sample Lesson Plan:
Sinking and Floating (continued)

*Lesson
Plan*

Explain:
I think the clay will sink
because . . .

_____
_____
_____
_____

Explain:
I think the clay will float
because . . .

_____
_____
_____
_____

Accommodations::

Accommodations for this example include reading the instructions with children who are English language learners and providing the option of answering orally in addition to writing the answer. Children with visual impairments will benefit from the tactile nature of the investigation. Large print instructions will also help. One possible modification would be requiring the children to identify the clay shape that is likely to float, rather than explain the properties of the shape that contribute to floating.

Gifted learners can be challenged to explore the concept of density. Give them a thin square of metal about 2 cm x 2 cm and about 1 cm thick. Note that the dimensions make it relatively easy to determine the volume (Length x Width x Height). You want the metal square to sink in water. Give them an equal size of a material that is less dense and will float, such as styrofoam. Ask them why equal volumes and area of styrofoam float and the metal sinks. Let the children try to explain the properties. Guide them to determine the volume and mass of each item, and recognize the mass per unit volume differs. Then have them compare it to the same mass per unit volume of water. Identify these ratios as densities. Provide a chart of substances and their densities relative to the density of water and ask the children to determine which items will float in water.

Element 2: Prior Knowledge: Describe Common Misconceptions about the Topic   No child is a blank slate. They have ideas about the world based on their prior experiences. Sometimes these ideas are accurate, but more often they are incomplete or tainted with misconceptions. Therefore, consider what you can reasonably assume about their knowledge of the subject and common misconceptions. This will become easier with experience and the longer you work with the children in your class. You can also access information on the Internet about common misconceptions (cf. links to misconceptions at MyEducationLab). In the sinking-floating example, it can be assumed that in previous lessons children have learned that certain materials float or sink. A common misconception about floating and sinking is that for an object to float, it must be made from a material that itself will not sink when placed in water.

Element 3: Performance Objectives   Performance objectives provide a clear statement of the behaviors that the children will exhibit to demonstrate their learning. The only way to assess learning is through their observable behaviors and performances. There must also be criteria associated with behaviors and performances to indicate satisfactory learning.

Performance objectives consist of three components: a condition for learning, an observable performance to indicate learning, and criteria to rate the level of performance.[8] Clear performance objectives will make it easier to assess the children's understanding at the end of the lesson using performance assessments.

Figure 4.4

Sample of a teacher's content outline

> 1. *An object will float if it displaces a mass of liquid equal to the object's mass.*
>
> 2. *The shape of an object affects the mass of liquid that it can displace.*
>   a. The greater the volume of the object, the more liquid it can displace.
>   b. The lower the volume of the object, the less liquid it can displace.
>
> 3. *Example:* clay ball and clay canoe
>   a. A clay ball will sink in water because its volume does not displace its mass in water.
>   b. A clay canoe will float in water because it does displace its mass in water.
>
> It often helps to reorganize the content to identify the important connections and contexts that need to be taught. This reorganization of content helps put the content in a logical framework for thinking about and teaching the content. It will also be useful to determine assessment strategies.
>
> 1. *Identify the elements*
>   1.1. Water
>   1.2. Objects that float or sink
>
> 2. *Properties of the elements*
>   2.1. Shape
>   2.2. Weight (mass)
>
> 3. *Identify the rules of interaction among the elements*
>   3.1. Objects float if they displace (push away) a mass of liquid that is the same as the mass of the object.
>   3.2. Objects sink if they displace (push away) a mass of liquid that is less than the mass of the object.
>   3.3. Shape is a factor that determines how much liquid an object can displace.
>   3.3.1. Shapes that take up more volume can displace more water
>
> 4. *Emergent properties*
>   4.1. The shape of a material can determine whether it sinks or floats.
>   4.2. Example
>   4.2.1. A ball of clay will sink, but a canoe shape displaces more water relative to its weight (mass) and will float.

Element 4: Concept Development   Safety: Concept development describes the presentation of the lesson to the students. Include safety notes throughout the lesson as reminders of necessary safety precautions. Read more on safety in the classroom in the section entitled "For the Teacher's Desk."

▶ *Engagement*

Recall from Chapter 2 that effective learning occurs when the context is meaningful. As with any good movie or novel, the writer must engage the attention of the audience quickly. As an elementary school teacher, you will find that the window of opportunity to capture and hold the children's attention usually closes quite quickly. You need to craft an engagement that not only piques the children's curiosity but also establishes a central question that creates a desire and need for deeper inquiry.

There are three main types of inquiry questions: information gathering, addressing the general question, "I wonder what happens when . . . ?" Such as, "I wonder what stages a caterpillar goes through to become a butterfly?" or "What phases does the moon go through over the course of a month?" Questions can be experimental, asking, "I wonder what would happen if . . . ?" As in, "I wonder what would happen if we put the plants in the closet?" Lastly, questions could address "How to do it" as in, "How can I build a better bridge?"

Discrepant events are counterintuitive experiences that pique curiosity and a desire to seek an explanation. They grab our attention and interest because the outcome is usually the opposite of what is expected. An example of a discrepant event is given in Figure 4.5.

▶ Exploration

Recall from Chapter 2 that exploration provides an opportunity for children to encounter and reflect on new content. Whatever strategy one chooses for the exploration, it should enable the children to be active participants in the learning experience such as describing changes, manipulating variables, or designing solutions. Exploration is the concept development stage during which a variety of teaching methods that you have been learning can be employed.

▶ Explanation

The explanation follows the natural flow of the inquiry lesson. It is tempting to simply tell the children the answer at this point. It is best to provide an opportunity for the children to communicate their explanation first, so they can make logical connections on their own. The explanation may be expressed in writing, through a diagram, orally, or kinesthetically using a simulation. You can reinforce their correct answers and challenge inaccuracies through questioning and concept attainment methods. It is at this point that you can become more didactic to explain the answer. Direct teaching during the explanation stage is meaningful because the children will have a genuine investment in the question and consequently will be more eager and receptive to the explanation.

▶ Elaboration

Elaboration challenges the children to deepen and reinforce what they have learned by applying the concept in a similar context.

Figure 4.5
Discrepant Event:
The Ping Pong Ball
and the Funnel

Present the children with a Ping-Pong ball and funnel. Put the Ping-Pong ball in the funnel with the stem pointing down. Ask the children to predict what will happen to the Ping-Pong ball when someone blows through the stem into the funnel. Most often children will predict that the ball will be pushed out of the funnel. In fact, the ball will remain in the funnel, no matter how hard you blow.
Explanation: Air exiting the stem into the funnel must travel faster to get around the ball. The fast-moving air around the bottom of the ball creates an area of lower pressure relative to the slower air movement above the ball, resulting in a higher pressure area above the ball, which pushes the ball down and keeps it in the funnel. This is an example of the Bernoulli effect.

Element 5:   Evaluation (Assessment)   "Did the children learn what you thought you taught?" Assessment is the opportunity to rejoice in the fruits of your labor. After all, you have worked hard to design and execute a learning experience for the children in your class that is thought provoking and productive.

There are several strategies for assessment that probe children's understandings and abilities at a variety of levels: nominal, descriptive, and explanatory. A more detailed description of these levels and assessment strategies will be addressed in Chapter 6.

Element 6: Accommodations   Accommodations are designed to provide all the children with the least restrictive environment for learning experiences. For example, teaching English language learners may require you to post word banks or provide supplemental instructions with illustrations and diagrams. Large print and seating near the front of the room may assist children with visual impairments. Accommodations usually benefit all children. Universal Design for Learning is a teaching strategy that facilitates learning for all children. It is based on the following:

> **Multiple means of representation** to give learners various ways of acquiring information and knowledge
>
> **Multiple means of expression** to provide learners alternatives for demonstrating what they know, and
>
> **Multiple means of engagement** to tap into learners' interests, challenge them appropriately, and motivate them to learn

Modifications differ from accommodations in that they alter curricular content by raising or lowering the performance expectations. Examples consist of more challenging work for gifted children or lower expectations for mentally disabled children.

Chapter 9 addresses accommodations in more detail.

Reality Check

One of my favorite activities in elementary school was making "Oobleck," a simple mixture of two parts cornstarch to one part water. It is a material that seems to have the properties of both a solid and a liquid. Perhaps your fourth-graders will enjoy it, too. But as a teacher, you recognize that although an activity may be fun there should be some benefit to learning in the activity. You do a quick Internet search and find the following explanation of Oobleck:

> When enough pressure is applied, the Oobleck acts like a solid. When little or no pressure is applied, it acts like a liquid. This is a result of long chains called *polymers* (*poly* = many, *mer* = part) that form when cornstarch is added to water. Anytime a polymer is added to a liquid, it slows down the reaction time of the liquid and makes it harder for the liquid to move. Cornstarch is a polymer that slows down the movement of water. If pressure is applied quickly, the cornstarch polymer gets tangled up and acts like a solid. If pressure is applied slowly, the polymers don't get as tangled, making the Oobleck act more like a liquid.[9]

Based on your knowledge of national and local science standards, what content could you justify teaching to your fourth-graders based on this activity?

Classroom Organization and Management

Go to **MyEducationLab**, select the topic Classroom and Community Resources, watch the video entitled "Using Centers 1," and complete the questions that accompany it.

I'm not going to provide an elaborate treatise on maintaining appropriate classroom behavior. The fact is, I have seen more *teachers* produce discipline problems than I have seen *children* cause them. If you are able to maintain appropriate behavior when you teach social studies, reading, math, or any other subject, you will be able to do so when you teach science. If you have problems with classroom control, science activities will neither solve your problems nor make them worse. Even so, you can take some steps that will help things go more smoothly for everyone. Appropriate classroom behavior is not hard to achieve; it just requires attention to a few common-sense matters.

• Distributing Materials

The attack of a school of piranha on a drowning monkey is a model of tranquility when compared with a group of 20 children trying to acquire a magnet from a tote tray containing 10 of them.

In order to distribute materials effectively, you need to devise techniques that are appropriate for your setting. In some settings, for example, two or three children can distribute materials to all the groups. Another technique is to have one child from each group come forward to acquire needed materials. Regardless of the procedure you employ, try to avoid having all the children get what they need simultaneously.

• Providing Work Space

"Please make him (her) stop bugging us, or I will wring his (her) neck."

This is a rather common classroom request (threat) among children involved in science activities. One way to diminish this type of problem is to give your learning groups some work space. This may be difficult if you have a small room, but you should try anyway. Movable bookcases, room dividers, and similar objects should be pressed into service to give groups of children semiprivate work spaces. Because science activities provide ample opportunities for social interaction among group members, there is little need for groups to interact with one another. Such contact is often counterproductive.

The most important element of a science work space is a flat surface. If you have the opportunity to select furniture for your classroom, choose tables and chairs rather than conventional desks. The typical classroom desk for children is designed for *writing*, not for doing science activities. If your classroom has desks with slanted tops, you will need to acquire tables, build your own tables, or use the floor as the place for science activities. Some teachers find that the inflexibility presented by traditional desks can be overcome by placing tables along the periphery of the room. Students can then carry out their science activities on the tables and use their desks during other instructional activities.

• Providing Clear Directions

"I didn't know what I was supposed to do with the ice cubes, so I put them down her back."

Children (and adults) seem to get into trouble when they don't understand what they are supposed to be doing. So, it should come as no surprise that problems arise in the classroom when children don't understand what your expectations are. If you learn to announce these expectations clearly and simply, you will find that misbehaviors decrease.

If the science activity the children are going to do requires procedures or materials they are unfamiliar with, you will need to model the use of these materials or procedures (except, of course, when the objective of the activity is the discovery of how to use them). *Children who do not know how to read a meterstick will use it as a baseball bat or sword rather than as a device for making linear measurements.* By taking a few minutes to teach children how to use materials and equipment properly, you can make the process of discovery more pleasant—for you and for them.

Summary

The success of an inquiry-based, discovery-focused classroom depends on your abilities to both plan and manage. The science curriculum for children typically consists of a number of learning units. Unit plans are long-term plans for science experiences that focus on particular topics. Daily lesson plans are single components of unit plans. This chapter suggests six elements in the lesson planning process and offers an example of each in the context of a complete lesson plan. Of course there are other lesson plan formats, but this will serve as a framework from which to begin the planning process. There will be several more examples of lesson plans in Part Two of this book. Hopefully, you will use this framework to create your own approach to planning lessons.

A classroom in which students carry out science activities as part of group work undoubtedly will face some classroom management challenges. Teachers can use various techniques to ensure that science time is rich in appropriate learning opportunities yet manageable, as well.

Going Further

On Your Own

1. How you plan for teaching will probably depend to a great extent upon your general outlook on the nature of teaching and how children learn. To bring these perceptions into focus, respond to each of the following statements:
   a. Careful planning is consistent with how I carry out the activities in my life.
   b. Planning can restrict flexibility.
   c. I never had a teacher who planned.
   d. Children will learn regardless of how much teachers plan.

2. Review the sample lesson plan in this chapter. Then select a science topic appropriate for the grade level you are interested in and develop a lesson plan. If possible, teach the lesson to a group of children or peers who role-play children. Assess the extent to which your lesson relates to the 5E learning cycle.

3. Sketch your vision of the ideal classroom in which to teach science. Label the special areas in your classroom. Note, in particular, the location and arrangement of classroom seating and work space. What advantage does your ideal classroom have over a conventional elementary school classroom? How could you use your ideas for classroom organization in a conventional classroom?

On Your Own or in a Cooperative Learning Group

4. Brainstorm a discrepant event to engage children in each of the following science topics. Write a performance objective for each activity. Be sure to include a condition, measurable performance, and criteria for scoring.
   a. Indoor Gardening
   b. Animals with Pouches
   c. The Changes in the Seasons
   d. Earthquakes
   e. Friction

5. Role-play a job interview between a school principal and a teaching candidate for either a self-contained classroom or a departmentalized school. During the interview, the "principal" should ask about the following:
   a. The teacher's awareness of the NSES
   b. The science content and experiences appropriate for children at that grade
   c. The planning style the prospective teacher would use
   d. The management strategies the teacher would use
   e. Ideas the teacher has for giving children opportunities to explore
   f. Alternate techniques the teacher could use to introduce a concept
   g. Ideas that the teacher has for helping children apply concepts to new situations

Resources for Discovery Learning

Internet Resources

To access these helpful websites, go to **MyEducationLab,** select Resources, and then Web Links. To learn more, click on the following link and you will easily be directed to each website.

- **Discovery Education:**
  http://school.discoveryeducation.com/

- **Discrepant Events Best Teaching Practices:**
  www.agpa.uakron.edu/k12/best_practices/discrepant_events.html

- **The Drinking Happy Bird University of Virginia Physics Department:**
  http://galileo.phys.virginia.edu/outreach/8thGradeSOL/Evaporation.htm

- **National Science Digital Library:**
  http://nsdl.org/

- **NyeLabs:**
  www.billnye.com

- **Science NetLinks:**
  www.sciencenetlinks.com

Print Resources

Suggested Readings

Ansberry, Karen Rohrich and Morgan, Emily. *Picture Perfect Science Lessons: Using Children's Books to Guide Inquiry.* Arlington, VA: NSTA Press, 2005.

Avraamidou, L., et al. "Giving Priority to Evidence in Science Teaching: A First-Year Elementary Teacher's Specialized Practices and Knowledge." *Journal of Research in Science Teaching* 42, no. 9 (November 2005): 965–986.

Cummings, Carol. *Winning Strategies for Classroom Management.* Alexandria, VA: Association for Supervision and Curriculum Development, 2000.

Fetters, Marcia, et al. "Making Science Accessible: Strategies to Meet the Needs of a Diverse Population." *Science Scope* 26, no. 5 (February 2003): 26–29.

Giacalone, Valerie. "How to Plan, Survive, and Even Enjoy an Overnight Field Trip with 200 Students." *Science Scope* 26, no. 4 (January 2003): 22–26.

Gooden, Kelly. "Parents Come to Class." *Science and Children* 40, no. 4 (January 2003): 22–25.

Ledoux, M., et al. "A Constructivist Approach in the Interdisciplinary Instruction of Science and Language Arts Methods." *Teaching Education (Columbia, S.C.)* 15, no. 4 (December 2004): 385–399.

Marble, S. "Inquiring into Teaching: Lesson Study in Elementary Science Methods." *Journal of Science Teacher Education* 18, no. 6 (December 2007): 935–953.

Melber, Leah M. "Tap Into Informal Science Learning." *Science Scope* 23, no. 6 (March 2000): 28–31.

Molledo, Magdalena. "The Resourceful Teacher." *Science Scope* 24, no. 6 (March 2001): 46–48.

Morrison, J. A., et al. "Using Science Trade Books To Support Inquiry in the Elementary Classroom." *Childhood Education* 84, no. 4 (Summer 2008): 204–208.

Redmond, Alan. "Science in the Summer." *Science Scope,* 24 no. 4 (January 2000): 28–33.

Roy, Ken. "Safety Is for Everyone." *Science Scope* 26, no. 5 (February 2003): 16–17.

Silverman, E., et al. "Cheep, Chirp, Twitter, & Whistle." *Science and Children* 44, no. 5 (February 2007): 20–25.

Sussman, Beverly. "Making Your Science Program Work." *Science Scope* 23, no. 6 (March 2000): 26–27.

Sutton, Kimberly Kode. "Curriculum Compacting." *Science Scope* 24, no. 4 (January 2000): 22–27.

Notes

1. *National Science Education Standards* (Washington, D.C. National Academies Press, 1996). Courtesy of National Academies Press.
2. National Research Council, *National Science Education Standards* (Washington, DC: National Academy Press, 1996), p. 6. Courtesy of National Academies Press.
3. Ibid., 104.
4. Ibid., 103.
5. James Zull, *The Art of Changing the Brain* (Sterling, VA: Stylus Publishing LLC, 2002).
6. National Research Council, *National Science Education Standards* (Washington, DC: National Academy Press, 1996).
7. More on science notebooks in Chapter 6: Assessment.
8. Robert F. Mager, *Preparing Instructional Objectives: A Critical Tool in the Development of Effective Instruction* (Atlanta, GA: The Center for Effective Performance, 1997).
9. Paul D. Reed, Polymers and You (CIBT-RTC October 2005). http://cibt.bio.cornell.edu/programs/archive/0510rtc/Polymers.pdf.

chapter 5

Strategies and QuickChecks

How can I effectively use cooperative learning, questioning and wait-time strategies, active listening, demonstrations, and textbooks in my classroom?

▶ **Getting Started**

My greatest challenge as a teacher is to refrain from telling my students everything—far more than they want to know. This problem seems to be a highly contagious ailment that can be transmitted from professor to student. I have reached this conclusion because I find that teachers in grades K–8 tell their students too much—usually more than the children really want to be told. A favorite story of mine concerns a first-grade child who asks a teacher to explain nuclear fusion. The teacher replies, "Why don't you ask your mother? She is a nuclear physicist." The child replies, "I don't want to know *that* much about it."

Perhaps it is just human nature to tell people more than they really want to know. In my case, it happens when I get excited about the content I am sharing; I want everyone to get the information quickly. When I work in science classrooms, I try to restrain

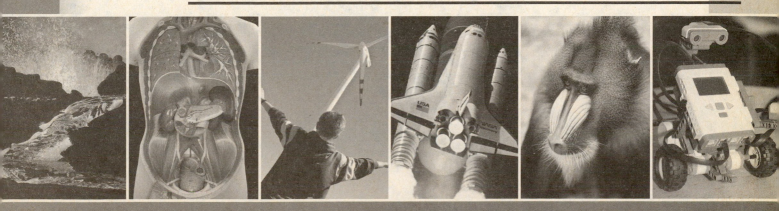

myself from talking so much because I know that I will enjoy watching children discover something special on their own, and I know that will happen only if I talk less. That smile or screech of excitement from a child who makes a discovery is powerful medicine that stops my wagging tongue.

How can we do more real science with children? Perhaps the first step is to talk less and to use more creative strategies that help children learn on their own—with our guidance, to be sure, but not with so much guidance that the smiles and screeches are lost.

Cooperative Learning Strategies

Go to **MyEducationLab**, select the topic Laboratory and Demonstrations, watch the video entitled "Cooperative Learning," and complete the questions that accompany it.

Each stage of the learning cycle can be enriched by the use of well-planned group work. One promising approach to improving the quality of group work is the use of *cooperative learning groups,* which consist of children who are, in fact, working *together* on a project. That is to say, they are supportive of one another and accountable for both their individual learning as well as the learning of every other person in their group.

Creating and Using Cooperative Learning Groups

Cooperative learning groups have very special characteristics that distinguish them from traditional classroom learning groups. Figure 5.1 makes a point-by-point comparison of nine of those characteristics, clearly contrasting these two approaches to group work.

In fact, these characteristics of cooperative learning groups emerge from three more fundamental elements, or strategies, of cooperative learning. If you can incorporate these strategies into your work with children before, during, and even after group work, you will increase the chances for successful group work. Here is a brief discussion of each:

1. *Teach for positive interdependence.* Help all members of each group understand that their success depends on the extent to which they agree on goals, objectives, and the roles each member is expected to carry out. They also need to agree in advance on an acceptable way to share available resources and information.

The success of a cooperative learning group depends on the success of each of its members.

78

Figure 5.1
What are the differences between a cooperative learning group and a traditional learning group?

Cooperative Learning Group	Traditional Learning Group
• Positive interdependence	• No interdependence
• Individual accountability	• No individual accountability
• Heterogeneous	• Homogeneous
• Shared leadership	• One appointed leader
• Shared responsibility for each other	• Responsibility only for self
• Task and maintenance emphasized	• Only task emphasized
• Social skills directly taught	• Social skills assumed and ignored
• Teacher observes and intervenes	• Teacher ignores group functioning
• Groups process their effectiveness	• No group processing

2. *Teach for individual accountability.* Help all members of each group understand that they are accountable not only for their own learning and behavior but also for helping other group members learn and work productively.

3. *Teach interpersonal and small-group skills.* If you expect children to work together and display appropriate group process skills, you will have to take the time to teach them those skills. Before group work, discuss group process skills such as sharing leadership, praising good work done by others, and active listening. Also teach children how to analyze how well the group process itself is going and how to modify the process to improve it.

▶ *Do It! Use the Cooperative Learning QuickCheck*

Figure 5.2 is a tool that you can use as you guide group work in your own classroom or as you observe another teacher's groups at work. Simply observe a group or a number of groups at work for a period of time, and use the points in the QuickCheck to help you determine the true nature of the group work that's occurring. You should check off (✓) each cooperative learning behavior that you observe. Think about whether you are observing a cooperative or a traditional learning group. Then use the results of your observation for guidance when you create and oversee future cooperative group work during science time.

Questioning Strategies

Go to MyEducationLab, select the topic Questioning Strategies, watch the video entitled "Questioning," and complete the question that accompanies it.

Every now and then, I visit a classroom that makes me feel like I've entered a time machine and been transported back to the days of the Spanish Inquisition. At those times, I feel like I'm an observer in an interrogation room—not a classroom. Questions, questions, and more questions!

Asking children a reasonable number of purposeful questions can be a helpful strategy. But too often, what I hear are rapid-fire questions that simply require recall and not much actual thought. In fact, sometimes children don't even have a chance to think about the possible answers before the next question is put forth.

Figure 5.2   Use this checklist to determine the level of cooperative learning in science group work.

Quick Check

Cooperative Learning QuickCheck

1. Does the group display *positive interdependence?*
   _____ Group members agree on general goals.
   _____ Group members agree on specific objectives.
   _____ Group members agree on roles for each group member.
   _____ Group members are sharing resources.
   _____ Group members each have a role that is integral to the completion of the task.

2. Does the group display *individual accountability?*
   _____ Group members try to keep the group on task.
   _____ Group members help one another complete tasks.
   _____ Group members try to keep their resource materials organized.

3. Does the group demonstrate *interpersonal and group process skills?*
   _____ Leadership is being shared among group members.
   _____ Group members praise each other.
   _____ Group members actively listen to one another.
   _____ Group members say and do things that keep the group moving ahead.

● Improving the Questions You Ask

Educational researchers have long been concerned about the quantity and quality of teacher questions. As a teacher, you have found or will soon find that it takes self-discipline to ask questions that actually stimulate thought and move children along the road to inquiry-based, discovery-focused learning.

Fortunately, you can take some practical steps to ensure that the time you spend probing what children actually know will be well spent. To begin, gather data about what you presently do in terms of question asking. You can do this by videotaping or audiotaping lessons or parts of lessons you teach to children or to peers. Then classify the types of questions you ask. One system for classifying questions has as its foundation the six cognitive levels—knowledge, comprehension, application, analysis, synthesis, and evaluation.

After carefully studying these six cognitive levels, Orlich and others proposed a more simplified three-category system for classifying questions.[1] The three categories of questions are as follows:

1. *Convergent questions* get children to think in ways that focus on basic knowledge or comprehension.

   Examples
   How did the yeast help our dough rise?
   What did the three-horned dinosaur eat?
   How was the plant cell different from the animal cell?
   How many planets orbit the sun?

2. *Divergent questions* get children to think about a number of alternative answers.

Examples

What are some ideas about what caused the dinosaurs to become extinct?

If you were a prey animal in the jungle, what could you do to keep safe from predators?

What are some ways we could reduce the amount of water and electricity wasted in our school?

3. *Evaluative questions* get students to offer a judgment based on some criteria.

Examples

If a power plant was going to be built next to your house, which one type of energy would you want it to generate?

If you could pick only three foods to take on a week-long camping trip, what would they be?

Where would be the safest place to be during an earthquake?

▶ *Do It! Use the Questioning QuickCheck*

I have used these three categories in creating a Questioning QuickCheck (see Figure 5.3). By counting the number of each type of question asked, you can analyze the tapes

Figure 5.3   Use this form to count questions by type during a live or recorded teaching episode.

Quick Check

Questioning QuickCheck

Date of episode _____   Start time _____   End time _____

Observe

1. *Convergent questions* get children to think in ways that focus on basic knowledge or comprehension.
   Tally of questions asked:

2. *Divergent questions* get children to think about a number of alternative answers.
   Tally of questions asked:

3. *Evaluative questions* get students to offer a judgment based on some criteria.
   Tally of questions asked:

Evaluate

1. How long did you observe, listen to, or watch the teaching episode? _____

2. How many of each type of question were asked?
   Convergent _____   .
   Divergent _____
   Evaluative _____

3. What was the total number of questions asked? _____

that you make of your own teaching or as you observe others teach. Clearly, to create an inquiry-based, discovery-focused classroom, a balance must be reached among the types of questions you ask. Using the Questioning QuickCheck will help you start that process.

Wait-Time/Think-Time Strategies

Have you ever heard of *wait-time* or *think-time?* Unfortunately, teachers' questioning behavior tends to follow a certain pattern: We ask a question, receive a response from a child, and then *immediately* react to the response and ask another question. The generally too-short gap between our question and the child's answer is known as wait-time or think-time. Experts tell us that that time is usually just two or three seconds long, if that. Regardless, it is too brief for the children to actually think deeply about one question before hearing its answer or yet another question.

● Allowing More Time

Allowing a very short wait-time/think-time turns your classroom into a game show of sorts, in which you are trying to catch the children and indirectly embarrass them. By increasing wait-time or think-time, you can produce some very positive results. In particular, by allowing more time between questions, you can change a traditional classroom into a richer environment for inquiry-based, discovery-focused learning.

Researchers Tobin and Capie, in building on the previous work of Mary Bud Rowe, describe the following benefits of increasing wait-time beyond three seconds:

1. The length of student responses increased.
2. The number of unsolicited but appropriate responses increased.
3. Failure to respond decreased.
4. Confidence, as reflected by a decrease in the number of inflected responses, increased.
5. The incidence of speculative responses increased.
6. The incidence of child-child comparisons of data increased.
7. The incidence of evidence-inference statements increased.
8. The incidence of questions asked by students increased.
9. There was an increase in the incidence of responses emanating from students rated by the teacher as relatively slow learners.
10. The variety in the type of verbal behavior of students increased.[2]

The pause provided by a sufficient wait-time seems to refresh and improve the learning process. Make a real attempt to slow down the pace of questioning in your classroom.

▶ *Do It! Use the Wait-Time/Think-Time QuickCheck*

The QuickCheck in Figure 5.4 lists a variety of strategies you can use in the classroom to improve your own wait-time/think-time.[3] Check off (✓) the strategies as you try them, and make note of which ones seem especially effective using an asterisk (*).

Figure 5.4   Use the strategies in this checklist to slow down the pace of questioning.

Wait-Time/Think-Time QuickCheck

1. *To improve wait-time/think-time:*

   _____ Prompt the children to think about the answer before answering.

   _____ Mentally count off five seconds after you ask a question.

   _____ As you wait, look around the room to observe any signs of confusion about the question.

   _____ If the child's answer is appropriate, praise him or her and then count off another five seconds mentally before asking another question.

2. *If the children don't respond:*

   _____ Ask the childen if they would like you to ask the question in a different way.

   _____ Repeat the question with some modifications.

   _____ If possible, represent the question graphically on a chalkboard, whiteboard, or transparency.

   _____ Try to ask a simpler form of the question.

   _____ Ask if anyone in the class can rephrase the question for you.

   _____ Ask if part of the question is too difficult, and modify it accordingly.

   _____ Use the think-pair-share technique. After the children have reflected individually, ask them to share their ideas with their neighbor and then report to the class.

3. *If the children do respond appropriately:*

   _____ Liberally praise the responding child or children.

   _____ Ask the child to elaborate on his or her answer.

4. *If the children offer a partial response:*

   _____ Focus on the adequacy of the answer and capitalize on it (for instance, by asking "Can anyone help Jamie's answer?")

   _____ Praise the act of responding, perhaps by saying "That was a very good try, Jamie."

Active Listening Strategies

"For the third time, you draw the food chain arrows so the arrow heads point to the living things that receive the energy. Why do I keep seeing people draw the arrows from the killer whale to the seal? Was anyone listening when we talked about the food chain?"

It's very frustrating when you suddenly realize that your students are not listening to you, their classmates, or even visiting speakers as intently as you might wish. To help them improve on this skill during science time, focus on the idea of *active listening*, which is the conscious effort to focus one's attention on what people are saying as they are saying it. This is an important life skill that children need to master—and *you* may need a little work on it yourself! (I am relatively easily distracted, since I find everything around me quite interesting, so I need to work on active listening, also!)

Increasing Active Listening

You can take some practical steps to increase active listening in your classroom:

1. *Restructure the physical setting to minimize distractions.* A classroom in which children are involved in hands-on activities will not be as quiet as a library. As you speak, there will be the bubbling sounds of the fish tank, the background noise of shifting chairs and desks, and so on. The first step in providing an environment in which active listening can occur is to compensate for background noise. Do this by having the children speak louder when asking or answering questions, by moving classroom furniture so that everyone can see the speaker, and by having the children look directly at and speak directly to the group or person they are addressing.

2. *Have children listen for key science words.* One way to keep their attention on the speaker is to listen for words such as *up, down, under,* and *above* that signal what is to follow. You will need to teach the children to use such terms as *observe, classify, graph, measure,* and *predict* and then to reinforce the use of these words through your praise. On a regular basis after a child has spoken or you have spoken, ask a question such as "Did you hear any key words when Emilio told us about last night's storm?" By teaching the children to listen for key words and what follows them, you and they will hear more of what is actually being said.

3. *Have children create questions for the speaker.* Challenge them to become such good listeners that you and they will be able to ask the speaker a question that uses some of his or her own words and ideas. For example, if Nadine is reporting the results of her group's work on rock classifying to the full class, ask the class at the end of the report if they have any questions for Nadine or her group. By doing this, you will help the children realize that they should be so attentive to the speaker that they can later ask good questions about what was said.

Figure 5.5 Use this checklist to apply specific strategies for improving the quality of listening in the science classroom.

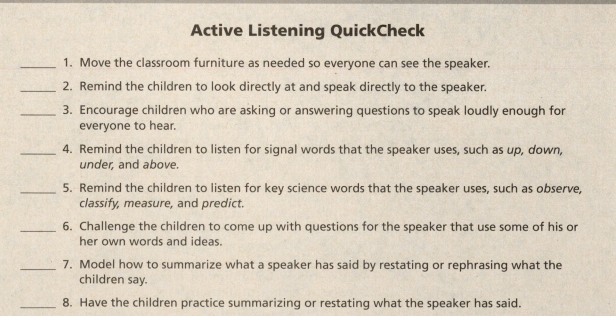

Active Listening QuickCheck

_____ 1. Move the classroom furniture as needed so everyone can see the speaker.

_____ 2. Remind the children to look directly at and speak directly to the speaker.

_____ 3. Encourage children who are asking or answering questions to speak loudly enough for everyone to hear.

_____ 4. Remind the children to listen for signal words that the speaker uses, such as *up, down, under,* and *above.*

_____ 5. Remind the children to listen for key science words that the speaker uses, such as *observe, classify, measure,* and *predict.*

_____ 6. Challenge the children to come up with questions for the speaker that use some of his or her own words and ideas.

_____ 7. Model how to summarize what a speaker has said by restating or rephrasing what the children say.

_____ 8. Have the children practice summarizing or restating what the speaker has said.

4. *Practice summarizing what the speaker has said.* When children speak or ask questions, listen so attentively that you can restate in summary form what they said. To do this, you have to use the natural gaps in a speaker's speech patterns to mentally summarize the key ideas as they emerge. Model this by occasionally restating or rephrasing a child's question in a shorter form and then checking with him or her to see if you have captured the point or question.

▶ Do It! Use the Active Listening QuickCheck

You can apply these four guidelines to a real classroom setting by using Figure 5.5, the Active Listening QuickCheck. It provides some very specific steps you can take to increase active listening. Check off (✓) each strategy as you try it.

Demonstrations

"*Do it again!*"

This exclamation should bring joy to your heart after you do a science demonstration for children. These three little words send a clear message that you have made contact with a child's mind.

● Presenting a Good Science Demonstration

In recent years, I have observed fewer and fewer demonstrations in elementary science classrooms. It seems that a long-overdue emphasis on having *children* do activities has taken an important job away from the *teacher:* showing children phenomena they cannot efficiently, effectively, or *safely* discover for themselves. Because it has enormous potential for focusing

Science demonstrations have enormous potential for focusing children's attention on specific phenomena.

attention on a given phenomenon, the science demonstration can be an important tool for promoting inquiry in children. A demonstration can raise many questions for children, which can then be addressed in greater detail by individual science activities.

Of course, demonstrations can be misused in the classroom. They should never replace children's involvement in science activities, and they should not be used solely to reproduce phenomena that children have already read about. Instead, demonstrations should be used to intensify children's curiosity about a unit to be studied; to clarify the confusion that may result from attaining contrary results by children who have carried out identical science activities; and to tie together various types of learning at the end of a unit. Be sure to consider safety precautions and maintain a safety zone for the students when using hot liquids or potentially hazardous materials.

Make the demonstration interactive. Although you may be manipulating equipment and materials, actively involve the children in the thought process of the demonstration. Ask them to make predictions, to seek explanations, and to make suggestions about how you might proceed with the demonstration. Interactive demonstrations provide a great opportunity for you to model thinking.

▶ Do It! Use the Demonstration QuickCheck

The chapters in Part Two of this book include elementary school demonstrations for the life, physical, and earth/space sciences. Other sources of science demonstrations are provided in the resources at the end of this book. Bear in mind that by using larger equipment or materials, you can transform virtually any science activity into a demonstration you feel the children should experience as a class.

A number of considerations must be made in order to present an effective demonstration. Use Figure 5.6, the Demonstration QuickCheck, to assess the effectiveness of the science demonstrations that you or others do. Check off (✓) each item that applies.

Figure 5.6   Use this checklist to evaluate a science demonstration for children that you observe or perform.

Demonstration QuickCheck

_____ 1. The teacher began the demonstration promptly; the children didn't have to wait an excessive amount of time while the teacher got prepared.

_____ 2. The demonstration was essentially simple and straightforward, not elaborate and complex.

_____ 3. All the children in the class could observe the demonstration.

_____ 4. It seemed as if the teacher had pretested the demonstration; there was no evidence that this was the first time it had been tried—for example, missing equipment, confusion in the sequence of steps.

_____ 5. The teacher was able to create a bit of drama by presenting purposely puzzling situations or outcomes that were unexpected to the children.

_____ 6. The demonstration did not endanger the health or safety of the children.

_____ 7. The demonstration seemed to fit the topic under study.

_____ 8. The demonstration was appropriately introduced, carried out, and concluded.

_____ 9. The children had an opportunity to ask questions, make statements, and give reactions.

_____10. The demonstration provided a significant learning experience for the children.

Make the Case *An Individual or Group Challenge*

● **The Problem**

A large class may make so many demands on a teacher's time and attention that some children who have a special aptitude for science may go unnoticed.

● **Assess Your Prior Knowledge and Beliefs**

Based on your personal experiences, comment on how much each of the following may increase the likelihood of a teacher's recognizing children with a special aptitude for science:

1. The group leader shares the results of a science activity with the class as a whole.

    _____

2. The teacher leads a discussion about a field trip the class has recently taken.

    _____

3. The teacher asks questions that will reveal the children's knowledge of a topic.

    _____

4. The teacher discusses the results of a demonstration.

    _____

5. The teacher helps a cooperative learning group summarize its findings.

    _____

6. The teacher praises a group that has completed its science activity before other groups.

    _____

7. The teacher asks groups to select their own leaders.

    _____

● **The Challenge**

It has become clear that you must find some way to reach those children who are not working to their full potential in science. You have decided to teach a few students in higher grades some basic questioning and cooperative group skills and then use these students as assistants. You have already decided to call the project "Science Buddies." What factors should you consider in the early stages of planning for this project?

Science Textbooks

The year was 1489. The city was Florence, Italy. A young man, just 14 years old, was walking through the work yard next to a cathedral that was being built. He came upon an enormous old block of poorly shaped marble resting in the weeds, which was called "The Giant" by marble workers and sculptors. Many had tried to make some use of it and failed. "It had lain for 35 years in the cathedral's work yard, an awesome ghostly reminder to all young sculptors of the challenge of their craft."[4]

Twelve years later, the same man rediscovered and very carefully studied the sleeping, malformed Giant. Now, at 26, he saw something in the marble that only he could release. That something would become known as *David,* and the man who stripped away the excess marble to reveal perhaps the most extraordinary sculpture known to humankind was Michelangelo. Within the imperfect, he saw what few others could see: potential.

Using Textbooks as Resources

Your science classroom will be filled with imperfect resources: computers with Internet access that may lock up just as your children reach the best part of your research assignment, stacks of videotapes of nature adventures that really don't fit your curriculum, and bookshelves of textbooks that seem far too dull for your active children. You can spend a great deal of time wishing that you had better resources, but doing so will make no difference at all.

Science textbooks, bought with taxpayer money and intended as useful resources, will probably be flawed in one way or another. Their limitations will be obvious to all, but their potential will be unseen by many. Jones tells us that "U.S. textbooks are about twice the size of textbooks in other countries, and this is one situation where bigger is definitely not better."[5] She goes on to cite another expert who comments on the fact that textbooks seem unfocused, repetitive, and lacking coherence.

Although modern textbooks have definite weaknesses, they also contain some resources that you, a discovery-oriented teacher, can make good use of—*if* you are creative. They contain science content written at particular grade levels and provide many hands-on science activities. In addition, they usually come with teacher's guides that include enrichment ideas.

The activities in a textbook series, of course, reflect a particular scope and sequence of science content. If you have the freedom and the desire to create your own science curriculum, the textbook can still be quite useful. By omitting some of the structure present in the textbook's directions to the children, you can modify the activities so that they place more emphasis on discovery learning.

Textbooks are typically divided into a number of *units,* or groups of chapters. If you look over the units and the teacher's guide that accompanies the book, you will find many helpful teaching ideas. You will also find that many of the suggestions can be applied to learning units that you devise on your own. Many teacher's guides for textbooks provide bulletin board ideas, suggestions for field trips, lists of audiovisual materials, lists of children's books, and other helpful information that you can use to enrich your learning units.

In sum, you should consider these criteria in determining the usefulness of a certain textbook:

1. Content
2. Reading level
3. Approach to instruction
4. Physical characteristics
5. Availability of supplemental materials

Figure 5.7   Use this checklist to assess the quality of science textbooks available for children at your grade level.

Textbook Quality QuickCheck

1. *Content*
   _____ Does the content easily correlate with National Science Education Standards, state standards, and local standards?
   _____ Are the inquiry process skills emphasized?
   _____ Are there unit, chapter, section, and lesson objectives, and are they clearly written?
   _____ Is the content accurate and up-to-date?
   _____ Are the units, chapters, sections, and lessons logically organized?
   _____ Are distinctions made between *fact* and *theory?*
   _____ Are connections made between science and technology and personal/social perspectives?
   _____ Are the accomplishments of women, individuals from diverse cultural backgrounds, and individuals with special challenges included?
   _____ Do the end-of-unit, -chapter, or -section questions go beyond simple recall?
   _____ Is the content relevant to students' daily lives?

2. *Reading Level*
   _____ Is the reading level appropriate for the intended grade level?
   _____ Will the material engage student interest?
   _____ Is new vocabulary clearly introduced and defined?
   _____ Is there a glossary?

3. *Approach to Instruction*
   _____ Does the book appropriately relate the reading of science content to inquiry-based, discovery-focused activities?
   _____ Can the science activities be done with readily available, inexpensive materials and equipment?
   _____ Are there suggestions for follow-up activities that students could carry out on the Internet, at home, or as special long-term projects?

4. *Physical Characteristics*
   _____ Does the book look interesting from the view of students at your grade level?
   _____ Is the size and font of the print appropriate for students at your grade level?
   _____ Are the photographs and artwork clear, purposeful, and engaging?
   _____ Are the charts and graphs labeled well, and do they clarify the text?
   _____ Is there an appropriate mix of photos and art representing females, males, students with challenges, and students from diverse cultural backgrounds?

5. *Availability of Supplemental Materials*
   _____ Does the teacher's guide (teacher's edition) seem useful in terms of providing help in planning lessons and units?
   _____ Are any of the following available?
   _____ Transparencies
   _____ Lab books, workbooks, or other student materials
   _____ Assessment materials
   _____ Videos/CD-ROMS
   _____ Related software
   _____ Correlated science materials and equipment kits

Textbooks can provide you and your children a general structure for science content and experiences, ensuring continuity both during a single school year and from year to year within a school. Keep in mind, however, that the extent to which textbooks lead to discovery learning will, in the final analysis, depend on you.

▶ Do It! Use the Textbook Quality QuickCheck

If you have access to a collection of modern textbooks that are used in an elementary or middle school, you will likely find it very useful to systematically analyze a few of them, using the five criteria just listed. Doing so will reveal a great deal to you about the content that is commonly taught at particular grade levels as well as the quality of textbook resources that teachers might use. Use Figure 5.7, the Textbook Quality QuickCheck (page 89), to guide your efforts, checking off (✓) each criterion that applies. You may wish to add additional criteria to the checklist as you put it to use.

Science Kits

You are likely to teach at a school that uses any one of several prepared science curriculum kits consisting of a series of modules comprised of equipment and materials with supportive student worksheets and teacher guides. Science kits often provide background for teachers, inquiry-based activities, assessments, and ideas for integration across disciplines.

Integration of the kits into your science class requires proper professional development and support from people who have used the kits in their classroom. It takes an initial investment of time and energy to become familiar with a kit's layout and approach. Kits, like textbooks, are not designed (or should not be designed) to be teacher-proof. Rather, they provide a framework that a good teacher will modify to fit his or her teaching style and students' needs.

● Using Science Kits Effectively in your Classroom

Keep It Simple   If it is your first time using the kit, begin with one module, preferably one on a topic with which you feel comfortable and that you enjoy. Once you get a feel for the teaching progression and layout of the module, other modules will be easier to implement.

Familiarize Yourself with the Kit   Spend some time unpacking the kit and reading through the manual to be sure the materials are sufficient and the progression of inquiry makes sense. Jones identifies material management and time management among the common challenges that teachers using kits encounter.[6] Therefore, familiarize yourself with the activities on your own prior to using them in class. Often kits go unused because some of the consumable materials are missing, therefore check and restock the kits after each use. Most consumables can be located and replenished easily (i.e., cotton balls, rice, tongue depressors).

Use the Kit as a Guide   Teaching science inquiry can be challenging if you are not comfortable with the science content or with the student-centered and sometimes chaotic dynamic of discovery learning. Science kits can be a welcome guide to keep you anchored the first time you teach a unit. Research suggests that science kits, by providing focus and structure, help teachers overcome the initial apprehension of teaching inquiry.[7]

Modify the Kit to Fit Your Needs   You don't have to do everything in the kit. Use the elements of the kit that suit your purpose without compromising the integrity and intellectual honesty of the lesson. As you become more familiar with the kit and its options, you will find yourself adapting it to fit your needs.

▶ *Do It! Use the Science Kit QuickCheck*

Science kits can provide a foundation for rich learning experiences. Good kits can introduce you to new teaching strategies as well as provide the basis for dynamic learning experiences for your students. Use the Kit QuickCheck in Figure 5.8 to assess science kits. Check off (✓) each criterion that applies.

Figure 5.8   Use this checklist to assess science kits.

Science Kit QuickCheck

1. Content

_____ What science topics does the kit address?

_____ Is the content appropriate for the grade level?

_____ Does the content address the NSES or the local standards?

_____ Is the content accurate and up to date?

_____ Is there a content background for teachers?

_____ Is it clear and informative?

2. Process

_____ Does the recommended teaching strategy include engagement and exploration activities?

_____ Do the activities connect meaningfully with the science content?

_____ Do the activities support inquiry?

_____ Is there evidence that students will use science process skills to create descriptive, explanatory, or experimental models?

_____ Are both formative and summative assessment strategies included?

_____ Are the student guides clear?

_____ Does the kit reflect principles of universal design for learning (see Chapter 9), providing multiple means of engagement, representation, and expression?

_____ Are there enrichment activities?

_____ Are there suggestions for interdisciplinary connections, e.g., to math and language arts?

_____ Is safety addressed? Are Material Data Safety Sheets provided as needed?

3. Materials

_____ Are the materials and equipment complete?

_____ Is the equipment in good working order?

_____ Are consumables inexpensive and easy to replenish?

Summary

Classroom teachers can use a variety of strategies to teach children science in an effective yet creative way. Cooperative learning groups can be used as an important part of any learning environment that encourages discovery learning. Teachers' use of questioning and wait-time strategies, ability to teach children to become active listeners, inclusion of science demonstrations along with hands-on activities, and creative use of textbooks and science kits can all serve to enhance and enrich the learning environment.

Going Further

On Your Own

1. Reflect upon the science activities you experienced in elementary school:
   a. Specifically, what activities do you remember? Why do you think you remember them?
   b. If you do remember activities, were they carried out by individual children or by groups? What do you think motivated the teacher's decision in this respect?
   c. While the activities were underway, were there any specific problems with work space, classroom behavior, or the availability of science materials? If so, what?
   d. Would you say that your teacher or teachers encouraged discovery learning?

2. Select a chapter from a conventional elementary school science textbook that contains some science activities. Develop a strategy for using the activities and text materials as the basis for a group of discovery-based lessons. How does your strategy compare with the more conventional use of chapters in science textbooks? Would your approach offer any cooperative learning possibilities?

3. How could you use some of the ideas in this chapter to create an ideal curriculum for children at the grade level you are most interested in? Be specific and focus upon the following:
   a. The content you would stress
   b. The concepts you would stress
   c. How the curriculum would reflect the teaching style you would use
   d. The use of cooperative learning groups
   e. The use of teacher demonstrations and hands-on student activities
   f. The use of effective questioning and wait-time strategies
   g. The use of textbooks as resources
   h. The use of science kits as resources

On Your Own or in a Cooperative Learning Group

4. With others, role-play the best and worst science demonstrations you have ever observed. What factors contributed to the quality (or lack thereof) of each? If you are doing this activity by yourself, respond in writing.

5. Select a topic commonly covered in elementary school science, and create five questions the teacher could use to help children make discoveries in this field of study. Also try to think of a demonstration that the teacher could use to raise questions among the children that might lead to discoveries.

6. Formulate a position on each of the following statements. You may wish to have a minidebate in which various members of the group adopt extreme positions.
   a. Discovery learning uses up valuable classroom time.
   b. Textbooks cannot be used with inquiry-based techniques.
   c. By asking questions, you can slow down a child's thought processes.

Resources for Discovery Learning

Internet Resources

To access these helpful websites, go to **MyEducationLab,** select Resources, and then Web Links. To learn more, click on the following links and you will easily be directed to the websites.

- **Curricular Companions:**
  www.keystone.fi.edu/matrix1.shtml

- **The Cooperative Learning Center at the: University of Minnesota**
  www.co-operation.org

Print Resources

Suggested Readings

Brune, Jeff. "Take It Outside!" *Science and Children* 39 no. 7 (April 2002): 29–33.

Corder, Greg, and Reed, Darren. "It's Raining Micrometeorites." *Science Scope* 26, no. 5 (February 2003): 23–25.

Fones, Shelly White. "Engaging Science." *Science Scope* 23, no. 6 (March 2000): 32–36.

Freedman, Michael. "Using Effective Demonstrations in the Classroom." *Science and Children* 38, no. 1 (September 2000): 52–55.

Galus, Pamela. "Reactions to Atomic Structure." *Science Scope* 26, no. 4 (January 2003): 38–41.

Irwin, Leslie, et al. "Science Centers for All." *Science and Children* 40, no. 5 (February 2003): 35–37.

Jones, M. T., et al. "Implementing Inquiry Kit Curriculum: Obstacles, Adaptations, and Practical Knowledge Development in Two Middle School Science Teachers." *Science Education* 91, no. 3 (May 2007): 492–513.

Kelly, Janet, et al. "Science Adventures at the Local Museum." *Science and Children* 39, no. 7 (April 2002): 46–48.

Krutchinsky, Rick, and Harris, William. "Super Science Saturday." *Science and Children* 40, no. 4 (January 2003): 26–28.

MacKenzie, Ann Haley. "Brain Busters, Mind Games & Science Chats." *Science Scope* 24, no. 6 (March 2001): 54–58.

Reeve, Stephen L. "Beyond the Textbook." *Science Scope* 25, no. 6 (March 2002): 4–6.

Souvignier, Elmar, and Kronenberger, Julia. "Cooperative Learning in Third Graders' Jigsaw Groups for Mathematics and Science with and without Questioning Training." *The British Journal of Educational Psychology* 77, no. 4 (December 2007): 755–771.

Stivers, Louise. "Discovering Trees: Not Just a Walk in the Park!" *Science and Children* 39, no. 7 (April 2002): 38–41.

Notes

1. Donald Orlich et al., *Teaching Strategies: A Guide to Better Instruction* (Lexington, MA: D. C. Heath, 1994), pp. 186–193.
2. Kenneth G. Tobin and William Capie, *Wait-Time and Learning in Science* (Burlington, NC: Carolina Biological Supply, n.d.), p. 2.
3. I drew ideas for the Wait-Time/Think-Time QuickCheck from a variety of sources that you may find of interest, including Robert J. Stahl (1995), "Using 'Think-Time' and 'Wait-Time' in the Classroom" (ERIC Digest no. ED370885); it can be found on the Internet at <www.ed.gov/databases/ERIC_Digests/ed370885.html>. Another useful source, which focused on college teaching assistants, is "Teaching Tips for TAs: WAIT-TIME" (June 14, 2000), published by the Office of Instructional Consultation, University of California, Santa Barbara, and located on the Internet at <www.id.ucsb.edu/IC/TA/ta.html>.
4. Robert Coughlan, *The World of Michelangelo* (New York: Time, 1966), p. 85.

5. Rebecca Jones, "Solving Problems in Math and Science Education," *The American School Board Journal* 185, no. 7 (July 1998): 18.

6. M. T. Jones, et al., "Implementing Inquiry Kit Curriculum: Obstacles, Adaptations, and Practical Knowledge Development in Two Middle School Science Teachers," *Science Education* 91, no. 3 (May 2007): 492–513.

7. Ibid, p. 509.

Assessment of Understanding and Inquiry

A good teacher asks, "How am I doing?"
A great teacher asks, "How are my students doing?"

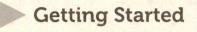 **Getting Started**

"What d'ja git?"
"She gave me a C!"

Would overhearing this exchange between two students—after you've taught a unit that took three weeks to plan and far too many afternoons shopping at discount stores for inexpensive activity materials—get your attention? And would it sting just a bit?

It would and should for two reasons. First of all, it would tell you that the end-of-unit test probably didn't assess whether your children actually learned some science. Second, it would tell you that your children have the extraordinary idea that

the teacher *gives* a grade. Notice the phrasing *She gave*. Does that imply, even slightly, that the student's grade was *earned*?

In this chapter, you will learn about a range of assessment techniques that will help you discover whether your children are actually learning science. Carefully studying these materials will help you create a classroom in which the children are more concerned about what they *learned* and less concerned about the gifts they think you give!

Two Approaches to Assessment: Formative and Summative

I do not recall where or when I heard the statement, "*A good teacher asks, 'How am I doing?' A great teacher asks, 'How are my students doing?'*" But a truly outstanding teacher should ask both questions. Formative and summative assessments are two approaches that help us focus on these two, very important aspects.

Formative assessment occurs during instruction to let us know whether the children are on the pathway to learning the intended content. It serves as a check on the execution of the lesson plan, answering the questions, "Are the children doing what you intended them to do?" and "Are there signs that the children are constructing the understanding and developing the concepts that you targeted for learning?" If the children are on track to learning, then you can continue the lesson as planned. If feedback from your formative assessment indicates that the children are not on track, then it is not too late for you to revise and adjust the lesson accordingly. A lesson plan is just that, a plan. The saying that even the best plans go astray is all too true when teaching. Formative assessment keeps you from being surprised when plans falter and provide you with time to adjust and salvage the lesson. In this respect, formative assessment addresses how you are doing as well as how your students are doing.

Summative assessment occurs after the intended learning has taken place. It answers the questions, "What did the students learn? Did they learn what I thought I taught?" It is a culminating activity during which students demonstrate their understanding of the content or skills that you intended to teach. Summative assessments are usually used for purposes of placement, grading, accountability, and informing parents and future teachers about student performance.

Teachers often ask me for a list of formative and summative assessment tools. Unfortunately, it is not that easy. Although some assessment tools are usually associated with one of the two approaches, often the methodologies overlap. Whether an assessment is formative or summative depends on how you choose to use the data.

I will resist the urge to classify any assessment methodology as strictly formative or summative. Throughout this chapter, we will consider several assessment methodologies and evaluate the strengths and weaknesses of each. It will be up to you choose the appropriate assessment strategies for your purposes.

The design of good assessment tools is made easier by stating clearly and concisely the content to be taught and establishing good performance objectives. You will be reminded to refer to both of these components in your lesson plan as you develop assessments.

● A Brief Comment on Performance Assessment and Authentic Assessment

Performance assessment and authentic assessment have very similar meanings. Performance assessment is a measure of assessment based on authentic tasks such as activities, exercises, or problems that require students to show what they can do.[1] Authentic assessments

Descriptions of Formative and Summative Assessment as Described by the National Research Council[2]

Formative assessment refers to assessments that provide information to students and teachers that is used to improve teaching and learning. These are often informal and ongoing, though they need not be. Data from summative assessments can be used in a formative way.

Summative assessment refers to the cumulative assessments, usually occurring at the end of a unit or topic coverage, that intend to capture what a student has learned or the quality of the learning, and judge performance against some standards. Although we often think of summative assessments as traditional objective tests, this need not be the case. For example, summative assessments could follow from an accumulation of evidence collected over time, as in a collection of student work.

present students with real-world challenges that require them to apply their relevant skills and knowledge.[3] The assessment strategies used for each type of assessment are often interchangeable. I consider authentic assessments a type of performance assessment, and consequently will address performance assessments in general. Let's begin by looking to the National Research Council as our guide.

The National Science Education Standards (NSES) Approach to Assessment

NSES

The NSES recommend assessing children in two broad areas: understanding and inquiry. *Understanding* means what you would expect it to mean—whether children comprehend the science ideas you are teaching. *Inquiry* focuses on whether children have the ability to actually seek their own explanations. The following sections will further clarify the intent of the standards as well as provide some practical examples.

● Assessment Strategies

Go to **MyEducationLab**, select the topic Assessment, watch the video entitled "Ongoing Assessment: Assessing Knowledge and Understanding," and complete the questions that accompany it.

Prompt and Rubric   Basic to the NSES approach to assessment is the use of prompts and rubrics. A *prompt* is a question or group of questions that includes a statement about a task to be done along with directions on how to do it. A *scoring rubric* (pronounced "roo-brick") is used to describe the criteria that should be used when assessing a child's performance.[4] Let's look at examples of the use of prompts and scoring rubrics in the classroom.

▶ *Example of a Prompt and Rubric*

Topic: Sound (for grades 1–3)

Content to be assessed: Sounds are caused by vibrations.

Performance objective: Given a drum, pencil, and rice, students will hit the drum with the pencil and explain orally that sound is produced by vibrations.

Prompt: "This little drum is made by stretching plastic wrap over a jar. I'd like you to tap the drum with the eraser, look at the plastic, and tell me what you see and what you hear. Then sprinkle some rice grains on the plastic and look at it as you tap it again."

Questions:

1. What do you observe when you hit the drum with an eraser?
2. What do you think causes sound?

Rubric:

3	2	1
Student's description of what was observed includes the plastic moves up and down, the vibration causes sound	Student's description includes a response with one correct observation	No response is given or incorrect responses are given

You could use this prompt and rubric as a formative assessment if it was administered during the lesson or as a summative assessment after the lesson.

Reality Check

Write a prompt and scoring rubric for the following content to be assessed:

Content: Energy from the sun is converted to food by plants. Animals such as mice and rabbits eat the plants to get their food. Animals such as snakes and hawks eat mice and rabbits. When living things die, they are broken down by organisms such as bacteria and fungi and returned to the soil where they can be used again by plants. When elements of the food chain are removed, the organisms that depend on them have to find other food sources or die.

Performance Objective: Given a food web diagram, students will explain what will occur if the mice are removed from the food web. The students will score at least satisfactory on the rubric that you will create. (Go to Rubrics and Scoring Guides on page 109 if you need help.)

Food Web

Go to **MyEducationLab**, select the topic Inquiry, watch the video entitled "Evaluation," and complete the question that accompanies it.

Performance Assessment

Inquiry is a central component of the [National Science Education] *Standards.* It involves developing descriptive models, explanatory models, and experimental models using science process skills such as asking questions, planning, designing and conducting experiments, analyzing and interpreting data, and drawing conclusions.[5] Your young students may be able to do all or part of the inquiry process on their own. You will need to assess the degree to which your students can carry out the process of inquiry, keeping in mind that the inquiry can be measured on a continuum from being highly directed to completely open ended. The more the students initiate questioning, exploration, data collection, data analysis, and conclusions on their own, the less directed the inquiry.

Because inquiry is a process, assessing students' ability to do inquiry frequently takes place over an extended time. Atkin, Black, and Coffey in *Classroom Assessment in the National Science Education Standards* suggest that, "The best way to support inquiry is to obtain information about students while they are actually engaged in science investigations with a view toward helping them develop their understandings of both subject matter and procedure."[6] Performance assessment strategies lend themselves to evaluation of students' abilities to inquire. Note that a collection of data from several assessment instruments over time will provide you with a good idea of what students can do with respect to inquiry.

As their name implies, performance assessments are based on observations of students as they demonstrate a specific task or problem-solving skill. They are usually evaluated using a rubric or scoring guide. The evaluator collects data about the student's procedures and conclusions through direct observation of behavior, written records such as notes, worksheets, lab reports, or products such as posters, role plays, and recordings.

▶ Example of a Performance Assessment

Topic: Light and plants (for young learners)

Engagement: What will happen if Mrs. Riley's plants are kept in the closet without light instead of in sunlight on the window sill?

Exploration: I will give each group two plants. You have one week to find out what will happen to the plants if they are kept in a closet without light. Use the following questions to guide your investigation:

1. Make a prediction that you can test.
2. Describe how you will test your prediction.
3. Carry out your test.
4. Make observations of your plants each day and record your observations in your science notebook, using words and drawings.
5. At the end of your test, state your results.

Explanation: Students will describe whether their evidence supports their prediction or does not support their prediction.

Scoring guide:

Performance	Criteria	Potential score	Student score
Prediction	Prediction is testable	1	
Test of prediction	Implies treatment	1	
	Implies control	1	
	Identifies observables (color, height . . .)	1	
Daily observations	Makes daily entries	1	
	Uses words to describe observables	1	
	Uses drawings to describe observables	1	
	Observations are accurate	1	
Results	Results are consistent with observations	1	
Explanation	Students relate that the presence of light is necessary for Mrs. Riley's plants to live	1	
Total score		10	

● Portfolios

A *portfolio* is an organized collection of a person's work that shows the very best that he or she can do. Although each piece placed in a portfolio can be assessed with respect to the degree to which the student achieved specific unit objectives, the portfolio as a whole will illustrate the child's progress.

You can learn a great deal by observing a child at work.

You may be wondering what specific examples of a child's science work should go in a science portfolio. Here are some products that could be included:

- Written observations and science reports
- Drawings, charts, and graphs that are the products of hands-on, discovery-focused activities
- Thank-you letters to resource people who have visited the classroom (e.g., beekeepers, veterinarians, health care providers)
- Reaction pieces, such as prepared written responses to science software, videos, discovery experiences, field trips, and websites
- Media products, such as student-produced science work in audio, video, or digital form

● Anecdotal Records

Name: Jimmy Green　　　Age: 8
Grade: 2　　　　　　　Date: May 5

This week Jimmy's group, the Science Stars, which was responsible for taking care of the aquarium, found a dead guppy. Jimmy volunteered to bury it in the school lawn. He told the group, "Even though it's dead, it'll help the grass grow."

A teacher's brief notes about a child's behavior can reveal a great deal about what the child has or has not learned. The notes, called *anecdotal records,* can help you assess how well individual children are doing. They can be particularly helpful when you wish to reflect upon and assess how well individual children are mastering inquiry process skills or developing desirable attitudes and values.

● Affective Development Checklists

"Boy, do I hate science!"

If you heard one of your students say this, what would you conclude about his or her affective development? Your only basis for assessing changes in *affect* is your observation of the affect-laden behaviors students exhibit. Their comments, smiles, frowns, in-class behavior, and out-of-class behavior reveal a great deal about how much they are developing favorable attitudes toward science and your teaching.

Figure 6.1 presents a list of behaviors that you may wish to draw on to create your own affective development checklist. Add your personal observations of student behaviors to create a more comprehensive list.

Figure 6.1　Draw from these behaviors to create an affective development checklist.

- Makes drawings and diagrams of science-related objects and events
- Is curious about new objects, organisms, and materials added to the classroom
- Talks about surprising things he or she notices in the environment
- Spends free time at the in-class science learning center
- Questions but is tolerant of the ideas of others
- Enters science fairs and school science expositions
- Brings science-related magazine pictures to class
- Checks science-related books out of the class or school library
- Reads science fiction
- Collects natural objects as a hobby
- Comments on science-related programs seen on TV

- Comments on science-related films
- Asks for class field trips to museums, planetariums, and so on
- Invents things
- Builds models
- Asks questions about science-related news stories
- Asks to do more science activities
- Asks to make or fix science equipment
- Volunteers to carry out demonstrations
- Asks to work on science-related bulletin boards
- Asks to distribute materials and equipment for activities
- Questions superstitions
- Asks to take care of classroom animals or plants

Science Conferences with Children

The words we speak tell a great deal about what we know and how we feel. The quickest and possibly most reliable way to find out if children in a discovery-oriented classroom are learning is to give them an opportunity to talk to you. If you learn to listen carefully and gently probe around the edges of a child's talk, you will discover whether he or she has grasped the real meaning of a food web, has had anything to do with creating the group's drawings showing the movement of the continents, or is becoming increasingly curious about the natural world.

Science Notebooks

Have you ever watched a child fish around in his or her desk to locate a bologna-stained sheet of paper that contains yesterday's science notes? Some teachers have found that a journal or notebook devoted only to science can be a great asset for children as well as a useful tool for assessing how well individual students are doing. I have noticed an increase in the use of science notebooks in elementary school science classes during the past few years. While it may seem like semantics, science notebooks can be distinguished from science journals in that science notebooks allow for more reflection and less structure than science journals typically do. Children are encouraged to include not only formal investigative elements, such as procedures, data, and results, but also their questions, predictions, reflections, and to express their feelings about science. Most importantly, notebooks provide a place for students to record new concepts they have learned or want to learn. Figures 6.2a and 6.2b show examples of entries in science notebooks. Here are some suggestions for implementing the use of science notebooks:

1. At the start of the year, ask each child to obtain a notebook he or she will devote exclusively to science. You may also wish to have the children construct their own science notebooks.

Figure 6.2   Examples of science notebook entries

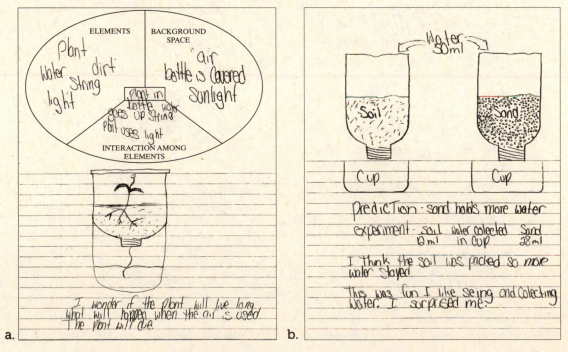

2. Encourage the children to design covers for their science notebooks. One way to do this is to have a general discussion about the major themes or units they will do during the year.

3. Encourage children to write in their notebooks each day, and provide time for them to do so. Offer some guiding questions, such as "What did you do? What did you learn? How do you feel about what you have learned?"

4. Schedule time at the end of each teaching unit for children to discuss some of the things they have written.

5. Consider using the science notebooks during parent-teacher conferences. Also consider putting the notebooks on display for Parents' Night or Back-to-School Night.

● Probes

Probes are similar to prompts and rubrics, but designed more specifically to uncover whether a student understands a particular rule of interaction that you targeted in the lesson. *Probes* include a simple question that seeks a two-part answer. The first part usually involves lower order thinking skills such as identification or naming. The second part of the probe requires students to demonstrate higher order thinking by stating rules of relationship between or among elements.

▶ *Example*

Is it a physical change or a chemical change?

The list below involves situations that cause changes in materials. Put a P next to the situations in which the materials in italics undergo a physical change and a C next to the situations in which the materials in italics undergo a chemical change.

_____ *Ice cream* melts in the sun

_____ *Wood* is cut to make sawdust

_____ A *car* rusts

_____ *Wood* is burned in a fire

_____ *Water* evaporates from a pan

_____ An *egg* is fried

Explain your thinking. Describe in writing a "rule" to decide if something undergoes a physical or chemical change.

● Children's Self-Assessment

As teachers, we may forget that children naturally reflect on how well they do in each activity that is a part of their science experience. And so it should seem logical to capitalize on self-reflection when you incorporate assessment into your classroom.

There are many ways to stimulate children's self-assessment. For example, before the children begin to write in their science notebooks, you might say, "So far this month, you have worked on two projects. One was building a flashlight, and the other was using a flashlight and mirrors to study how light behaves. What did you learn in each project?" The children's responses will represent their efforts to assess what they have done. This is important information to you as a teacher.

● Concept Mapping

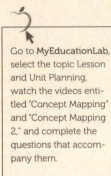

Go to **MyEducationLab**, select the topic Lesson and Unit Planning, watch the videos entitled "Concept Mapping" and "Concept Mapping 2," and complete the questions that accompany them.

A family is seated around the dinner table. The dad passes a bowl of reconstituted instant mashed potatoes to his son and asks, "So, what did you learn in science today?" The child responds, "Nuthin."

How can this be? That child spent the entire day in a lovely, pastel-walled classroom overflowing with books and science materials, was taught by knowledgeable and motivated teachers, had access to a variety of resources (including four or five computers with Internet access), took an around-the-school-yard nature field trip with his class, and also attended a special all-school assembly with Dr. Science, who performed demonstrations that flashed, popped, and banged. Yet the child answered his dad's question with "Nuthin." What went wrong?

The answer is simple: The child doesn't really know what he learned. By that, I mean that the child has had no opportunity to make what he learned *explicit*. He probably learned many things today, but he has not brought them to the forefront of his consciousness and tied them all together. Consequently, both the child and his dad finish their meal thinking that the day was as bland as those mashed potatoes.

One way to help a child assess self-learning is to have him or her make a concept map after an inquiry-based experience. You can even use a concept map as a personal unit-planning device. Even so, I am presenting it here as an assessment tool, so you can see what children have learned in a concrete way. They will literally draw you a picture!

A *concept map* is a diagram that represents knowledge by identifying basic concepts and topics and showing how these items are related. Such a map is created using these two symbols:

1. *Node*—A shape (typically a circle or oval) that contains a word or phrase to represent the item of content knowledge.

2. *Link*—A line with an arrowhead at one or both ends that's used to connect the nodes and to show the relationship between them. A single arrowhead indicates that one node leads to or is part of another. A double arrowhead indicates that nodes are reciprocal or mutually supportive of each other.

Figure 6.3   This concept map represents what one child learned in a school yard field trip to observe types of living things.

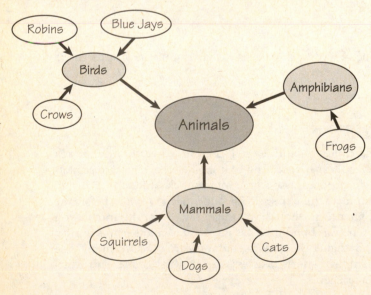

Figure 6.3 shows the concept map a child drew after going on a school yard field trip to observe types of living things in the environment. Starting with "Animals" in the center of the page, the child branched out to classes of animals, such as "Mammals" and "Birds," and then became even more specific by noting types of animals within each class, such as "Dogs" and "Squirrels" under "Mammals." Note that all of the arrows point the same way: back to "Animals."

By studying a child's concept map, you can assess what he or she has really learned during an experience and how he or she has tied specific pieces of knowledge together. The child will benefit from creating the map because he or she will make what might have been abstract or general more concrete and specific. As a result, the child will have a much fuller knowledge of what was learned—and it won't seem like "Nuthin"!

Traditional Assessment Techniques

● End-of-Chapter Homework

"*. . . and then do numbers 1 through 5 on the last page.*"

Does this bring back a few classroom memories? Giving children an end-of-chapter homework assignment is a common way for teachers to discover whether the children remember what they have read. When you make such an assignment, you believe that children will read the chapter first and then answer the questions. Perhaps in elementary and middle school, you read your science chapters before you did your homework. If so, I congratulate you! If you didn't, this is a good opportunity to consider what traditional end-of-chapter homework does and doesn't accomplish.

▶ What Does It Accomplish?

An end-of-chapter assignment tells the children that you are serious about the content you are teaching. It forces them to look at and, if you are fortunate, read text material, if only to find answers to the questions they have been assigned. This type of assignment provides you with one small indicator of how serious a child is about his or her schooling. The actual appearance of a textbook in the home also tells parents that the child is doing something in science class. Finally, homework assignments that are *not* done provide you with a reason for talking with a child and the child's parents about his or her effort.

▶ What Doesn't It Accomplish?

End-of-chapter homework does not tell you much about what children know, and it doesn't tell you if they like science. Completed homework seldom reveals any understanding of information beyond the recall level of the cognitive domain. End-of-chapter homework will probably not pique children's interest to the point that they will want to learn more about the topic.

Using End-of-Chapter Homework Effectively   Before making the assignment, talk with children about the purpose of the homework and the reading they have done. Use statements such as "You know this first chapter on living things told us about the differences between living and nonliving things. The questions at the end will help you find out if you remember and understand some of the big ideas." After this introduction, give children a few minutes of class time to begin the assignment. Doing so will increase the probability that children will do the homework and possibly make the experience somewhat more meaningful to them.

● Quizzes

Do you still live in fear of the "pop" quiz? Does your heart flutter a bit just hearing the term *quiz*? Quizzes are a part of the classroom assessment process from elementary school through graduate school, and their effect on students seems to remain rather constant. A quiz takes little time and is usually used as a quick assessment of whether students remember or understand factual information or concepts.

▶ What Do They Accomplish?

Quizzes tell teachers whether children can think fast and have a sufficient command of writing to get their responses on paper before time is up. They are easy to grade and provide a snapshot of the student's recall of information. They also serve to keep children "on their toes," but they should not divert teachers from the science experiences that should be taking place in the classroom.

▶ *What Don't They Accomplish?*

Quizzes do not tell teachers much about in-depth understanding. Children's lack of success on quizzes may not reveal a deficit in knowledge or understanding but rather a deficit in being able to express themselves quickly.

Using Quizzes More Effectively Quizzes should be used in moderation. If you wish to find out whether children are learning, giving a quiz now and then that is focused on the important ideas of a science unit can provide some information about student progress. Doing so can also help you discover that you need to modify your teaching or help a particular child before a unit is completed.

● Tests

Given the large numbers of children in most classrooms, most teacher-developed tests are composed of short-answer questions and some multiple-choice items. At the end of the test, there may be a few so-called essay questions. In inquiry-based classrooms, teachers who use tests are likely to include some questions dealing with how science activities were conducted and what was learned from them.

▶ *What Do They Accomplish?*

Test results tell children, parents, and you how well the children answered the questions that were asked. Test results give children a way to assess their own progress and a way to compare themselves to others. They give you a neat and tidy way to get information to use for grading. They also tell you which children in the class are good test takers. That information is important if you want to teach children skills that will be useful in later life.

If you create a test with questions that discover more than children's recall abilities, you may get more useful information. The test results may reveal whether children understood concepts, were able to apply what was learned, and were able to analyze the science phenomena studied. If, however, the test consists solely of recall questions, only the children's memory will be assessed.

Traditional assessment may not reflect all of the learning that occurs in a discovery-based science classroom.

▶ *What Don't They Accomplish?*

Tests tell you only what children know and understand about the particular questions you asked. Very few tests assess how well children can express their thoughts. Questions that elicit this information are challenging to create, require many minutes for children to complete, and demand that the teacher spend a considerable amount of time outside class carefully reading each response, reflecting on the work, offering written feedback, and assigning grades.

Tests probably do little to motivate children to think about science as an interesting subject area or to increase their career awareness. Nor does success on science tests indicate that children like science, are interested in science, will engage in free reading about science topics, will watch televised science programs, or even will become interested observers of the natural world.

Using Tests More Effectively   As you prepare a test, try to cross-reference each item to one of the cognitive, affective, or psychomotor objectives of the teaching unit. By doing this, you can measure student progress over all of the unit's objectives. To help you assess student achievement on the objectives of the unit and the quality of the questions you have asked, after the test, prepare a chart on which you will record the number of children who answer each question correctly.

Library Reports

Can you recall going to the school library or media center to do research on a topic for a science report? Perhaps you remember poring through encyclopedias and other reference books to find information on such topics as whales, volcanoes, tornadoes, and rockets. A great deal can be learned through library work that is related to the science experiences that occur in the classroom.

▶ What Do They Accomplish?

Science library reports are common assignments in elementary and middle school and provide students with information and ideas that can round out what they have learned through hands-on activities, demonstrations, and class discussions. Library reports can lead children to think about topics and questions that were not considered during class. They can also help improve a child's grade for a marking period by making up for low quiz or test grades.

▶ What Don't They Accomplish?

When used in the traditional manner, library reports do little to extend and enrich the basic knowledge, skills, and attitudes emphasized in a discovery-focused classroom. They do not present children with an opportunity to touch science materials or to move through the full learning cycle. In the best circumstances, library reports tell you whether children can look up information in reference books and summarize what they have learned.

Using Library Reports More Effectively   In order for library reports to be meaningful, they should engage children in a quest that resolves some issue or problem. Therefore, if the children are engaged in inquiry-based science experiences related to the life cycle of insects, you might say, "I would like you to do work in the learning center that will help you answer the question 'Why don't we ever see baby butterflies?'" This type of assignment captures the same curiosity that you are hoping to capitalize on with hands-on discovery science. Children should be going to the library or learning center to learn how to use books and media as *tools* that are as essential to the pursuit of science as microscopes and metersticks.

Activity Write-Ups

How will you know that children are learning, fitting new learnings into previous knowledge, and constructing new meanings? You can discover this by observing them, by listening to them, and by reading what they have written in their activity write-ups.

▶ What Do They Accomplish?

Having children synthesize and share what they have learned in activity write-ups tells them that you believe thinking, talking, and writing about what they have experienced is important. Listening to a child's observations of water droplets forming on an ice-filled glass or reading a list of written observations gives you valuable information about the learning that is occurring in your classroom.

▶ What Don't They Accomplish?

A variety of problems can arise when you use activity write-ups. The most obvious one is that a child may have completed an activity successfully but not be a good writer. Under these circumstances, a poor report may tell you more about his or her language arts abilities than science abilities. If you rely only on activity write-ups, children with language difficulties will be unable to express what they have learned.

By necessity, the activity write-up is a very brief sketch of the work the child has done. While it will tell you a good deal about the results of a child's experimentation, it will tell you little about all the experiences he or she may have had as the activity was carried out.

Using Activity Write-Ups Effectively   When you look at or listen to a child's activity write-up, you need to be able to assess whether the efforts reflect the child's or the group's work on the activity. To help you make this assessment, take some time to explain to the children the importance of clearly identifying all the group members involved in preparing the report.

Another component of assessing the quality of a write-up is determining whether an incomplete report shows a lack of effort on the child's part or a limitation in his or her ability to use language. The only way to make this distinction is to ask the child clarifying questions.

● Standardized Tests

Go to **MyEducationLab**, select the topic Assessment, watch the video entitled "Standardized Tests," and complete the questions that accompany it.

If you walk down a school hallway and notice that it is strangely quiet, that the children are seated quietly at their desks, and that the public address system is not blaring messages, chances are the children are taking a standardized test. For some reason, standardized tests create a time of palpable quiet and anxiety.

In addition to the usual battery of IQ tests and personality inventories, some school districts have children take achievement tests in a variety of subjects. If you teach in a school that requires a standardized science achievement test, you may find that *you* are more concerned about the results than the children are.

▶ What Do They Accomplish?

A standardized achievement test in science compares how much the children in your class know compared to children nationwide, as reflected in norms. If the children in your class do well, it may make you feel very successful. If they do poorly, you may feel obliged to rethink what and how you are teaching. The results provide teachers, administrators, and members of the community with an opportunity to compare the success of their children to that of children around the country.

▶ What Don't They Accomplish?

If you have been teaching science using a hands-on, discovery-focused approach, you may have good reason to be anxious when the children in your class are expected to display a command of the basic subject matter on a standardized test. After all, teaching science in a hands-on fashion may not provide the background in science knowledge that children from more traditional textbook-oriented classrooms have. On the other hand, the children in your class will probably have acquired many inquiry process skills and have developed a favorable attitude toward science. Standardized achievement tests will not reveal your success in helping children grasp central science concepts through hands-on experimentation.

Using Standardized Achievement Tests More Effectively   First, help children understand that the results of a standardized test will not measure all that they have learned. If, for example, your class has carried out a hands-on unit on the use and waste of water in your school, explain to the children that they should not expect to see questions about it on the test. Point out that some of the science units they have studied have given them a lot of information that will not be measured. Emphasize that they should not feel bad if many of the things they have learned are not on the test.

Also, take some class time before the test to teach basic standardized test-taking strategies. The children likely will take many standardized tests while they are students and when they pursue employment. Investing time and energy to improve test-taking skills may annoy you because of your own feelings about testing, but it may help children become more successful test takers.

Rubrics and Scoring Guides

Go to **MyEducationLab**, select the topic Assessment, watch the video entitled "Forms of Assessment," and complete the questions that accompany it.

Most of the assessment strategies presented to this point are fine for collecting data in the form of student outcomes. Frankly, collecting student work is relatively easy compared to analyzing student outcomes and making judgments about a student's performance. For each assessment strategy, you will need to make a tool to analyze the outcomes. Most often you will use an answer key or a rubric.

Answer keys are helpful when clearly defined answers are required. The students either name the parts of a flower or they don't. Rubrics, on the other hand, provide a guide for you to evaluate less structured and more open-ended responses typical of students seeking to provide explanations. They are often helpful when assessing process rather than factual content. There are two basic forms of rubric: analytical and holistic. Analytical rubrics specify performances for each criterion. They provide more detail about a student's performance. Holistic rubrics provide a general assessment based on all the criteria at once. They do not disaggregate performance on each criterion and are better for quick evaluations of student work.

I rewrote the rubric used earlier for Mrs. Riley's plants using all three forms. Note that rubrics all include criteria, performance for criteria, and a rating scale. They differ by degrees of specificity.

Analytical List: Lists desired performance for each criterion

Criteria	Performance	Potential score	Student score
Prediction	Prediction is testable	1	
Test of prediction	Implies treatment	1	
	Implies control	1	
	Identifies observables (color, height . . .)	1	
Daily observations	Makes daily entries	1	
	Uses words to describe observables	1	
	Uses drawings to describe observables	1	
	Observations are accurate	1	
Results	Results are consistent with observations	1	
Explanation	Students relate that the presence of light is necessary for Mrs. Riley's plants to live	1	
Total possible score		10	

Analytical Continuum: Specifies levels of performance for each criterion

Criteria	Meets criteria 3 pts	Satisfactory 2 pts	Needs improvement 1 pt
Prediction	Clearly stated, testable	Stated but not clearly testable	Difficult to discern prediction
Test of prediction	Demonstrates experimental model: Clearly implies treatment Experimental control Variable control Identifies observables (color, height . . .)	Implies treatment Suggests an awareness of controls but does not clearly discern variables or observables	Does not suggest an awareness of an experimental model
Daily observations	Evidence of descriptive modeling, addresses elements, rules of interaction, and background space Makes comprehensive daily entries Uses drawings to describe observables Observations are accurate	Makes daily observations Observations are generally accurate Intermittently supported by text or drawings Moderate evidence of descriptive modeling	Sporadic entries Little or no evidence of descriptive modeling
Results	Results are consistent with observations	Results exhibit some inconsistencies with observations	Results are inconsistent with observations
Explanation	Explanatory model based on descriptive model	Explanatory model partially based on descriptive modeling	Explanatory model is unrelated to descriptive model
	Students relate that the presence of light is necessary for Mrs. Riley's plants to live	Students relate light to plant growth in general without expressing cause and effect related to Mrs. Riley's plants	Students demonstrate no awareness of the relationship of light to plant growth
Total possible score	15		

Holistic Rubric: Does not list specific levels of performance for each criterion. It provides a general assessment based on overall criteria

Meets criteria
- Makes a clear and testable prediction
- Designs a solid experiment with appropriate controls and variables
- Records accurate and informative daily observations
- Results are consistent with observations
- Explanation is consistent with observations

Satisfactory
- Prediction is stated but not testable
- Experimental design has most of the controls and variables
- Observations are fairly consistent and descriptive
- Results are mostly consistent
- Explanation relates light to plant growth

Needs improvement
- Prediction is difficult to discern
- Demonstrates little awareness of experimental design
- Exhibits minimal descriptive modeling
- Results are largely inconsistent with observations
- Does not articulate a connection between plant growth and light

Reality Check

It is your first parent conference night. You are well prepared, having displayed student work for the parents, being sure to include a sample from every child in your class. You have portfolios for each student as well as their grades on all the assignments to date. Although you look forward to meeting the parents of your students, you are also a bit anxious. It will be easy to report to the parents of the students who are doing well, but what do you say to the parents of the children who seem to be struggling? You are particularly concerned about explaining Amanda's performance in science to her parents. You search for a way to describe her performance in a manner that will be informative and constructive. While reviewing Amanda's portfolio, you realize that she has done well on matching and fill in the blank sections of probes and that she is often but not always able to link ideas on concept maps and diagrams, but she does not perform well on performance assessments that require her to generate explanations. Based on the following guide, what can you tell Amanda's parents about the level of understanding exhibited by Amanda?

Level of understanding	Assessment strategies	Comments
Nominal	Matching Fill in blank Vocabulary quiz	Demonstrates ability to identify and associate elements and concepts Answers often memorized No indication of deep understanding
Descriptive	Concept map Diagram Essay Poster Lab report Activity write up	Demonstrates ability to express rules of interaction/connections among elements
Explanatory	Performance assessment Lab practical Model Simulation	Demonstrates ability to propose an explanation or demonstrate ability based on the rules of interaction among the elements of the system

   Sample response: Amanda does well identifying scientific terms and recognizing most of the main concepts. Her concept maps and diagrams demonstrate that she is able to recognize the fundamental relationships and main connections among most of the science concepts. She is off to a good start. The next step for Amanda is to use her ability to create good descriptive models and recognize important connections to generate responses to open-ended questions more independently. I will continue to help her make the transition to this higher level of mastery by providing her with opportunities to use her concept maps, which she does quite well, as a guide to generate answers to open-ended questions. You can support her in this at home by suggesting that she make a concept map when she is working on a response to an open-ended question and help her use the concept map by pointing out connections that lead to an explanation. We should see her progress in her responses to open-response questions on standardized testing this spring.

Summary

A teacher asks, "Did I teach you that?"

Now comes the real challenge: How do you create a meaningful assessment system that will tell whether your students understand the science content and can conduct inquiry?

Use as your foundation the major approaches to assessment discussed in this chapter. Then consider your curriculum—specific units you teach or observe being taught. With that material in mind, try to answer the question, "What is the ideal way to assess whether children are understanding and inquiring successfully?" Certainly, the answer must lie in your clever integration of assessment strategies plus your familiarity with what you teach.

Assessment lets you know the impact of the many hours spent planning and agonizing to get a lesson or unit just right. Good assessment begins with the identification of clear and concise content to be taught and an awareness of the student behaviors and outcomes that you will measure to indicate learning. Remember there is no one-size-fits-all assessment strategy. Use a variety of traditional and performance assessments to meet your needs. For example, suppose a child does poorly on a quiz but evidence from formative assessments such as science notebooks and probes suggests that the child is more proficient than the quiz suggests. You can follow up the quiz with a student conference to gain better insights about the child's understanding and level of mastery. Use the guide in Figure 6.4 to help you plan your assessment. Many other questions will also likely come to mind as you reflect on the results you acquired by using the guide.

The "bottom line" for assessment is that you need to use a variety of measures because you will have a variety of students in terms of achievement levels, aptitudes, and attitudes. If you are able to assess students' performance well and then use that information gathered sensibly, your students will become better students and you, of course, will become an even better teacher.

Figure 6.4   Use the guide to help you plan your assessment.

- Know what you intend to teach
    - Look to the content to be taught for guidance

- Decide which of your assessments will be formative or summative
    - On the path to learning (formative)
    - Mastery of content (summative)

- Know which student performances indicate learning
    - Look to your performance objectives for guidance
    - Be sure that the criteria are measurable

- Choose assessment strategies that meet your needs

- Develop a rubric that you can use to analyze student outcomes

Going Further

On Your Own

1. Imagine that you are an elementary- or middle-grade science teacher who has just received a $1,000 grant to improve the strategies and techniques used to assess children in science. What would you spend the money on? Explain your rationale.

2. Select a science topic you might teach to chilnden at a grade level of your choice. For that topic, suggest a specific subject for an age-appropriate, inquiry-based project. Then briefly describe how you would apply the strategies suggested by the NSES to determine whether the children were successful in completing the project.

On Your Own or in a Cooperative Learning Group

3. Create a poster listing five techniques children should use to prepare for a traditional science unit test. Highlight techniques that you or members of your group learned through direct experience as students.

4. Imagine that you and some other teachers have decided to give a Back-to-School Night presentation that will provide the rationale for using science portfolios in place of traditional assessment techniques. Prepare a PowerPoint presentation that you could use as part of the presentation.

5. On a sheet of newsprint, have your group identify one science topic at a grade level of interest. Under that topic, list three or four "content points" that children should understand by the time the unit has been completed. Show that you can implement the techniques suggested by the NSES for gauging how well children understand the content points. Identify a prompt and a scoring rubric that a teacher could implement to assess understanding.

Resources for Discovery Learning

Internet Resources

To access these helpful websites, go to **MyEducationLab**, select Resources, and then Web Links. To learn more, click on the following links and you will easily be directed to each website.

- **Association for Supervision and Curriculum Development:**
  www.ascd.org/portal/site/ascd

- **Authentic Assessment Toolbox:**
  http://jonathan.mueller.faculty.noctrl.edu/toolbox/index.htm

- **Science Notebooks in K12 Classrooms:**
  www.sciencenotebooks.org/

- **Trends in International Mathematics and Science Study:**
  nces.ed.gov/timss

- **Programs for International Student Assessment**
  www.nces.ed.gov.surveys/pisa

Print Resources

Suggested Readings

Barton, James, and Collins, Angelo. *Portfolio Assessment.* White Plains, NY: Dale Seymour, 1997.

Brown, Janet Harley, and Shavelson, Richard. *Assessing Hands-On Science.* Thousand Oaks, CA: Corwin Press, 1996.

Classroom Assessment in the National Science Education Standards. Washington, D.C. National Academy of Science, 2001.

Coray, Gail. "Rubrics Made Simple." *Science Scope* 23, no. 6 (March 2000): 38–49.

Craven, John A., and Hogan, Tracy. *Science Scope* 25, no. 1 (September 2001): 36–40.

Davis, Elizabeth A., and Kirkpatrick, Doug. "It's All the News: Critiquing Evidence and Claims. *Science Scope* 25, no. 5 (February 2002): 32–37.

Demers, Chris. "Beyond Paper-and-Pencil Assessments." *Science and Children* 38, no. 2 (October 2000): 24–29, 60.

Eberle, F. et al. "Formative Assessment Probes." *Science and Children* 45, no. 5 (January 2008): 50–54.

Enger, Sandra, and Yager, Robert. *Assessing Student Understanding in Science.* Thousand Oaks, CA: Corwin Press, 2001.

Franklin, John. "Assessing Assessment." *Curriculum Update* (Spring 2002): 1–8.

Gandal, Matthew, and McGiffert, Laura. "The Power of Testing." *Educational Leadership* 60, no. 5 (February 2003): 39–42.

Goodnough, Karen, and Long, Robin. "Mind Mapping: A Graphic Organizer for the Pedagogical Toolbox." *Science Scope* 25, no. 8 (May 2002): 20–24.

Guskey, Thomas R. "How Classroom Assessments Improve Learning." *Educational Leadership* 60, no. 5 (February 2003): 6–11.

Jabot, M., et al. "Mental Models of Elementary and Middle School Students in Analyzing Simple Battery and Bulb Circuits." *School Science and Mathematics* 107, no. 1 (January 2007): 371–381.

Neill, Monty. "The Dangers of Testing." *Educational Leadership* 60, no. 5 (February 2003): 43–45.

Olson, Joanne K., and Cox-Peterson, Anne M. "An Authentic Science Conference." *Science and Children* 38, no. 6 (March 2001): 40–45.

Otero, V. K., et al. "Preservice Elementary Teachers' Views of Their Students' Prior Knowledge of Science." *Journal of Research in Science Teaching* 45, no. 4 (April 2008): 497–523.

Pelligrino, James W. "Knowing What Students Know." *Issues in Science and Technology* 19, no. 2 (Winter 2002–2003): 48–52.

Sclafani, Susan. "No Child Left Behind." *Issues in Science and Technology* 19, no. 2 (Winter 2002–2003): 43–47.

Shepardson, Daniel P., and Britsch, Susan J. "Analyzing Children's Science Journals." *Science and Children* 38, no. 3 (November/December 2000): 29–33.

Smith, Deborah C., and Wesley, Ann. "Teaching for Understanding." *Science and Children* 38, no. 1 (September 2000): 36–41.

Stavy, Ruth, and Tirosh, Dina. *How Students (Mis-) Understand Science and Mathematics.* New York: Teachers College Press, 2000.

Stearns, Carole, and Courtney, Rosalea. "Designing Assessments with the Standards." *Science and Children* 37, no. 4 (January 2000): 51–55.

Sunda, Ruth. "Thinking about Thinking—What Makes a Good Question?" *Learning & Leading with Technology* 30, no. 5 (February 2003): 10–15.

Varelas, Maria, et al. "Examining Language to Capture Scientific Understandings." *Science and Children* 38, no. 7 (April 2001): 26–29.

Ward, Robin E., and Wandersee, James. "Roundhouse Diagrams." *Science Scope* 24, no. 4 (January 2000): 17–27.

Waters, M., et al. "Science Rocks! A Performance Assessment for Earth Science." *Science Activities* 45, no. 1 (Spring 2008): 23–28.

Notes

1. Association for Supervision and Curriculum Development. www.ascd.org/portal/site/ascd (accessed 05-26-08).

2. J. Myron Atkin, Paul Black, and Janet Coffey, eds. *Classroom Assessment in the National Science Education Standards.* (Washington, D.C.: National Academy of Science 2001), p. 25. Reprinted with permission from the National Academics Press, Copyright © 2001, National Academy of Sciences.

3. Funderstanding. www.funderstanding.com/index.html (accessed 05-26-08).

4. For a detailed discussion of the use of prompts and scoring rubrics, see National Research Council, *National Science Education Standards* (Washington, DC: National Academy Press, 1996), pp. 91–98.

5. J. Myron Atkin, Paul Black, and Janet Coffey, eds. *Classroom Assessment in the National Science Education Standards* (Washington, D.C.: National Academy of Science, 2001) p. 60.

6. Ibid., p. 25.

chapter 7

Integrating Science

*How can I integrate inquiry-based science
with other subjects in a child's school day?*

▶ Getting Started

Sarah was excited to finally have her own classroom. As a student teacher she always felt like a guest, no matter how gracious an effort her cooperating teacher made to help Sarah feel welcome. Sarah knew and the students knew that it really was not her class. Today she had a totally different feeling as she entered the school as a full-fledged faculty member. There were still several weeks remaining before the first class, but she wanted to begin planning the curriculum and preparing the room for that first day in September. As she entered the room she noticed a vase of flowers on the desk. She was very lucky to have such a thoughtful mentor teacher. This was going to be a wonderful year. Next to the vase lay the district curriculum frameworks. Her mentor teacher suggested that she familiarize herself with the frameworks before planning the curriculum. The document seemed awfully thick as Sarah lifted it and began to read through it. An hour later, her initial excitement dampened, Sarah wondered how she was ever going to cover all the content. There were standards for language arts, history and social science, mathematics, science, as well as health, art, and English language proficiency. Sarah knew that each subject was not a separate entity, at least not in real life, and that she had to integrate the

content not only to cover it, but also to enrich the learning experience for her students. However, integration is easier said than done. She was going to need some help.

The good news for Sarah and all teachers is that human knowledge is interconnected. In fact, the same strategies for discovery and inquiry used in science apply across disciplines. The historian seeking to explain the causes of the American Revolution would ask about the key issues, how they are related, their contexts, and how they merged to create conditions ripe for a revolution. The literary agent reviewing a book might ask about the characters, how they are related, and how the time period or social context come together to form the plot. These are nothing more than versions of the more general fundamental questions of inquiry: What are the elements, rules of interaction, and background space that lead to the emergent properties of the system? This way of thinking connects learning in different domains to a common process of inquiry and discovery.

Go to **MyEducationLab**, select the topic Cross-Curricular Connections, watch the video entitled "Integration," and complete the question that accompanies it.

As you plan science units, remember that science experiences can draw together a variety of subjects, acting as a kind of "superglue" that connects the learning in a range of areas and shows how human knowledge and experience fit together to form a larger, more meaningful whole. So let's consider some practical things you can do to integrate science with other subjects.

Project 2061

Implications for Integrating Science across the Subject Areas

Project 2061 provides strong guidance for integrating science with mathematics and technology, using particular themes. And you can use these themes to find ways of integrating science with other subjects in the curriculum (something that Project 2061 does not do directly).

Here are the themes that Project 2061 provides for tying together science, mathematics, and technology:

- Systems
- Models
- Constancy and change
- Scale

Using "Systems" as a theme, for example, you would teach children that a whole object, event, or interaction is made of parts, that those parts relate to each other, and that those parts affect the whole. Using the theme of "Models," you would teach that models are either real things or ideas that are used as tools to understand the world. The theme of "Constancy and change" addresses those ideas and discoveries that have withstood the test of time along with the nature of change and how small changes can have large effects. Finally, in teaching the theme of "Scale," you would help children see that things that differ from one another in terms of size, weight, or any other variable may also behave differently.

Specific recommendations for implementing these four themes are available at the Project 2061 website: **www.project2061.org/.**

Science and the Language Arts

"That cloud looks like a pregnant polar bear."

Children have a natural inclination to react to the world around them, and they absorb information from what they see, hear, taste, and touch as well as what they read. They can also respond in many ways, talking, writing, and drawing about what they absorb. Like scientists, children develop a repertoire of specific reading and writing process skills that enable them to carefully observe and react to what they experience through their senses. The next few sections will describe techniques you can use to help children expand both their science and their language arts abilities.

● Selecting Trade Books That Stimulate Inquiry and Discovery

Do you love books? I certainly hope so! One feature of your classroom should be an extensive collection of books that motivate children to think and engage in inquiry-based, discovery-focused science.

Trade books are volumes distributed by commercial publishers that do just that. They are not textbooks. Instead, they present about scientific adventures, the lives of scientists, science careers, and provide factual material about stars, planets, dolphins, the rain forest, and much more.

How can you select the best possible trade books for your children? Try using the following criteria, which were suggested by a distinguished panel of teachers and other science educators:

- The book has a substantial amount of science content.
- The information presented is clear, accurate, and up-to-date.
- Theories and facts are clearly distinguished.
- Facts are not oversimplified so as to make the information misleading.
- Generalizations are supported by facts, and significant facts are not left out.
- The book does not contain gender, ethnic, or socioeconomic bias.[1]

I won't provide you with a list of recommended science trade books, because so many new ones appear each month. Instead, I'll direct you to two excellent and easily accessible sources that *will* provide you lists of the very best modern trade books for children and youths:

1. An annual article in *Science and Children* whose title is always "Outstanding Science Trade Books for Students K–12"
2. The Internet site www.nsta.org, where you may select the feature "NSTA Recommends"

● Three Integrating Techniques

As the children entered the classroom on Monday morning, their exclamations could be heard the length of the hallway. "Wow!" "What happened here?" "It's beautiful!"

Over the weekend, their fourth-grade teacher had transformed the classroom into a tropical rain forest. The children knew that this was going to be no ordinary day. But their teacher was no ordinary teacher.[2]

Indeed, any teacher who finds creative ways to cross subject matter barriers using language arts as the bridge is special. You can be such a teacher if you focus on actively finding techniques to tie science and language arts together. Rakow and Vasquez, who described the fourth-grade teacher in the preceding excerpt, suggest three ways to do this:

1. *Literature-based integration* is simply the use of modern nonfiction science books, such as the trade books just discussed, to help children acquire science-related information. Additionally, for those children who might benefit from getting science information through a story line, many fictional books by authors such as Eric Carle and Tomie dePaola have science information and concepts threaded through them.

2. *Theme-based integration* is instruction in which a major theme or concept becomes the foundation for a learning unit that cuts across subject lines. Think in creative ways as you identify a theme such as "Ecosystems," "Space Neighbors" for astronomy, or "Animals with Pouches" for the life sciences.

3. *Project-based integration* involves children in actually carrying out a long-term activity in which they investigate a real-world problem. Here are a few examples of science-related projects that provide excellent opportunities to tie language arts development to science content:
   - Discovering the amount of paper wasted each day in a classroom or school and communicating ideas to others that will help solve the problem
   - Discovering how much water is wasted at school water fountains each day or week and communicating ideas to others that will help stop the waste
   - Discovering how well school hot lunch offerings and student choices match proper nutrition guidelines and communicating ideas to others that will help children choose better lunches[3]

Science-related projects provide excellent opportunities for integrating the language arts.

Weaving It All Together with Language Arts

Class time overflows with children dictating stories, chanting, singing, speaking, writing, constructing "big books," and the like. These experiences help children develop and improve their language arts skills.

Language arts teaching strategies can be easily adapted to enrich and extend children's science experiences. Writing stories about butterflies and rockets, making "big books" about insects, and writing and singing songs about saving the earth's natural resources are activities that involve children in a variety of science topics and help develop their language arts skills.

I hope that you will create appropriate ways to develop each component of the language arts through science. In the sections that follow, you will find some very specific ways to achieve a science/language arts synergy.

Extending the Basics: Vocabulary, Comprehension, and Writing

Using Descriptive Modeling to Build Vocabulary　Someday, somewhere, some child will come up to you, look you straight in the eye, and ask with a giggle, "What grows down while growing up?" And you will enjoy not only the joke but also what telling it has to say about that child's ability to use language.

Unfortunately, for many children, words and their meanings are *not* sources of jokes and riddles. For these children, words are mysterious combinations of ink marks that make little sense and create little pleasure. If you are not alert to the need to teach and reinforce reading skill development, the printed page of a science book can serve as a source of frustration for a child with limited vocabulary skills.

Reality Check

When developing theme-based science units, avoid broad topics such as, "The Rain Forest," or the "Oceans of the World." Rather, identify a science concept and essential question that will serve as the focus of inquiry, such as "Rain forests and oceans: How can they both be ecosystems?" This theme develops the concept of ecosystems, rather than the rain forest or ocean as entities in and of themselves. Most of your students will live neither in the rain forest nor the ocean, but all will live in an ecosystem.

Below are broad topics for theme-based integration. Rewrite each with an essential question that reflects a science concept.

Theme	Essential question
Volcanoes	
Adaptation	
Minerals	
Earthquakes	
The solar system	
Life cycles	

Descriptive modeling provides a meaningful context for children to use words and consequently build their vocabulary. Here are some specific strategies that you can use to help children broaden their vocabulary through descriptive modeling:

1. Provide a list of descriptive terms that children can use while developing their descriptive models.

2. Post new science words and their definition as they emerge in class on a piece of newsprint or poster board to create word banks. Keep the word banks posted in the room for children to refer to during the unit.

3. Look through science trade books and elementary science textbooks before the children work with them *to identify terms that may be too difficult to learn from the context,* and then preteach those words.

4. *Pronounce science vocabulary words with children* before they reach them in their science materials.

5. *Have each child develop a personal word card file* that lists and defines each new science word. Each card should include the word, the sentence in which the word was found, a phonetic respelling of the word, and, if appropriate, a drawing or diagram showing the object or concept that the word defines.

Comprehension   The quest to seek explanations makes science a compelling backdrop for comprehension. If children are engaged and invested in finding an answer, then they will be more motivated to read for understanding.

You can help children build their comprehension skills in science by focusing their attention on prereading experiences. Before the children begin reading a specific text, trade book, or Internet article, focus your discussion of the material around three magic words:

1. *What?* When you distribute trade books, text material, or resource material on a science topic, take the time to discuss exactly what you expect the children to do with it. Describe how much time they will have and what they are expected to produce as a result of the reading.

2. *Why?* Take the time to explain to children why they are going to do the assignment. Do your best to describe how it will relate to work they have done before and work that will follow.

3. *How?* Describe how you expect children to learn from the material they are reading. You might say something like this: "Here are some topics you can use to organize the information you get about the planets from your reading: What is the planet's size compared to Earth? What is the surface like? How long is a day on the planet? Why don't you list them in your science notebook before you start reading. That way, you will have a specific place to put the information that you find in the book."

Writing

> *Writing is like talking to your best friend.* —Eric, a first-grader
>
> *Writing is a dance in the sun.* —Christi Ann, a second-grader
>
> *Writing is meeting the person in me I never knew.* —Mike, a seventh-grader[4]

This excerpt from *Reading and Learning to Read* tells a lot about the power you give children when you help them learn how to move their thoughts to a page. Science classrooms that provide children with opportunities to explore the natural world are places that provoke thought and thus create an unending array of possibilities for communication through the powerful medium of the written word. When you are teaching science, you are offering the possibility of many "dances in the sun."

You are quite fortunate when you teach children science because the breadth of content, processes, and affect that you teach is well matched by the range of writing forms that elementary school children need to practice. In *Language Arts: Learning Processes and Teaching Practices,* Temple and Gillet suggest that there are six basic writing forms:

Description	Expression	Persuasion
Exposition	Narration	Poetry[5]

Here are some examples of how you can help children develop their abilities with each writing form. I am sure that you can suggest many others.[6]

- *Description.* Have the children describe in detail an animal they observe on a class trip to a zoo.
- *Exposition.* Have the children explain how to make a flashlight lamp light using just one battery, one wire, and one bulb.
- *Expression.* Have the children write thank-you letters to a park ranger who visited the class to talk about protecting the natural environment.
- *Narration.* Have the children write stories about an incident in the life of a young girl who decides to be the first astronaut to set foot on the planet Mars.
- *Persuasion.* Have the children write scripts for a children's television commercial that will convince others to eat more green, leafy vegetables.
- *Poetry.* Have the children observe and draw a seashell and then write poems that use at least three of the observations they made about the shell.

Science and Mathematics

"Whose mine is it?" asked Milo, stepping around two of the loaded wagons.

"BY THE FOUR MILLION EIGHT HUNDRED AND TWENTY-SEVEN THOUSAND SIX HUNDRED AND FIFTY-NINE HAIRS ON MY HEAD, IT'S MINE, OF COURSE," bellowed a voice from across the cavern. And striding toward them came a figure who could only have been the Mathemagician.

He was dressed in a long flowing robe covered entirely with complex mathematical equations and a tall pointed cap that made him look very wise. In his left hand he carried a long staff with a pencil point at one end and a large rubber eraser at the other.[7]

This excerpt from *The Phantom Tollbooth* comes from the part of the book in which Milo, the watchdog Tock, and the Dodecahedron are about to find out where numbers come from.

"So that's where they come from," said Milo, looking in awe at the glittering collection of numbers. He returned them to the Dodecahedron as carefully as possible but, as he did, one dropped to the floor with a smash and broke in two. The Humbug winced and Milo looked terribly concerned.

"Oh, don't worry about that," said the Mathemagician as he scooped up the pieces. "We use the broken ones for fractions."[8]

The journey of Milo and his friends to the numbers mine has always struck me as an excellent frame of reference for both understanding the difficulties children may have with mathematics and helping them overcome those difficulties. Some children view numbers as squiggly lines on paper that have no basis in reality. For all they know, numbers come from number mines! Although there are many aspects of elementary school mathematics that can be reinforced, extended, and enriched as children do science, three are particularly important: computational skills; data collection and expression; and logical reasoning.[9]

● Computational Skills

Figure 7.1 provides examples of various ways in which computational skills can be practiced and put to real work during science. As you look over the figure, see if you can think of other ways to have children work on computation as they carry out science activities and projects.

● Data Collection and Expression

> Zing! Another rubber band flies across the science classroom. Is this a sign of unmotivated students in an undisciplined classroom? Not this time. This otherwise unruly behavior is actually part of a hands-on activity that teaches students the basics of graphing and experimental design.[10]

Although I definitely don't suggest this particular activity for either brand-new or veteran teachers with limited classroom management skills, I share it with you to focus attention on what a creative science teacher can do to build a child's science/math skills. Even though shooting rubber bands will not be your first choice as an activity to use when your school principal is observing your magnificent teaching talents, it does provide a good data-collection and data-expression experience. Notice the true sophistication of the activity:

> In this experiment the independent (or manipulated) variable is the width of the rubber bands and the dependent (or responding) variable is the distance they fly. Does the width of a rubber band affect the distance it travels? Ask students to write a prediction using an if-then sentence format that states how the independent variable will affect the dependent variable. Once they have constructed a prediction, let the rubber bands fly![11]

Figure 7.1

A variety of science activities can be done to improve math computational skills.

Computational Skill	Science-Teaching Example
• Counting	Determine the number of pieces of litter on the school lawn.
• Addition	Keep track of the number of birds that visit a feeder.
• Subtraction	Measure children's heights at the beginning and end of the year and calculate growth.
• Multiplication	Estimate the number of birds in a flock on the school lawn by first counting a small group and then multiplying by the number of groups.
• Division	Do a school survey of animals in classrooms, and find the average number in each.
• Working with fractions	Place half a collection of seeds in moist soil and half in dry soil, and compare their relative growth.
• Working with decimals and percentages	Study the list of ingredients and the nutrition chart on a box of sweetened cereal, and figure out what part of the weight of the cereal is sugar.

Even if you are not quite ready (or will never be ready) to extend science through rubber band shooting, you can do equally interesting, if not equally exciting, activities that lead to data collection and expression. For example, you can have the children observe changes in the level of water in an open container. Begin by having a child place a mark on the container to show the present water level. The children can then mark the level each day for several days. At the end of the time, the children can measure the distance from the first mark to the new marks and make graphs to show the changes.

Can very young children express data through graphs and charts? They certainly can! By cutting paper strips that represent the distance from the water level to the original mark in the preceding example, the measurement for each day can be recorded. The paper strips can then be placed in sequence to produce a rudimentary graph of changes in water level.

Make the Case *An Individual or Group Challenge*

● **The Problem**

As a result of their school and real-world experiences, children may conclude that science is an isolated and complex branch of human knowledge.

● **Assess Your Prior Knowledge and Beliefs**

Check your beliefs and knowledge about the following:

1. Children in the elementary grades learn that science is separate and different from other subjects.

   strongly disagree   disagree   agree   strongly agree

2. Children in the elementary grades learn that science is difficult.

   strongly disagree   disagree   agree   strongly agree

3. In the middle grades, children experience science as a separate subject.

   strongly disagree   disagree   agree   strongly agree

4. In the middle grades, children learn that science is a difficult subject.

   strongly disagree   disagree   agree   strongly agree

5. Science activities in most elementary- and middle-grade textbooks and resource books connect science to other school subjects.

   strongly disagree   disagree   agree   strongly agree

● **The Challenge**

Before being interviewed for a teaching position, you review the science curriculum and notice that it includes sample science activities. At the end of each activity is the side heading "Connections," which suggests how to relate the activity to other subjects. During the interview, the interviewer tells you, "We are so excited about our new curriculum. It is really interdisciplinary. I think you've had a chance to look it over. What do you think of it?" How would you respond?

Following the data-gathering process, the children can be led through a discussion of the lengths of their paper strips. Their understanding of math concepts can be probed and developed with questions such as these:

1. Can you explain why the strips are different lengths?
2. How much longer is the longest strip than the shortest?
3. How do the changes shown by your strips compare with those shown by other children's strips?

Logical Reasoning

An important goal of mathematics education for children is to develop an understanding of the logical structure of mathematics. In practice, this means a child is able to look at collections of items and make statements about them and the outcomes of grouping and regrouping them. This is the mathematics of sets and subsets, open sentences, and the commutative, associative, and distributive properties. Science experiences can provide children with opportunities to put their understanding of mathematical concepts to work. You could, for example, have the children in your class do these activities:

1. Group collections of plants into sets and subsets.
2. Devise a system for classifying organisms into the set of all plants and the set of all animals.
3. Identify the similarities and differences of various elements of the set of all birds and fish.
4. Use a list of characteristics to determine whether an organism is part of such subsets as fish, birds, and reptiles.

Science and the Social Studies

"After analyzing what kind of garbage was in and around the creek (like grocery carts, litter, and car tires), the students agreed that the source of the trash was from various people and places. When the students had decided who was responsible, it was more difficult for them to decide who should help with their cleanup. How could they ask people in the apartments to come clean up the creek safely and without offending them?"[12]

Social studies and science can easily be integrated, because societal problems, in many cases, lend themselves to real-life inquiry-based experiences for children. The outdoor experience just described shows how challenging children with meaningful projects can tie together science and social studies. And in doing so, it can raise important issues about individual and societal attitudes and values.

Attitude and value development is an important dimension of social studies that can easily be integrated with science. Children who learn that questions of values cut across content areas are more apt to appreciate the significance of such topics. Here is a sampling of the types of questions you can use to stimulate attitude- and value-based science discussions and to generate ideas for activities and projects that relate science and social studies:

1. Should animals be kept in zoos?
2. Should cities and towns have animal control officers?

Figure 7.2
Many social
studies topics can
be extended
through science
activities.

Social Studies Topic	Related Science Concept
• The natural resources of a country	The sun as the original energy source in the solar system
	The protection of air and water resources
	The use of alternative energy sources
• The history and development of a country or part of the world	Contributions made by specific scientists and inventors
• The employment of North Americans in diverse occupations	Career awareness for occupations in science and technology
• The structure of the family and other social groups; the interaction of group members	The effect of improved technology on providing increased leisure time
• The production, transportation, and consumption of goods and services	The improvement of the quality and quantity of agricultural products through selective breeding and food preservation technology

3. Should a factory that provides many jobs for people but also pollutes the town's air and water be closed down?

4. Should people be required to wear seat belts?

5. Should commercials for sugar-sweetened cereals be shown during Saturday morning children's shows?

As with any science lesson or unit, clearly identify the targeted scientific content to be taught. If you prepare a science unit on pollution, consider the science behind the pollution. For example, if you choose a lesson on oil pollution, address the effect of oil on the capacity for bird feathers to repel water or on the density of oil compared to water. When children address legal and social issues such as whether there should be offshore oil drilling, encourage them to use reasoning based on the science rather than pure emotion.

Also see Figure 7.2, which shows how a number of social studies topics can be extended through related science content. Integrating these two content areas will help children realize the science/social studies connection.

Science and Art

Recently, I began to plan a unit on the human body. In an art unit that I had done a few years ago, the class used fabric crayons to make a wall mural for display in the hall. So I decided to use these crayons to make ourselves walking, anatomically correct models of the digestive and respiratory systems.[13]

Jackie Moore, the teacher who came up with this clever idea, goes on to explain that first she had each child bring in a white, cotton-blend T-shirt. The fabric crayons were

Figure 7.3
These sample activities integrate art and science.

> • *Tree Stump Rubbings:* Place paper on a smooth, recently cut tree stump, and rub the paper with a pencil. Follow-up activities may include discussions about climatic changes, as reflected in changes in the annual ring pattern, and how to find the age of the tree.
>
> • *Leaf Rubbings:* Place paper over a variety of leaves, and rub the paper with the side of a crayon. Follow-up activities can include observation of leaf veins in the print and discussion of the variety of leaves found or defects in leaf surfaces as a result of insect activity.
>
> • *Native Crafts:* Use natural objects to make sculptures, including mobiles or stabiles, and pictures. Examples include stone people, acorn people, apple-head dolls, fruit and vegetable prints, dried flowers, and shell sculptures.
>
> • *Sand Painting:* After studying the origin and characteristics of sand, dye the sand to use in sand paintings. This can be integrated with social studies, since it is an activity that comes from the heritage of native North Americans.
>
> • *Moving Sculpture:* Build simple circuits to operate sculptures that have moving parts as well as blinking lights.

used to draw the systems and organ labels on paper, and the drawings were then ironed on the shirts. She describes the culminating activity this way:

> To show off our beautiful bodies all my 125 students wore their shirts on the same day. Quite a sight to behold! Interestingly enough, the students do better on questions dealing with these two systems than on any of the other systems that we study.[14]

This activity shows how you can easily encourage children to use art with science and thereby help them see the relationship between art and science. There are many other activities that you can use to accomplish this. Use those described in Figure 7.3 to get you started on developing your own strategies for relating science and art.

Science and Music

Music has become so much a part of our daily lives that we are sometimes oblivious to it, but the children that you teach are not. Even very young children are able to hum, dance, whistle, and sing a multitude of breakfast cereal commercials and know some of the words and phrases of the most popular songs on MTV. Music has had a profound impact upon our culture, and we should be able to take advantage of its ability to attract and hold a child's attention when we teach science.

Hapai and Burton have prepared a helpful resource book called *BugPlay* that offers many strategies for integrating one common science topic—insects—with the rest of the school curriculum. One of my favorite songs from this book, and a favorite of children for obvious reasons, is "Cock-a-Roaches."[15]

Another strategy for relating music and science is to locate music that was composed to express feelings about topics that you are covering in science. For example, if you teach the four seasons, you can fill your classroom with selections from Vivaldi's Concerto in F Minor, op. 8, no. 4, "Winter," from *The Four Seasons.*

Science and Health and Physical Education

The sun is shining. Feel its warm glow on your seed bodies. Now it's raining . . . a gentle rain. You are beginning to grow ever so slowly. Feel your sides enlarge. What are you growing into? A dandelion? A flower? A blade of grass? A young sapling? Feel your arms and fingers stretch into leaves, petals, or branches. S-T-R-E-T-C-H. Reach for the sky. Reach for the sun. Now there's a wind, a gentle breeze. Now there's a rainstorm. Move as a flower, plant, or tree would move in a rainstorm. Now the sun is peeking out from behind a cloud. Fill your body with its wonderful warmth. Breathe in the air . . . in and out . . . in and out.[16]

Wouldn't doing this activity be a nice way to review some of the concepts taught in a unit on green plants while helping a child develop his or her motor skills? The concepts that underlie physical education activities for children are clearly related to many of the topics of elementary school science.

The physical education component of a child's day focuses on such matters as engaging in recreational activities that may be carried out over a lifetime, improving general health, and developing strength and coordination through a variety of movement activities. Thus, much of what is done during a modern physical education class actually is related to common science vocabulary terms, such as *time, space,* and *force.* Whether children become aware of this relationship is certainly a debatable question.

To build your own bridge between physical education and science, you need to establish a working relationship with your school's physical education teacher. If you teach in a self-contained classroom, strive to develop each curriculum—science and physical education—in a way that emphasizes and extends the concepts common to both.

Reality Check

Choose one or all of the integration challenges below:

1. During art the children mix magenta, yellow, and cyan paint to get a variety of colors. Some of the children, who are in the school musical, have noticed that different colored lights are used to make different colors on stage. But they noticed that the stage lights are colored red, green, and blue rather than magenta, yellow, and cyan like the paint in art class. They are confused and ask you why the stage lights don't mix the same colors as the paint. How can you use the children's curiosity to integrate science and art? Hint: go to www.omsi.edu/visit/tech/colormix.cfm.

2. How would you integrate a social studies unit on the Pilgrims with a science unit on the weather?

3. The children are having a kick ball tournament in physical education class. There is a controversy brewing about how much air to put in the ball. Some argue that the harder the ball, the farther it will go. Others argue that ball will travel farther if it is softer. How can you take advantage of this disagreement to deepen the children's science content and or process knowledge?

Teaching the Science of Art, Music, and Physical Education

Although the previous sections addressed strategies for using art, music, and physical education to teach science, also consider the perspective of teaching the science of art, music, and physical education. Art, music, and physical activity have a wealth of scientific principles embedded within them. For example, what makes color? How can the stage lighting in a play make a red dress look black? Prisms, rainbows, chromatography, reflection, absorption, spectrum, and primary colors are all associated with learning the science of color. The same idea applies to music, which of course is sound consisting of vibrations, frequency, and intensity.

Summary

Inquiry and discovery are at the heart of science experiences for children and can also serve as the "glue" that ties together various subjects during the school day. Science experiences offer many opportunities to build and extend language skills. Math experiences for children—including computation, data collection and expression, and logical reasoning—can be easily tied to science work, as can activities in subjects such as social studies, art, music, health, and physical education. There is great potential for the teacher who is willing to invest the energy to integrate science across disciplines. Consider not only teaching science using art, language arts, math, social studies, and physical education, but also teaching fundamental concepts of science inherent in these subjects.

Going Further

On Your Own

1. Identify a reading or language arts activity that you could have children do when they are learning about each of these topics:
   a. The seasons
   b. Sound energy
   c. Endangered animal species
   d. Rocks and minerals
   e. The role of technology in their lives

   For each activity, suggest whether you would do it at the beginning, middle, or end of a unit of study.

2. What special techniques might you use to help poor readers read science materials successfully? How could you help children with writing problems improve their written communication skills while they learn science? Be specific in your responses, citing techniques that could be used with a wide variety of science content.

3. Can you recall a science experience that you had as an elementary school child that integrated at least one other content field? If you can't recall such an experience, try to recall a science activity that could have been related to another content field with minimal teacher effort. What benefits could result from such an integrated activity?

4. The study of current events can provide many opportunities to relate science and social studies. Identify a recent news story that had a significant scientific or technologic dimension. For this current event, describe a scientific principle that you could teach and a series of classroom activities that would provide children with experiences that highlight the relationship of science and social studies.

5. Select a topic in science that could be used as a theme in a variety of subject areas. If you are working with a group, have each person play the role of the teacher of a specific subject in a departmentalized elementary or middle school. Discuss how a group of teachers at the same grade level might plan a teaching unit that integrates the subject areas. (If you are doing this on your own, prepare a written statement that highlights possible comments each teacher might make.)

6. Interview a teacher who works in a self-contained classroom. During the interview, determine the following:
   a. The major science topics emphasized during the year
   b. The science processes that are emphasized

c. The extent to which the topics are enriched as a result of his or her efforts to relate other subjects to science

7. Interview a teacher in a departmentalized elementary or middle school. During your discussion, determine the following:
   a. The major topics and processes emphasized during the year
   b. The approximate length of a science class
   c. Whether other teachers at the grade level are aware of the topics dealt with in the science curriculum
   d. Whether all the teachers at the grade level ever work together to plan and teach units with interdisciplinary themes

Resources for Discovery Learning

Internet Resources

To access these helpful websites, go to **MyEducationLab,** select Resources, and then Web Links. To learn more, click on the following link and you will easily be directed to the website.

- **Association for Supervision and Curriculum Development:**
  www.ascd.org/portal/site/ascd

- **NSTA Position Statement: Science/Technology/ Society: A New Effort for Providing Appropriate Science for All**
  www.NSTA.org/about/positions/sts.aspx

Print Resources

Suggested Readings

Akerson, Valerie. "Teaching Science When Your Principal Says 'Teach Language Arts.'" *Science and Children* 38, no. 7 (April 2001): 42–47.

Ansberry, Karen R., and Morgan, Emily. *Picture Perfect Science Lessons: Using Children's Books to Guide Inquiry.* Arlington, VA: NSTA Press, 2005.

Barman, Charles, et al. "Assessing Students' Ideas about Plants." *Science and Children* 40, no. 1 (September 2002): 25–29.

Burns, John E., and Price, Jack. "Diving into Literature, Mathematics, and Science." *Science Scope* 26, no. 1 (September 2002): 15–17.

Butzow, John, and Butzow, Carol. *Science through Children's Literature.* Englewood, CO: Libraries Unlimited, 2000.

Fioranelli, Debra. "Recycling into Art." *Science and Children* 38, no. 2 (October 2000): 30–33.

Freedman, Robin Lee Harris. *Science and Writing Connections.* White Plains, NY: Dale Seymour, 1999.

Keena, Kelly, and Basile, Carole G. "An Environmental Journey." *Science and Children* 39, no. 8 (May 2002): 30–35.

Kupfer, Joseph H. "Engaging Nature Aesthetically." *Journal of Aesthetic Education* 37, no. 1 (Spring 2003): 77–89.

Lee, Michele, Lostoski, Maria, and Williams, Kathy. "Diving into a Schoolwide Science Theme." *Science and Children* 38, no. 1 (September 2000): 31–35.

Minton, Sandra. "Using Movement to Teach Academics: An Outline for Success." *Journal of Physical Education, Recreation and Dance* 74, no. 2 (February 2003): 36–40.

Mixing It Up: Integrated, Interdisciplinary, Intriguing Science in the Elementary Classroom. Arlington, VA: NSTA Press, 2003.

Morris, R. V. "Social Studies around the Blacksmith's Forge: Interdisciplinary Teaching and Learning." *The Social Studies (Washington, D.C.)* 98, no. 3 (May/June 2007): 99–103.

National Science Teachers Association (NSTA), Children's Book Council Joint Book Review Panel. "Outstanding Science Trade Books for Students K–12." *Science and Children* 39, no. 6 (March 2002): 31–38.

Nikitina, Svetlana. "Movement Class as an Integrative Experience: Academic, Cognitive, and Social Effects." *Journal of Aesthetic Education* 37, no. 1 (Spring 2003): 54–63.

Rogers, M. A. P., et al. "Connecting With Other Disciplines." *Science and Children* 44, no. 6 (February 2007): 58–59.

Shaw, E. L., et al. "From Boxed Lunch to Learning Boxes: An Interdisciplinary Approach." *Science Activities* 42, no. 3 (Fall 2005): 16–25.

Silverman, E., et al. "Cheep, Chirp, Twitter, & Whistle." *Science and Children* 44, no. 6 (February 2007): 20–25.

Terrell, Arlene G. "Leaders, Readers, and Science." *Science and Children* 39, no. 1 (September 2001): 28–33.

Young, Rich, Virmani, Jyotika, and Kusek, Kristen M. "Creative Writing and the Water Cycle." *Science Scope* 25, no. 1 (September 2001): 30–35.

Notes

1. National Science Teachers Association (NSTA), Children's Book Council Joint Book Review Panel, "Outstanding Science Trade Books for Students K–12," *Science and Children* 39, no. 6 (March 2002): 33.

2. Steven J. Rakow and Jo Anne Vasquez, "Integrated Instruction: A Trio of Strategies," *Science and Children* 35, no. 6 (March 1998): 18.

3. Ibid., 19.

4. Jo Anne L. Vacca, Richard T. Vacca, and Mary K. Gove, *Reading and Learning to Read* (Boston: Little Brown, rpt. 1991), p. 127.

5. Charles Temple and Jean Wallace Gillet, *Language Arts: Learning Processes and Teaching Practices* (Glenview, IL: Scott, Foresman, 1989), p. 231.

6. You may wish to refer to the presentation of a sample unit on space exploration, which shows a detailed integration of the language arts with a science topic, in Susan I. Barcher, *Teaching Language Arts: An Integrated Approach* (New York: West, 1994), pp. 351–367.

7. From *The Phantom Tollbooth* by Norman Juster, copyright © 1961 and renewed 1989 by Norton Juster. Used by permission of Random House Children's Books, a division of Random House, Inc.

8. Ibid., 180.

9. AIMS Activities that Integrate Math and Science and GEMS (Great Explorations in Math and Science) are two interesting curriculum development projects involved in the preparation of teaching materials that cut across the traditional boundaries of mathematics and science. To receive overviews of available integrated activities from these projects, write to AIMS Education Foundation, P.O. Box 8120, Fresno, CA 93747, and GEMS, Lawrence Hall of Science, University of California, Berkeley, CA 94720.

10. Richard J. Rezba, Ronald N. Glese, and Julia H. Cothron, "Graphing Is a Snap," *Science Scope* 21, no. 4 (January 1998): 20.

11. Ibid.

12. Kelly Keena and Carole G. Basile, "An Environmental Journey," *Science and Children* 39, no. 8 (May 2002): 32.

13. Jackie Moore, "Iron-On Respiratory System," *Science and Children* 28, no. 1 (September 1990): 36.

14. Ibid.

15. From *BugPlay,* © 1990 Addison-Wesley Publishing Co., Menlo Park, CA.

16. Milton E. Polsky, "Straight from the Arts," *Instructor* 99, no. 7 (March 1990): 57.

Using Technology to Enhance Science Learning

What comes first, content or technology?

▶ ## Getting Started

And now please welcome President Abraham Lincoln.

Good morning. Just a second while I get this connection to work. Do I press this button here? Function-F7? No, that's not right. Hmmm. Maybe I'll have to reboot. Hold on a minute. Um, my name is Abe Lincoln and I'm your president. While we're waiting, I want to thank Judge David Wills, chairman of the committee supervising the dedication of the Gettysburg cemetery. It's great to be here, Dave, and you and the committee are doing a great job. Gee, sometimes this new **technology** does have glitches, but **we couldn't live without it, could we?** Oh—is it ready? OK, here we go (http://norvig.com/Gettysburg/).[1]

Go to http://norvig.com/Gettysburg/ to see the PowerPoint presentation Lincoln might have made had the technology been available in 1863. Having seen the Power-Point presentation, do you think this Gettysburg Address would have had the same enduring effect to honor the men and women who fought in the battle as Lincoln's original speech? Hardly. The point of course is that technology for its own sake

has just as much potential to destroy the message as it does to enhance it. Although technology has wonderful potential for education, it must be used in the service of education and not simply because it is available. Sometimes drawing a graph with paper and pencil is a much more powerful learning tool than creating an Excel spreadsheet. Above all remember that you, the teacher, will always be more important than the technology.

This may seem like an ominous beginning for a chapter on the use of technology in the science classroom, but it is meant to put the use of technology in perspective. Used properly, technology has much to offer to the enrichment of science education. Technology can be a powerful educational tool, the potential of which we will explore in this chapter.

What Does Technology Really Mean?

Before beginning the chapter, we need to clarify what is meant by technology. Most often technology is thought of in the context of computer use in the classroom. However, educational technology has been around much longer than computers. Instructional technology consists of the tools used to enhance learning. In science, technology has always played a pivotal role by enabling scientists to deepen their descriptive models through the development of increasingly refined instruments that allow them to see the world more clearly. From a simple magnifying glass to the Hubble telescope, technology has expanded our ability to understand the world and the universe. This chapter will address the interface of computer technology with science education to advance the children's understandings of scientific process, concepts, and skills. Note that assistive technologies designed specifically to assist students with learning disabilities will be addressed in Chapter 9.

Technology: Why Use It?

In general, technology is familiar to children; it is fun and here to stay. I recognize that you may be teaching children who do not have access to computers at home. However, they will need to be users of technology in the twenty-first century, which is a reason to use technology appropriately in your classroom.

Technology can be engaging. It provides a window to a variety of virtual experiences that pique curiosity and can be used to inspire questions. It has the power to connect children with a community of learners, including peers as well as experts in the fields of science. Roblyer (p. 18) notes that technology enhances instructional methods by providing immediate feedback, visual demonstrations, and self-paced learning.[2]

As science educators, we recognize that science consists of both systematic processes and the collective explanations generated by the community of scientists using those processes. Computer technology assists science by providing tools that enhance inquiry through data collection, calculation, analysis, storage, and retrieval. It also provides dynamic modeling through simulations as well as dialogue and information gathering. Evidence suggests that technology enables the development of higher order thinking skills when students use technology to problem solve.[3] Keep in mind that as children use technology to explore scientific concepts, they are also improving their technological skills that are essential for the information age of the 21st century.

Figure 8.1   Questions for Judging the Credibility of an Educational Website

- Is it hosted by a reputable science or education organization? i.e., college, university, or government agency?

- If it is not hosted by known credible institutions, does the site reference credible institutions?

- Is the information presented consistent and valid with your understanding of the topic?

  If you suspect the validity of the information provided on the site, can you cross-reference the information with known reliable sources?

- Is it a safe website for children?

  Does it provide links to questionable sites with inappropriate themes?

  Does it solicit information from students? If so, what information?

- What does it have to offer educationally?

  Does it provide solely nominal information such as definitions and descriptions?

  Is it supported by graphics that clarify ideas?

  Is the text well written and developmentally appropriate for your students?

  Does the site provide opportunities for the children to interact with knowledge?

- Interactive simulations?

  Does the site provide opportunities for children to manipulate variables or discover how to do something?

  Does the simulation invite students to think about choices? Does it challenge them to use higher-level thinking skills?

Information Gathering

Go to **MyEducationLab**, select the topic Technology, watch the video entitled "Technology," and complete the question that accompanies it.

The Internet offers a seemingly infinite source of information. The challenge is to find good, manageable sources of information. Although there are many good sites run by individuals, I suggest using government websites such as NASA (www.nasa.gov) or the United States Geological Survey (www.usgs.gov). These sites frequently have sections dedicated to science education that include lesson plans, simulations, and links to other reputable sources. Other reliable sources include academic institutions such as universities and colleges, as well as museums and science centers such as the Boston Museum of Science (www.mos.org) and the Exploratorium (www.exploratorium.org). Figure 8.1 lists questions to consider when evaluating the educational value of a website.

Science WebQuests

You can incorporate information gathering into an inquiry experience for students using WebQuests. WebQuests engage students by creating a need to gather, analyze, and synthesize information that addresses a specific problem or challenge. A WebQuest should not generate a list of factoids that are simply copied from a website, nor should a WebQuest merely direct students to visit websites. WebQuests should actively involve students with content at the websites. Bernie Dodge, at San Diego State University, pioneered the development of WebQuests. You can find examples and templates for creating WebQuests at The WebQuest Page www.webquest.org/index.php.

Although there are several suggested templates for creating WebQuests, I find it helpful to follow the same 5E instructional strategy used in this book. The exploration uses the Internet as a tool to encounter new knowledge through information/data gathering, simulations, or virtual experimentation. The steps in the formation of a WebQuest are outlined below, followed by an example in Figure 8.2.

1. *Engage:* Set the context, pique interest, provide background information, and identify the challenge

2. *Explore:* Guide the students to websites where they encounter new information and interact with new knowledge

   a. The exploration can be guided using hyperlinks embedded in a procedure using software such as PowerPoint, Inspiration, or similar software.

   b. Or, the exploration can be presented in text format as exemplified in Figure 8.1

3. *Explain:* Provide students with an opportunity to articulate their responses to the challenge. Consider requiring the use of presentation software as an explanation tool

4. *Elaborate:* Provide an opportunity to transfer or apply the new knowledge

5. *Evaluate:* Assess the degree to which the students met the criteria of the learning objectives

Ask a Scientist

There are several online sites where children can ask a scientist for advice or for the answer to a puzzling question. This is helpful especially after the children have worked with a concept and generated meaningful questions. It is not helpful for children to use Ask a Scientist as a first resort. Wait until they have tried to seek an explanation and use Ask a Scientist sites for clarification. By asking someone, presumably an expert, there is the added motivation to develop a coherent, well-articulated question. Evidence suggests that children are much more motivated to express themselves well when they know other people outside the classroom will see their work.[4] Keep in mind that most scientists who respond on these sites are volunteers. It is unlikely that they will be able to address every question, and some of the more routine questions will be found in the FAQs. Therefore, be sure the students put some time into developing their questions to utilize this resource effectively. Suggest the following guidelines to students for preparing Ask a Scientist questions:

• Do your best to research the topic in the library or on the Internet. Check the FAQ section of the site if there is one. You may find others have asked the same or a similar question.

• Tell the scientist what you have learned in your basic research. Include your grade level in your e-mail.

• Don't be surprised if scientists give suggestions about how to discover an answer rather than answer your question directly. They are trying to help you learn how to inquire.

• Reply to the scientists who answered your question to thank them and let them know you received their responses. You may have a follow-up question.

Ask a Scientist links can be found on MyEducationLab.

Figure 8.2 Sample WebQuest   *WebQuest*

Engagement:

You are going camping with family and friends in the Grand Canyon in June after school gets out. The trip involves hiking several miles over the course of seven days. You need to pack as lightly as possible. Rather than take a camping stove and bottles of gas (wood for burning is scarce) you and your friend think that you can build a solar oven to do your cooking. Do you think this is a good idea? Explain your decision based on how solar ovens function and the properties of the Grand Canyon. To answer these questions, you will need to learn more about the Grand Canyon and how solar ovens work.

Exploration:

1. Go to http://solarcookers.org/basics/how.html to learn about how solar ovens work.

    a. Find the four principles of solar ovens. Record them in your science notebooks. (Upper elementary school students can go to http://tamaradwyer.com/solcook/phys_sci.html for a detailed description of the solar oven science.)

2. Based on your understanding of how solar ovens work, **explain** whether you think the Grand Canyon is a good place to use solar ovens.

    a. Go to weather-2-travel.com/climate-guides/index.php?destination=grand-canyon-az and www.thetrain.com/grandcanyon/climate/. Use the climate data that you find to support your answer. Record your answer in your science notebook.

3. Based on your understanding of how solar ovens work, draw a picture in your science notebook of what your solar oven might look like. Describe how each part of your solar oven would work. Remember to consider the four principles of solar ovens in your picture and explanation.

Explanation:

1. Do you think it is a good idea to try to use solar ovens during your camping trip in the Grand Canyon? Explain your decision based on what you learned about the function of solar ovens and the properties of the Grand Canyon in June.

    a. Discuss this in your group. Ask one person from each group to share the group's opinion. The other members in the group must be prepared to support the opinion with evidence.

2. Share your solar oven drawings with your group members. Combine your ideas to draw, on a poster board or PowerPoint presentation, your group's design for a solar oven.

Elaboration:

Go to www.solarnow.org/pizzabx.htm and use the directions as a guide to make a solar oven. You can change the directions if you think you can make a better solar oven than the one suggested. Try to make your solar oven reach a temperature of 100°F (38°C).

Evaluation:

1. Give each student a diagram of a solar oven with each part labeled. Ask them to describe in writing the function of each labeled part in the solar oven.

2. Bring their solar ovens outside on a sunny day and place a thermometer in each solar oven. Challenge the students to get the temperature of their solar ovens to 100°F (38°C), using only solar energy.

Figure 8.3
Computer probe interface

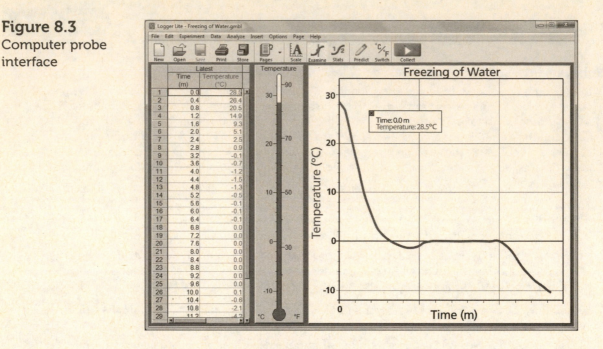

Real-Time Data Collection

Computer Probe Interfaces   The science classroom in particular benefits from interfaces between computers and sensors that can collect a range of data such as motion, temperature, speed, distance, blood pressure, and a host of other observables. The software accompanying the probes allows students to visualize their own data immediately and manipulate variables to deepen their understanding of complex concepts and relationships. (See Figure 8.3.) As an example, students can graph and compare the rate of temperature change in their solar ovens or see the relationship between distance and time using a motion detector to track a rolling ball. The probes are simple to use and usually plug into the USB ports on both Mac and PC computers.

Digital Microscopes   Microscope interfaces with the computer are particularly helpful for projecting real-time micro images on a screen using an LCD projector. Like the probes, the microscopes come with software that makes it easy to project images up to 200X magnification, although I rarely need above 60X (Figure 8.4). Some software allows you to record video or still images and even time lapse events. Digital microscopes are particularly helpful for assuring that the entire class is looking at the same micro image when developing a particular concept.

Figure 8.4   **Fire ant magnified**

Virtual Imaging Tools such as telescopes and microscopes extend our senses and abilities to make observations and construct descriptive models. Online tools enable children to see far out into the galaxy or peer into the often bizarre world of the microcosm. Other tools allow children to extend their abilities to make connections among a host of variables and imagine what properties emerge when they all interact at a unique time and place. These tools provide windows to new perspectives on the world and universe. One relatively new site is the World Wide Telescope, created by Microsoft (www.worldwidetelescope.org). "The WorldWide Telescope (WWT) is a Web 2.0 visualization software environment that enables a computer to function as a virtual telescope—bringing together imagery from the best ground and space-based telescopes in the world for a seamless exploration of the universe."[5] You will need to download supporting software from the site to use the World Wide Telescope. The directions are clear and downloading is relatively easy. When you succeed, you will have a portal into the galaxies to explore with your students.

Authentic Science Experiences

There are several Internet sites that provide students opportunities to be involved in authentic research. Authentic research involves students in collecting, sharing, and analyzing data associated with real-world investigations. The questions and data collection methods are usually determined by the organization hosting the site. Students participate in some form of data collection or investigation and share their data and conclusions with peers virtually on the Internet. Participation on these sites will require time on your part to enroll your class and become familiar with the logistics and procedures. Like anything else, it gets easier after you have done it once. Some sites require that teachers participate in a workshop in order to have total access to the sites.

The Global Learning and Observations to Benefit the Environment (GLOBE, www.globe.gov) is one example of an authentic learning site. Be prepared to spend some time becoming familiar with the site and all it has to offer to you and your students. In some respects, it is a one-stop site for integrating computer technology into your science curriculum. It enables your class to participate in environmental studies at the appropriate developmental level with school children of all ages from around the world. It is authentic in the respect that students can be directly involved in asking questions, collecting data, accessing data, analyzing data, and submitting data online for the GLOBE community to share. Inquiry-based guides and assessment tools are available as well as simulations that can be used to deepen students' descriptive models and allow them to manipulate variables to seek explanations. Teachers need to attend special workshops in order to fully participate in the program.

Tutorials and Games

Tutorials and games can be valuable for reviews and self-paced learning. Games like hangman, crossword puzzles, etc., are useful for reviews but usually do not inspire higher-level thinking. Tutorials provide young children with self-paced learning like www.edheads.org/activities/simple-machines/index.htm. Others help students associate properties with concepts such as simple circuits. See, for example, www.deltamicro.co.uk/primary_online/circuits.html.

Simulations

Computers and the Internet enable children to extend their mental models. Great thinkers such as Einstein, da Vinci, and Galileo are thought to have had the ability to imagine the interaction of several variables at once and how they all come together to explain a phenomenon. Most of us can do this to some extent, but computers enhance our ability to create models and predict the interactions among many variables. The weather is a good example of how several rules of interaction come together at a given time and place. Computer models greatly enhance our ability to predict the weather by predicting the interactions among these multiple variables.

Simulations allow students to manipulate variables and see how the interactions among variables change the system. They help students understand complex relationships such as speed and distance or succession in ecosystems. Simulations are also helpful because they allow students to visualize phenomena that would be inaccessible or otherwise dangerous, such as launching rockets or mixing chemicals. Lastly, they allow students to deepen their descriptive models, formulate hypotheses, make predictions, design experiments to test their predictions, and revise their explanations, thereby completing the progression of inquiry. There are several simulations available on the Internet. Registration and a fee are required for some, but there is often a free trial period. Many sites, such as Explorelearning (www .explorescience.com/), include assessments and lesson plan supplements that accompany the simulations.

Using Technology to Communicate Results

An essential element of science is peer review. Science advances through sharing insights and discoveries that other scientists build upon. Teaching students to communicate their ideas, discoveries, and questions is an integral component of science education. Presentation software such as PowerPoint provides students with tools to present their results and data. Simple line graphs, bar graphs, and pie charts can be constructed using programs such as Excel. Digital cameras are wonderful tools for recording images that can be printed or displayed electronically. I encourage students to record changes throughout the seasons of a particular tree or ecosystem with digital cameras. One caution with graphic presentations such as PowerPoint is the tendency to spend more time on design than substance. There are so many options available with respect to fonts, colors, and animations that students can easily spend most of their time deciding on design elements rather than thinking about the substance of the presentation. Therefore, I urge you to set limits by restricting the range of fonts, colors, and design elements that students can use in a report. This is not an unrealistic requirement because scientists frequently follow rigid guidelines for publishing and presenting at conferences.

Interactive Whiteboards

Computer-generated presentations offer great graphics and images, but it is difficult to spontaneously add a student's insights and observations to the presentation during the class. It is at those times that I long for good old overhead projectors with clear acetate film that I can write on to incorporate class responses in real time. Interactive whiteboards provide a much needed bridge between static presentations and the real-time ebb and flow of the classroom. As the term implies, interactive whiteboards enable various modes of instructional technology to be seamlessly integrated into class lectures and demonstrations. Whiteboards enable the user, teacher or student, to control the computer from the whiteboard rather than using a keyboard or mouse. Touching the whiteboard is the equivalent of clicking on the object with the mouse. Writing tablets allow notes to be made directly on the white board, saved, and distributed electronically or in print. Interactive whiteboards bridge the gap between prescribed presentations and real-time student-teacher interactions.

Interactive whiteboards provide several benefits for teachers and pupils. Whiteboards are similar to other presentation tools insofar as teachers can prepare graphics, text, and media files in advance. Software for whiteboards continues to grow, enabling teachers to incorporate a variety of media into their whiteboard presentations. The greatest benefit may be in the opportunity for students to receive immediate feedback while working on activities at the board. The appropriate software provides feedback that allows them to take risks and test ideas that they can immediately revise and develop in real time to deepen their understanding.[6]

Summary

Instructional technology as used in this chapter refers to the use of computers and the Internet as tools to enhance science education. Both provide rich opportunities to deepen children's understanding of science and the processes of science. The Internet provides a portal into vast stores of information and data collection techniques that advance descriptive models and simulations to run virtual experiments and enrich explanatory models. Authentic learning experiences via the Internet enable students to participate in meaningful data collection and motivate them to a higher level of accountability through interaction with a community of peers and scientists. Students can dialogue with members of the scientific community through Ask a Scientist sites and have access to cutting edge images and data through sites such as the World Wide Telescope. Probes and microscopes that interface with computers allow students immediate access to data supporting discoveries and construction of knowledge. Interactive whiteboards provide a teaching tool that integrates the tools of technology in a seamless and effective manner in the classroom.

All this technology is wonderful, but it is only as effective as the teacher who uses it wisely to serve the goals of learning and not simply because the technology is available. Using technology effectively for learning takes time and effort. Used appropriately, technology can unlock exciting and fruitful learning opportunities for you and your students. Even if you are uncertain about your ability to incorporate technology meaningfully in the classroom, don't be afraid to try it. As Napoleon Hill (1883–1970) said, "Don't wait. The time will never be just right." But do remember, as with any powerful technology, it must be used judiciously. Often a sketchpad and a pencil are all the technology needed to discover the wonders of the world.

Going Further

On Your Own

1. Choose a topic from the National Science Education Standards. Design a WebQuest for students for the topic.

2. Identify the major classroom management problems you feel might result from having technology in the classroom. Briefly describe what preventative steps a teacher might take to minimize such problems.

3. At the beginning of the chapter, the point was made that technology should serve education rather than drive education. Create a set of guidelines for determining when it is appropriate to use technology for science education.

On Your Own or in a Cooperative Learning Group

4. Try to achieve consensus among your group members as you prepare one response to each of the following questions:

a. What are the long-term benefits of having a classroom in which children are able to link to the outside world through computer networking?

b. What are the negatives for children and teachers who use this networking capability?

5. Visit an elementary school science class and note whether and how any of the technologies mentioned in this chapter are integrated into the science learning experience. Describe how the technologies were beneficial or not beneficial to the learning experience.

6. Interview practicing elementary school teachers about their views on the use of technology to teach science.

7. Imagine that you are writing a technology grant for your elementary school. Describe the rationale you would provide to justify the use of technology in the science classroom and how you intend to use technology to enrich the science curriculum.

Resources for Discovery Learning

Internet Resources

To access these helpful websites, go to **MyEducationLab,** select Resources, and then Web Links. To learn more, click on the following links and you will easily be directed to each website

- **Ask a Scientist:**
  www.askascientist.com

- **Bugscope:**
  http://bugscope.beckman.uiuc.edu/

- **Cornell University Library:**
  www.library.cornell.edu/olinuris/ref/webcrit.html
  and www.library.cornell.edu/okuref/research/webeval.html

- **Explore eLearning:**
  www.explorescience.com/

- **Howard Hughes Medical Institute (HHMI):**
  www.hhmi.org/askascientist/

- **NASA Kids Club:**
  www.nasa.gov/audience/forkids/kidsclub/flash/index.html

- **The Noon Day Project:**
  www.k12science.org/noonday/

- **Project RoadKill:**
  http://roadkill.edutel.com

- **Square of Life:**
  www.ciese.org/curriculum/squareproj/proj_inst.htm

- **TeAchnology:**
  www.teach-nology.com/web_tools/web_quest

- **Topmarks Educational Search Engine: Primary Interactive Whiteboard Resources:**
  www.topmarks.co.uk/Interactive.aspx?s=science

- **US Department of Energy:**
  www.newton.dep.anl.gov/aasinfo.htm

- **WebQuest.org:**
  http://webquest.org/index.php

- **Wonderful World of Weather:**
  www.k12science.org/curriculum/weatherproj/index.html

Notes

1. Peter Norvig. http://norvig.com/Gettysburg. Reprinted with permission.
2. M. D. Roblyer, *Integrating Educational Technology into Teaching* (Upper Saddle River, NJ: Pearson, 2007.)
3. Research by the Center for Applied Research in Educational Technology (CARET, http://caret.iste.org/).
4. M. Cohen, & M. Reil. "The Effect of Distant Audiences on Children's Writing." *American Educational Research Journal* 26, no. 2 (summer, 1989): 143–159.
5. World Wide Telescope. www.worldwidetelescope.org. accessed 05-24-08.
6. *Getting the Most from Your Interactive Whiteboard: A Guide for Primary Schools.* Millburn Hill Road, Science Park: Coventry, UK British Educational Communications and Technology Agency (Becta), 2004, pp. 10–11.

chapter 9

Adapting the Science Curriculum

How can I adapt the science curriculum for children from diverse cultural backgrounds, children with special needs, and children with special gifts and talents?

▶ **Getting Started**

You notice that Donny rarely interacts with the other students in the classroom. He prefers to keep to himself and read even during recess and group work. Lauren excels at anything hands-on, yet she can't seem to sit still during quiet reading times and is a distraction for other students. Carla, your straight A student, often looks bored during class. It does not seem as though you can challenge her enough. Francis is reading two levels below grade level, and Julia's Individualized Education Plan (IEP) requires modifications to the curriculum. Meanwhile, there are five other students for whom you need to make accommodations. How do you meet the needs of all these children in the same class?

This chapter will help you prepare science learning experiences for all children in your class. I hope it will prepare you to say to every child who enters your classroom, "Hello, I am glad you are going to be in my class. This is the place where *everyone* learns."

The "Digital Divide": A Cautionary Tale

A classroom computer that's connected to the Internet is a special "window on the world." It can bring children the images of young hawks being fed and raised, cavorting rain forest animals, and a dolphin giving birth. Children who don't have this "window"—due to the fact that they attend underfunded schools or live in homes that lack the resources or inclination to own a computer—see none of these virtual real-world wonders.

As you study this chapter, which focuses on the unique needs of special children, keep in mind that not all children have access to the technology that will bring these wonders and other advantages to their lives—now or in the years ahead. And when these children encounter one more thing that divides them from the larger society, they may become more removed, more distant, and even alienated from their schooling.

As you teach *all* children through the medium of science, try to bring to bear as much technology as your school has to offer. If you can help children cross the "digital divide," you will be doing much to broaden their self-confidence, their career aspirations, and ultimately their horizons.

Children from Diverse Cultural Backgrounds

● Getting Science Reading Materials for Non-English Speakers

Las Cremalleras Tienen Dientes Y Otras Preguntas Sobre Inventos

If English is your only language, you must really be puzzled by the above quote! Even if you have studied the language used, my guess is that you only partially understand it.

I will give you the translation later in this section, but for now, I want you to think about what it's like for a non-English-speaking child, likely new to the United States, to see books and headings that look as forbidding as the quote above looks to *you*. Add to this language confusion the idea that the quote probably has something to do with science, a potentially difficult subject, and you should more fully appreciate the challenge that science time must be for non-English speakers as well as their teachers.

In a perfect world, all teachers would be fluent in at least one other language. But unless you were fortunate enough to be raised in a bilingual home, the odds of your being able to communicate effectively with a newly immigrated non-English-speaking child are slim, at best. Even if you are fluent in a second language, the odds are still not in your favor (or more importantly, the child's), since that language may not be Spanish, Cantonese or **Mandarin Chinese**, Bosnian, Laotian, Cambodian, or Vietnamese—the home languages of many new arrivals to the United States.

Your success in helping non-English-speaking children learn science and expand their abilities with English will depend in part on whether you can bring to your classroom resources in other languages. However, these resources are meant to serve as a bridge to the ultimate goal of science and English-language proficiency. Children should be gradually weaned from their dependency on translations.

One way to find such materials is to contact community groups that represent speakers of various languages and find out what science resources might be borrowed from scientifically literate community members. Another strategy is to contact a local university to see if undergraduate or graduate students studying a given language would be available to make translations from English. Finally, if you are a world traveler, you might consider visiting one or more of the countries represented by your students. During your visit, you may be able to acquire resource materials that can be put to good use in your classroom.

Are you still curious about the quote presented at the start of this section? It's the title of a book for children that, roughly translated from Spanish, reads, *I Wonder Why Zippers Have Teeth and Other Questions about Inventions*. It is one of many Spanish language science books available from the Center for the Study of Books in Spanish for Children, which maintains a database of thousands of titles with brief descriptions. (See the Notes at the end of the chapter for the center's Internet address.)[1]

Isabel Schon, an expert in the use of books for children in Spanish, makes the following point about the availability of books in Spanish. But I think what she says can be applied to books in other languages as well:

> Encouraging young Spanish speakers into the world of science is becoming easier every day. The ever-increasing number of high-quality, informative, and appealing books being published in Spanish make the observation, identification, description, experimental investigation, and/or theoretical explanation of phenomena much more rewarding.[2]

● Reinforcing Reading and Language Arts Skills

Hands-on, discovery-based science experiences can be great confidence builders for children from diverse cultural backgrounds, even if their present reading and language arts skills in English are weak. Your challenge as a teacher is to remember that you can use a child's success in science as a starting point to build a positive attitude toward school. Let's take a unit on weather as an example. Here are some very specific ways to extend the unit to the areas of reading and language arts, which can be applied to any science unit:

1. Use daily weather observations by students to create a language experience chart. You may have learned this technique in reading and language arts methods courses or workshops. To make such a chart, transcribe the children's oral observations onto a large sheet of paper, and have them read and discuss the material.

2. Have cooperative learning groups make model weather instruments and maintain their own language experience charts. You or a child with advanced writing abilities can transcribe the observations to the chart.

3. Expect children to make labels for the parts of their model weather instruments.

4. Expect children to keep personal logs of their daily weather observations, and occasionally read to them from their logs.

5. Have children record their individual weather reports on audiocassette tape or videotape.

6. Read or have one of the children read weather-related passages from children's books.

7. Encourage children to cut out weather-related headlines from a daily newspaper, and read them to the class.

8. Using suggestions from the class, write short poems about weather on chartpaper.

9. Have the children create dictionaries of weather terms, including pronounciation hints and drawings.

10. Have the children create a school weather report and present it on the school public address system every morning.

These techniques will be most effective if they are rooted in your belief that children from diverse cultural backgrounds who have language difficulties need every possible opportunity to practice the skills of reading, speaking, and writing. Two other techniques are especially helpful for children who are not fluent in English in the classroom: peer tutoring and parent/classroom connections.

● Organizing Peer Tutoring

The key to success in peer tutoring lies in the selection of the tutors. Ideally, tutors are good students who are fluent in both languages, who understand the content you are teaching, and who possess those special personal characteristics that permit them to function as positive, supportive tutors.

Peer tutors also need some help from teachers. If possible, you should provide them with materials that display and explain science concepts in the child's native language as well as in English. If you happen to be fluent in the native languages of the children in your classes, you may wish to prepare alternative materials similar to those shown in Figure 9.1.[3] Children who speak only English may enjoy the challenge of trying to explain what the foreign terms on such diagrams mean.

● Fostering Parent/Classroom Science Connections

Science time can be a learning experience that fully and appropriately involves the parents of children from diverse cultural backgrounds. Reaching out to these parents is well worth the effort, even though time and energy are at a premium for modern parents and teachers. You may need the assistance of someone who is fluent in the child's home language to use the following ideas:

1. Send a letter to parents at the beginning of the year explaining what science time for students will be like. Write the letters in English and in the children's home languages, and send both copies to parents.

2. Send home a monthly science newsletter in the children's home languages that includes examples of students' work.

3. Call five parents a week to make contact for future communication.

4. Invite parents to school for a Science Open House, and invite school professionals who speak the home languages to be present.

5. Prepare home study science activity sheets in children's home languages.

6. Send a letter to parents asking for volunteers to accompany the class on field trips or to come to class when science activities are done. If you are not fluent in children's home languages, having a helper who can communicate in more than one language can be a boon.

For additional ideas on how to meet the special needs of minority and bilingual children in the classroom, contact one

Figure 9.1 With a little effort, you should be able to find drawings that are labeled in children's native languages.

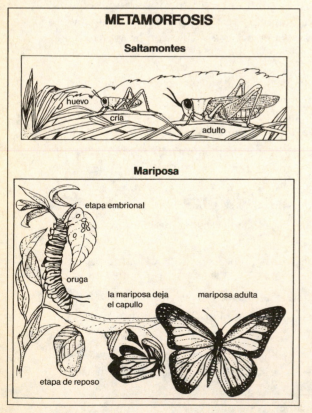

of the bilingual educational multifunctional support/resource centers listed in the For the Teacher's Desk section at the end of this book. As you review the listing, notice that the resource centers provide services for specific geographic regions.

Children with Special Needs

Go to **MyEducationLab**, select the topic Students with Special Needs, watch the simulation entitled "Assessing the General Education Curriculum," and complete the questions that accompany it.

Perhaps we, as teachers, should take a vow with respect to children who have impairments—namely, that we will not give these children additional challenges while they are in our care. My language may seem a bit strong, but it is possible to put these children at even greater risk when we make *content* adjustments when we should be making *methodology* adjustments. Children with disabilities need to learn the same things as other children, but they may need to learn these things in different ways or at different rates. Every child needs opportunities to explore, to inquire and acquire knowledge and skills, and to discover and apply what he or she has learned.

The Inclusion Challenge

The 1975 Education for All Handicapped Children Act (P.L. 94–142), renamed in 1991 the Individuals with Disabilities Education Act (IDEA) requires a free and appropriate education with related services for each child in the least restrictive environment possible. In response, some children with special needs have been moved from traditional special education or resource rooms to regular classrooms in a practice known as *inclusion* or *mainstreaming*. Although educating these children in classrooms with their agemates may seem like a good idea, actually doing it can be a difficult, intense process. In too many

Make the Case *An Individual or Group Challenge*

● **The Problem**	Because technological innovations occur so rapidly these days, it is difficult for teachers to select the best classroom technology for children with impairments.
● **Assess Your Prior Knowledge and Beliefs**	Based on your personal experience in science classrooms, assess your present knowledge about the classroom devices that could help you achieve the fullest possible participation of children with these impairments:

1. Hearing_____

2. Visual_____

3. Orthopedic_____

● **The Challenge**	Four engineers have formed a company to design and manufacture instructional equipment for children with impairments. They have asked you to suggest ideas for new devices or for improvements in existing devices that would assist these children in a hands-on, discovery-based classroom. What will you suggest?

All children—including those with special needs—need opportunities to explore, acquire knowledge and skills, and apply what they have learned.

cases, it's assumed that the physical placement alone is enough and that good things will automatically happen for everyone involved. It isn't quite that easy, however, especially in a science program designed to provide appropriate inquiry-based experiences for everyone. The strategies discussed in the next few sections will help you ensure that every child who is *physically* included in your classroom will be *educationally* included as well.

The Range of Disabilities

Disability is a term that encompasses a variety of physical and cognitive needs. It includes learning disabilities such as dyslexia, emotional or behavioral issues including attention deficit disorder, and physical disabilities that limit mobility or sensory perception. The literature includes English language barriers as disabilities as well. It is well beyond the scope of this text to address each disability separately. However, there are guiding principles that can inform your curriculum design and teaching to make your classroom a rich learning environment for all students.

Guiding Principles for Inclusion: Differentiated Instruction and Universal Design for Learning

Differentiated Instruction

Clearly not all students learn in the same manner. A one-size-fits-all approach to teaching and learning simply does not suffice to provide all students with opportunities to reach their fullest potential. Differentiated learning recognizes that students benefit when they have multiple options for learning. Consequently, teachers are challenged to be flexible in their approach to teaching the same content using a wide variety of teaching strategies to accommodate children with different learning modalities and needs based on cognitive, emotional, and physical abilities. Admittedly, this is quite an overwhelming charge. There is often, though not always, only one teacher for a classroom of students. Even with the assistance of others in your classroom, you still need to plan in order to differentiate instruction. Have no illusions that this is easy, but it is a worthy and attainable goal. One approach to assist you in planning for and providing differentiated learning is a strategy called Universal Design for Learning (UDL).

Universal Design for Learning

Go to **MyEducationLab**, select the topic Technology, watch the video entitled "Lesson on Birds," and complete the questions that accompany it.

UDL has its roots in architectural design strategies that include access to buildings for people with disabilities. Briefly stated, rather than create separate ramps for wheelchair users, UDL incorporates the ramps as the main access for all users. It has been found that ramps and similar accommodations such as curb cuts and audio signals at crosswalks benefit all users, not just those with disabilities.

The same approach applied to curricula and teaching strategies results in a flexible classroom environment that accommodates a wide range of learners. UDL incorporates multiple learning modalities, including visual, auditory, kinesthetic, and tactile, to provide access to learning for a variety of student needs relating to learning styles, cultural backgrounds, languages, and disabilities. There are three guiding principles to UDL:

- Provide multiple means of engagement.
- Provide multiple means of representation (and/or participation).
- Provide multiple means of expression.

Note that the principles of UDL coincide nicely with the 5E instructional strategy. Engagement is apparent, whereas exploration requires representation of concepts, and explanation calls for multiple means of expression.

The science classroom/lab affords several opportunities to implement these three principles. Each principle requires you to consider a variety of ways that students with different learning styles can access learning experiences. Adapting your curriculum to the principles of UDL can be a liberating experience that gives you license to think creatively. For example, to teach the properties of sound to students who are hearing impaired you could have them feel vibrations representing frequency and intensity through different media. But don't make this a separate activity for the hearing impaired; incorporate it into the lesson for the entire class. The wonderful outcome of UDL is that a variety of access points to the curriculum will benefit all students.

Some general strategies for each principle are given in the Figure 9.2. The value of UDL is in using a variety of strategies to access the same learning experience. For example, you may choose to engage students by putting two tomato plants on the table—one that is full of foliage, erect, and bright green, the other that has few leaves, limp, and pale green—and ask why the plants are different. At the same time, you can post the question on the board. Project a closeup of the plants on a screen using a live video projection (or prepared photos from a digital camera, which are easy to upload) and/or handout pictures of the two plants. Ask the children to prepare a descriptive model using a think-pair-share strategy. Post a word bank of descriptors on the board with pictures next to the descriptors. Let the children touch the plants to feel differences as well. Note that students with visual impairments benefit from close-up views of the plants provided by photos, video, and feeling the plants. Hearing-impaired students can rely on text and peer sharing, while English language learners benefit from word banks supplemented by pictures as well as think-pair-share strategies.

Figure 9.2   Strategies for UDL

1. Multiple means of engagement
   - Read aloud
   - Read with the text projected on the board
   - Supplement text with pictures, graphics, and video, audio
   - Music related to topic
   - Simulation
   - Role play (i.e., students role-play water molecules during phase changes)

2. Multiple means of representation and participation
   Representation
   - Word bank posted in classroom
   - Ideas bank posted in classroom
   - Electronic version of the text (varying text sizes, read aloud with text-to-speech)
   - CD-ROM or online encyclopedia with images and spoken text
   - Music for reflection time
   - Links to foreign language websites on the subject
   - Printed and electronic concept map with images, text, and hyperlinks
   - e-text outline of lecture content with main ideas highlighted
   - Tool to translate words or connected text into other languages
   - Graphic highlighting of important ideas (on screen or on paper)
   - Digital photograph collection
   - Concept maps
   - Time lines

   Participation
   - Cooperative groups with assigned tasks complementary to abilities
   - Stations
   - Role plays
   - Manipulatives

3. Multiple means of expression
   - Writing
   - Discussion
   - Role play
   - PowerPoint
   - Poster
   - Concept map
   - Play
   - Song
   - Art

Science also involves laboratory investigations at the bench as well as in the field. Making these inquiry experiences available to a range of abilities can be enhanced by resourcefulness and technology. Not all students will be able to collect pond samples, for example, but they can decide where to take the samples and work with a partner who can collect the samples for them.

Technology provides unique access to data collection and analysis. Examples include:

- Meters and probes with audible readout (e.g., enabling a light probe to emit a tone that increases in pitch proportionally to changes in light intensity)
- Talking thermometers, balances, and calculators; laboratory glassware with raised numbers
- Electronic note takers and portable word processors
- Digital voice recorders
- Adequate lighting and magnification
- Digital cameras[4]

Accommodations and Modifications

These terms are used to describe the general strategies that support inclusion in classroom practice. These strategies differ significantly in the type of support we provide for students with disabilities and the expectations we have for students with disabilities.

- **Accommodations**

    Services or support provided to help a student fully access the subject matter and instruction as well as to validly demonstrate what he or she knows. An accommodation *does not change the content* of instruction nor the performance expectations.

- **Modifications**

    Curriculum modifications made when a student either is taught something different from the rest of the class or is taught the same information but at a different level of complexity. A modification *does change the content* of instruction and the performance expectations.[5]

Reality Check

You have initiated an outdoor education program at your school. Your fourth-grade class has decided to integrate their history unit about the Pilgrims with science by planting a Three Sisters Garden of corn, beans, and squash. One of your performance objectives is for the students to gather descriptive information about the life cycle of plants over the course of the project. You organize the class of fifteen students into five groups of three. The class consists of seven boys and eight girls. Two of the boys have been diagnosed with attention deficit hyperactivity disorder. One girl is legally blind, another girl has a learning disability and is reading at the first-grade level, and one girl is an English language learner. Identify two strategies to differentiate learning for this class using the principles of universal design.

Teamwork Is Essential

Most of us are not qualified to identify a learning disability, although years of experience working with children will make you sensitive to the practical implications of processing problems. One of the most important steps you can take to effectively include students with disabilities in your classroom is to work with the special education team. Leverage their expertise and experience to understand the needs of the child and the strategies that best serve the student. Communicate your observations about the student(s) in your classroom and seek the team's advice. Consult the child's IEP to identify the accommodations and/or modifications that are mandated by the plan. Work with paraprofessionals if they are present in the classroom for particular students. Invite them to discuss the needs of the child with whom they are working and seek their input about the child's attitude and performance. They may have insights from working closely with the child that they can share. Also speak with the child's guardians to better understand the needs of the child in your classroom. Use all the resources available to you in order to create the optimal learning environment for all your students.

● Science Experiences for Children with Visual Impairments

Children with visual impairments don't need to be placed in special classrooms. A visual impairment affects only the *manner* through which knowledge enters a child's mind; it should not, in any way, affect the *nature* of the knowledge you select for the curriculum. (I am, of course, using *knowledge* in its broadest sense to include skills, attitudes, values, and so forth.)

But if you do not modify the curriculum, then what do you do? The answer is straightforward. You modify equipment, materials, and experiences that are visually based by incorporating the use of touch, hearing, and smell.

Science Reading Materials   One convenient approach to delivering printed science information to children with visual problems is to have sighted students with good oral-reading skills audiotape books, chapter sections, newspaper stories, and other printed materials. This can be an ongoing class project, in which children take turns preparing instructional materials. Another strategy is to have the school purchase large-type books, talking books, and braille books (if your children have braille reading skills). (See the Notes at the end of the chapter for major sources of such materials.)[6]

An outcome of The Individuals with Disabilities Education Act was the establishment of the National Instructional Materials Access Center. It makes the conversion of print instructional materials in specialized formats such as braille, audio, or digital texts available to distributors. Resources such as the Louis Database of Accessible Materials (www.aph.org/louis/index.html) enable you to search for available instructional print materials for the vision impaired.

Science Activities and Equipment   Some children with visual impairments have a degree of residual vision; that is, they may be able to distinguish light areas from dark areas and to differentiate shapes. To capitalize on these abilities, speak with the child, the child's parents, and perhaps the child's physician (with parental permission, of course) to get ideas about how to modify equipment for him or her.

A small digital recorder can be an important addition to your classroom equipment. It can take the place of a notebook by permitting the child to record the results of science experiences. The recording procedure will also help the child understand that you are holding him or her as accountable as the other students for taking and maintaining notes. Also consider the increasing availability of voice recognition software to assist children with disabilities that make writing challenging.

Look for ways to provide appropriate tactile experiences for children with visual impairments. I have used interlocking snap beads to represent DNA molecules. Each shape represented a different nucleotide. Staples or liquid glue can be used to raise the print of graphs or diagrams. The AAAS (1991) recommends the use of technology to facilitate observations and data collection such as talking thermometers, timers, and calculators.[7] Familiarize visually impaired students with the location of emergency exits, eye washes, and emergency showers with respect to their work space.

Here is a challenge for you: How would you have a child with a visual impairment observe a fish in an aquarium? Because aquarium fish usually are not noisy creatures and are tucked in water, which is itself encased in glass or plastic, this problem may seem insurmountable—but it isn't. If you place within the aquarium a slightly smaller plastic aquarium that has holes drilled in it, the child will be able to lift and tip the inner aquarium until most of the water drains into the larger aquarium. The fish will become trapped in the water that remains at the bottom of the inner aquarium. Use caution handling the fish. As any good fisherman knows, do not touch the fish with dry fingers. Be sure the child's hands are wet with the water in which the fish is kept. Encourage the child to treat the fish gently and to stroke it along the grain of the scales. Alternatively, use an anatomically correct model or professionally mounted fish for the child to touch in order to get a sense of the fish's external structure.

As the aquarium question illustrates, the real challenge to a child's learning may be the difficulty the teacher has in finding a way around or through a seemingly insurmountable problem. You are not completely on your own, however, as you think through these problems. Through research in specialized catalogs and your personal contacts with special education personnel, you will discover that adapted equipment is available to help children and adults with visual impairments measure such variables as elapsed time, length, volume, mass, and weight.

There should be an "eleventh commandment" for teachers who work with children who have visual impairments: Do not be meek in your demeanor as you go forth to make requests for special adapted materials and equipment. Your efforts to accommodate the special needs of children will be rewarded in many ways. The children will learn, and their peers will gain important knowledge and attitudes about people who may seem different but, in fact, are not.

● Science Experiences for Children with Hearing Impairments

Mainstreamed children with hearing impairments range from those who do not require a hearing aid to those who have no hearing. Some of these children will be skilled lip readers, some will be adept at sign language, and some will have neither of these skills.

Children who have hearing impairments can benefit greatly from the multisensory, hands-on approach to science used in any discovery-oriented classroom. Your principal challenge will be helping these children participate fully in the experiences. Written or pictorial directions for activities and assignments, directions on task cards, and even acting out the steps of an activity will prove helpful. In the upper-elementary grades and in the middle grades, you may wish to have children take turns taking notes from your oral presentations and sharing them with students who have hearing impairments.

The child with a hearing impairment should have an unobstructed view of you and the location where you carry out demonstrations. This will allow the child to search for visual cues to supplement any information that you transmit orally. As you carry out demonstrations, explain content, and give directions, try to position your head so that the child can read your lip movements and facial expressions. You may want to remind the child's classmates to do the same.

Children with hearing impairments benefit greatly from participating in multisensory, hands-on science activities.

When working with a child who has a hearing impairment, be careful not to form an opinion about his or her intellectual abilities based only upon listening to his or her speech. The inability to articulate properly results from not having a model for the spoken words and does not indicate intellectual ability. By encouraging the child's oral responses, you will provide him or her with an opportunity to build self-confidence and practice articulation.

● Science Experiences for Children with Physical Impairments

Physical impairments may range from mild to severe and differ widely in origin. Some physical challenges may result from accidents and diseases, and some may be congenital. As a science teacher, your concern should focus on the specific problems that the child may have as the class does hands-on activities. Think about whether the child has problems grasping objects, moving, stopping, or remaining steady. Also keep in mind the space needed for children with crutches, the room required for a wheelchair to navigate, and the access available at some field trip sites.

As you consider these matters, you may find that you have to make accommodations in the classroom for a child with a physical challenge or adaptations to the science materials and equipment that he or she will use. For example, you may need to arrange seating so that a child in a wheelchair has ready access to all parts of the room. Or you may need to be sure that a child who has a problem moving quickly has a work space that is close to the distribution point for science materials. Of course, the accommodations needed will vary with each child.

A child's physical challenge can provide a growth experience for the classroom if you capitalize on the opportunities it provides for building a sense of community among all the children. By helping children interact positively with *all* their peers, you not only help the child with a physical impairment but also the entire class.

Science Experiences for Children with Emotional Problems

Some children display emotional behaviors that interfere with their ability to function well academically or with their personal and social development in the classroom. These children may have little self-confidence, be frightened easily, be depressed, be disobedient or defiant, or simply spend their time daydreaming. The child with emotional problems acts the way he or she does for a reason. Unfortunately, the reason may have eluded even the most skilled school psychologist or psychiatrist.

The causes for the behavior you observe will probably lie outside your ability to remediate. However, the science activities you offer can serve an important therapeutic function. They can enable the child to manipulate and control variables and thus give him or her a unique opportunity to operate in responsible ways. This often benefits all children as well as those with attention deficit disorders to remain stimulated.

The 5E instructional strategy is designed to engage students in thought-provoking hands-on activities. If children can find success through such activities, they will gain self-confidence and pride in accomplishment. You may not be able to remedy children's basic emotional problems, but you can create an environment that can enhance feelings of self-worth.

As a teacher of science in a regular classroom, you should help your students welcome and encourage any child with emotional problems who joins the class for the day or a portion of the day. Remember, children with emotional problems need ever-increasing contact with children who display appropriate behaviors. Some teachers may be concerned that the rest of a class will learn inappropriate behaviors from a mainstreamed child with emotional problems. If this occurs, it may be that the teacher has been unable to create a total classroom environment that values and affirms productive and appropriate social behaviors.

Learning Disabilities

Learning disabilities (LD) are neurologically based processing problems. These processing problems can interfere with learning basic skills such as reading, writing, or math. They can also interfere with higher-level skills such as organization, time planning, and abstract reasoning. The types of LD are identified by the specific processing problem. They might relate to getting information into the brain (Input), making sense of this information (Organization), storing and later retrieving this information (Memory), or getting this information back out (Output). Thus, the specific types of processing problems that result in LD might be in one or more of these four areas.[8] Work closely with the special-education team and keep in mind the principles of differentiated learning and UDL as you address the LD needs of students in your class.

Children with Special Gifts and Talents

Many of the children in our schools have extraordinary intellectual abilities, and many have other abilities that are far more advanced than those of their agemates. In fact, it is estimated that between 3% and 5% of the school-age population fits this definition. How can you tell which children have special abilities? The following definition may help:

> Children capable of high performance, including those with demonstrated achievements or ability in any one or more of these areas—general intellectual ability, specific academic aptitude, creative or productive thinking, leadership ability, visual and performing arts, or psychomotor ability.[9]

Also keep in mind that gifted and talented children may come from diverse cultural backgrounds or they may have impairments, as discussed in previous sections of this chapter. Think of your classroom as a garden in which each gifted and talented child can blossom. Science can provide these children with unique opportunities to design and carry out explorations of their environment. Because gifted and talented children may move very quickly through the planned learning experiences you provide for your class, the challenge is to keep them growing and blossoming. You will need to find ways to extend and enrich your science activities so that these children do not become bored.

The National Association for Gifted Children recommends that an effective approach to programming for gifted learners should be seen as a combination of three elements: accelerative approaches, in which instruction is matched to the competence level of students; enrichment approaches, in which opportunities for the investigation of supplementary material are given; and individualization, in which instruction is matched specifically to the learner's achievement, abilities, and interests.[10]

Acceleration often refers to specialized courses or grade skipping, both of which are probably beyond the scope of your responsibilities as a classroom teacher. However, you can enrich and individualize instruction in your classroom using differentiated instruction that addresses gifted and talented students.

● Day-to-Day Enrichment Activities

Here are some enrichment activities you may wish to use even if your school has a standard science curriculum or a specific set of textbooks or other resource materials:

1. Get single copies of advanced levels of the materials for each child you think will benefit from such materials or activities.
2. Each time the class begins a new unit of work, have conferences with your gifted children to identify enrichment readings and activities for them to work on in the course of the unit and establish a schedule of follow-up conferences.
3. Develop strategies that will enable these children to share their readings and related experiences with the rest of the class.
4. In general, expect these children to participate fully in all regular activities, but try to put their special gifts and talents to use as they go beyond the basic curriculum.

● Challenge Projects

Gifted and talented children are a special joy to teach because many are able to function with considerable independence in the classroom. This capacity for independent, self-directed work is well suited to long-term science projects. I call such activities *challenge projects*. Here are a few examples:

Can You Make:
A sundial and use it as a clock?
A model wind-speed indicator?
A water filter using sand and pebbles that will clean up muddy water?
A compound machine from a group of simple machines?
A working model of a liquid-based fire extinguisher?
A simple battery-operated electric motor?
A balance that really works?
A clay contour map of the school grounds?

All challenge projects should begin with a teacher/student conference that focuses on the child's interest in and capacity to undertake various projects.

Integrate the enrichment activities and challenge projects into the curriculum. Avoid activities that are add-ons or busy work. Rather, make the learning experience one that genuinely deepens understanding, and make it optional yet available to all students. For example, suppose you were teaching a lesson on heat exchange using the freezing of water as an example. Provide an option for all students to calculate the latent heat of ice using the relationship expressed as

Heat gained by ice + Heat gained by water from melted ice =
Heat lost by container + Heat lost by water

$$m_i L_i \quad + \quad m_{wi} c_w \Delta T \quad = \quad m_c c_c \Delta T \quad + \quad m_w c_w \Delta T$$

where m = mass, i = ice, w = water, wi = water from melted ice, c = container.

Solve for L to get the latent heat of ice.

Provide resources for the students to investigate the kinetic molecular theory.

Responding to the special needs of gifted and talented children will provide you with many opportunities to stretch your own intellectual and imaginative abilities. You will find helping these children to reach their full potential is an extremely enjoyable part of teaching.

Summary

Teachers need to know how to use and provide access to the latest classroom technology so that special-needs children are not limited in their progress as a result of the "digital divide." Science time should be seen as an opportunity for all children to practice their reading and language development skills. Inquiry-based, discovery-focused activities, and the stimuli such activities provide, can help children from diverse cultural backgrounds increase their language skills as they learn science.

Children with special needs—whether visual or physical impairments, hearing problems, or emotional problems—must participate as fully as possible in the science activities that take place in the classroom. Your response to their special needs requires both an understanding of the unique challenges they offer and the ability to develop a variety of ways to make the curriculum accessible to them.

Gifted and talented children also have special needs. The science curriculum for these children should include various enrichment activities, challenge projects, and other opportunities to use their unique talents and abilities.

Use the principles of UDL to guide differentiated instruction as you plan the appropriate accommodations to your curriculum and teaching. Work with members of the special education team to provide meaningful and effective inclusion for all students in your class.

Going Further

On Your Own

1. If you have a disability or were an ELL in elementary school, comment on any special challenges you had to overcome to be a successful student in science class. If you feel that there were no such challenges, note whether this was due to special circumstances, such as a particularly responsible and encouraging teacher, parental support, and so on. If you do not have a disability or were not an ELL in elementary school, interview someone who is and record his or her responses to these questions.

2. How serious is the problem of science career awareness for children from diverse cultural backgrounds? Would broader media coverage of minority-group members in scientific fields counterbalance the

underrepresentation of such individuals in curricular materials? What do you see as the teacher's role in building scientific career awareness?

3. Identify a science activity you would do with children, and then describe how you would adapt it to the needs of a child with a visual or hearing impairment.

4. Write a sample letter that you could use to establish communication among yourself, a scientist living in the community, and a gifted child with a strong interest in science. In the letter, highlight the benefits that both the child and the scientist would enjoy.

5. Use the principles of UDL to develop an inquiry-based learning experience for a fifth-grade class of 20 students. The class consists of one student with a hearing impairment, one student with a learning disability, and two gifted students. The IEP for the LD student recommends the following strategies and accommodations:
   Repeat and clarify directions.
   Preview and review vocabulary.

Use a multimodal approach with audio and visual supplements. Always relate classroom activities to timetable and agenda.

6. Role-play the following situations with your group. When you are done, discuss each situation:
   a. A parent/teacher conference regarding a gifted child whose parent is dissatisfied with your response to the child's special abilities. This parent is particularly concerned about accelerating the child's learning in both science and mathematics.
   b. Same as in "a," except the child has a hearing or visual impairment.
   c. A conference in which the teacher encourages the parents of a child with a physical impairment to allow the child to participate in a field trip to a water treatment plant.

If you are doing this activity by yourself, write a brief description of what might take place in each of these three conferences.

Resources for Discovery Learning

Internet Resources

To access these helpful websites, go to **MyEducationLab,** select Resources, and then Web Links. To learn more, click on the following links and you will easily be directed to each website

- **CAST Teaching Every Student:**
  www.cast.org/teachingeverystudent/

- **Center for Applied Special Technology:**
  www.cast.org/research/udl/index.html

- **Differentiated Instruction:**
  www.frsd.k12.nj.us/rfmslibrarylab/di/differentiated_instruction.htm

- **Learning Disabilities Association of America:**
  www.ldanatl.org/aboutld/teachers/index.asp

- **National Association for Gifted Children:**
  www.nagc.org/

Print Resources

Suggested Readings

Allan, Alson. "The Minority Student Achievement Network." *Educational Leadership* 60, no. 5 (December 2002/January 2003): 76–78.

Bernstein, Leonard, et al. *African and African-American Women of Science.* Saddle Brook, NJ: Peoples Publishing Group, 1998.

Bernstein, Leonard, et al. *Latino Women of Science.* Saddle Brook, NJ: Peoples Publishing Group, 1998.

Bernstein, Leonard, et al. *Multicultural Women of Science.* Saddle Brook, NJ: Peoples Publishing Group, 1996.

Buck, Gayle A. "Teaching Science to English-as-Second-Language Learners." *Science and Children* 38, no. 3 (November/December 2000): 38–41.

Burgstahler, S. *Universal Design of Instruction (UDI): Definition, Principles, and Examples.* Seattle: DO-IT, University of Washington, 2008.

Carolan, J., et al. "Differentiation: Lessons from Master Teachers." *Educational Leardership* 64, no. 5 (February 2007): 44–47.

Cassano, Paul, and Antol, Rayna A. "Integration and Integrity." *Science Scope* 24, no. 7 (April 2001): 18–21.

Cawley, John F., Foley, Teresa E., Miller, James. "Science and Students with Mild Disabilities Principles of Universal Design." *Intervention in School and Clinic* 38A, no. 3 (January 2003): 160–171.

Curriculum Access and Universal Design for Learning. ERIC/OSEP Digest #E586 ERIC Clearinghouse on Disabilities and Gifted Education **ERIC Identifier:** ED437767 **Publication Date:** 1999-12-00 **Author:** Orkwis, Raymond

Delisle, J. R. "For gifted students, full inclusion is a partial solution." *Educational Leadership* 57, no. 3 (November 1999): 80–83.

Farenga, Stephen J., et al."Rocketing into Adaptive Inquiry." *Science Scope* 25, no. 4 (January 2002): 34–39.

Fetters, Marcia, Pickard, Dawn M., and Pyle, Eric. "Making Science Accessible: Strategies to Meet the Needs of a Diverse Student Population." *Science Scope* 26, no. 5 (February 2003): 26–29.

Flores, M. M. "Universal Design in Elementary and Middle School." *Childhood Education* 84, no. 4 (Summer 2008): 224–229.

Garrett, Michael Tlanusta, et al. "Open Hands, Open Hearts: Working with Native Youth in the Schools." *Intervention in School and Clinic* 38, no. 4 (March 2003): 225–235.

Gooden, Kelly. "Parents Come to Class." *Science and Children* 40, no. 4 (January 2003): 22–25.

Hall, T. (2002). *Differentiated instruction.* Wakefield, MA: National Center on Accessing the General Curriculum. Retrieved [insert date] from http://www.cast.org/publications/ncac/ncac_diffinstruc.html

Hehir, T. "The Changing Role of Intervention for Children with Disabilities." *Principal (Reston, Va.)* 85, no. 2 (November/December 2005): 22–25.

Hehir, Thomas. "Confronting Ableism." *Educational Leadership* 64, no. 5 (Feb 2007): 8–14.

Hrabowski, Freeman A., III. "Raising Minority Achievement in Science and Math." *Educational Leadership* 60, no. 5 (December 2002/January 2003): 44–48.

Krutchinsky, Rich, and Harris, William. "Super Science Saturday." *Science and Children* 40, no. 4 (January 2003): 26–28.

Lord, Thomas R., and Clausen-May, Tandi. "Giving Spatial Perception Our Full Attention." *Science and Children* 39, no. 5 (February 2002): 22–25.

Nitzberg, Joel, and Sparrow, Judith. "Parent Outreach Success." *Science and Children* 39, no. 3 (November/December 2001): 36–40.

Pemberton, Jane B. "Integrated Processing: A Strategy for Working Out Unknown Words." *Intervention in School and Clinic* 38, no. 4 (March 2003): 247–250.

Rolon, Carmen A. "Educating Latino Students." *Educational Leadership* 60, no. 5 (December 2002/January 2003): 40–43.

Schon, Isabel. "Libros de Ciencias en Espanol." *Science and Children* 37, no. 6 (March 2000): 26–29.

Schon, Isabel. "Libros de Ciencias en Espanol." *Science and Children* 38, no. 6 (March 2001): 23–26.

Schon, Isabel. "Libros de Ciencias en Espanol." *Science and Children* 39, no. 6 (March 2002): 22–25.

Talanquer, Vicente, and Sarmiento, Griselda. "One Foot = One Cenxocoalli: Measuring in the Pre-Hispanic World." *Science Scope* 25, no. 7 (April 2002): 12–15.

The Templeton National Report on Acceleration. *A Nation Deceived: How Schools Hold Back America's Brightest Students.* Vol. I. Edited by Nicholas Colangelo, Susan G. Assouline, Miraca U. M. Gross. 2004. The Connie Belin & Jacqueline N. Blank International Center for Gifted Education and Talent Development. Iowa City: Iowa.

The Templeton National Report on Acceleration. *A Nation Deceived: How Schools Hold Back America's Brightest Students.* Vol. II. Edited by Nicholas Colangelo, Susan G. Assouline, Miraca U. M. Gross. 2004. The Connie Belin & Jacqueline N. Blank International Center for Gifted Education and Talent Development. Iowa City: Iowa.

Williams, Gregory J., and Leon Reisberg. "Successful Inclusion." *Intervention in School and Clinic* 38, no. 4 (March 2003): 205–210.

Winebrenner, S. "Gifted students need an education, too." *Educational Leadership* 58, no. 1 (September 2000): 52–56.

Notes

1. You may reach the Center for the Study of Books in Spanish for Children at www.csusm.edu/campus.centers/csb.
2. Isabel Schon, "Libros de Ciencias en Espanol," *Science and Children* 35, no. 6 (March 1998): 30.
3. Many major publishers of educational materials prepare direct translations of some or all of their elementary- and middle-grade science books. I extend my thanks to Holt, Rinehart and Winston for their permission to reproduce Figure 9.1, which first appeared in J. Abruscato et al., *Ciencia de Holt*, Grade 5 Teacher's Guide (New York: Holt, Rinehart and Winston, 1985), p. TM10.
4. From Cynthia Curry, Libby Cohen, and Nancy Lightbody. "Universal Design in Science Learning." *The Science Teacher* 73, no. 3 (March 2006): 32–37.

5. Lauren Katzman (personal communication, April 15, 2007).

6. Sources of materials, such as large-type books, talking books, and braille books are the American Printing House for the Blind (Box 6085, 1839 Frankfort Avenue, Louisville, Kentucky 40206) and The Lighthouse for the Blind and Visually Impaired (1155 Mission Street, San Francisco, California 94103).

7. American Association for the Advancement of Science. "Laboratories and Classrooms in Science and Engineering." (Washington, DC: 1991) [ED 373 997].

8. Learning Disabilities Association of America. Types of Disabilities. www.ldanatl.org/aboutld/teachers/understanding/types.asp. Downloaded (06-03-08).

9. Dorothy Sisk, *What If Your Child Is Gifted?* (Washington, DC: Office of the Gifted and Talented, U.S. Office of Education, n.d.).

10. National Association for Gifted Children. www.nagc.org/. (accessed 06-03-08).

For the
Teacher's Desk

Your Classroom Enrichment Handbook

Position Statements of the National Science Teachers Association (NSTA)
    Women in Science Education
    Multicultural Science Education
    Substance Use and Abuse
    Science Competitions

Keeping Living Things . . . Alive
    Living Materials in the Classroom
    The Plant Picker

Safety Management Helper
    Safety Checklist

Materials to Keep in Your Science Closet
    Primary Grades
    Middle Grades

The Metric Helper

Content Coverage Checklists
    The Earth/Space Sciences
    The Life Sciences
    The Physical Sciences

Your Science Survival Bookshelf
    The Bookshelf
    The Magazine Rack

Your Science Source Address Book

Free and Inexpensive Materials

The "Wish Book" Companies

Bilingual Child Resources

Special-Needs Resources

Science Teachers Associations

NASA Teacher Resource Centers

Position Statements of the National Science Teachers Association (NSTA)*

Women in Science Education

The continuing policy within NSTA is, and has been, to involve and encourage all teachers and members of the scientific community, regardless of sex, to participate in all organizational activities.

As teachers, however, our responsibility for contributing to the development of the science skills and interests of women lies principally in the classroom. Three elements within the educational system have subtle but significant roles in supporting or negating our efforts in this regard. They are (1) the development and use of criteria for the selection of student-used materials, e.g., textbooks, films, filmstrips, to ensure the equitable portrayal of girls and boys, women and men involved in science; (2) the support of guidance departments that encourage students to develop to their full potential and to advise them of the course options available to them in school and the career options available to them after school; (3) the encouragement and guidance provided by the teacher regarding student achievement and careers in science; and (4) the inclusion of appropriate role models.

Because of the importance of these three elements, NSTA takes the following positions:

I. Any teacher whose charge includes the responsibility of evaluating or selecting instructional materials should demand that the materials (a) eliminate sex role stereotyping and (b) reflect a realistic female/male ratio in relation to the total number of people portrayed. Materials should be rejected by the teacher if they do not meet the above two criteria.

II. Science teachers must exert their influence to encourage guidance counselors to treat female students identically to male students relative to career opportunities and program planning. Science teachers can assist guidance counselors in this endeavor by providing them with detailed updated information and data on the interests and abilities of specific female students.

III. Science teachers must consciously strive to overcome the barriers created by society which discourage women from pursuing science for its career opportunities and for the enjoyment it brings to involved students.

—Adopted by the NSTA Board of Directors, July 1985

Multicultural Science Education

Science educators value the contributions and uniqueness of children from all backgrounds. Members of the National Science Teachers Association (NSTA) are aware that a country's welfare is ultimately dependent upon the productivity of all of its people.

*The position statements on pages 160–162 are reprinted courtesy of the National Science Teachers Association, Arlington, VA www.nsta.org/position.

Many institutions and organizations in our global, multicultural society play major roles in establishing environments in which unity in diversity flourishes. Members of the NSTA believe science literacy must be a major goal of science education institutions and agencies. We believe that ALL children can learn and be successful in science and our nation must cultivate and harvest the minds of all children and provide the resources to do so.

Rationale

If our nation is to maintain a position of international leadership in science education, NSTA must work with other professional organizations, institutions, corporations, and agencies to seek the resources required to ensure science teaching for all learners.

Declarations

For this to be achieved, NSTA adheres to the following tenets:

- Schools are to provide science education programs that nurture all children academically, physically, and in development of a positive self-concept;
- Children from all cultures are to have equitable access to quality science education experiences that enhance success and provide the knowledge and opportunities required for them to become successful participants in our democratic society;
- Curricular content must incorporate the contributions of many cultures to our knowledge of science;
- Science teachers are knowledgeable about and use culturally-related ways of learning and instructional practices;
- Science teachers have the responsibility to involve culturally diverse children in science, technology and engineering career opportunities; and
- Instructional strategies selected for use with all children must recognize and respect differences students bring based on their cultures.

—Adopted by the NSTA Board of Directors, July 2000

Substance Use and Abuse

Rationale

There is abundant evidence that the general public considers substance abuse a major problem. Students have revealed the same concern in surveys conducted nationwide. NSTA endorses the efforts of many school systems to conduct programs to help students understand the problem.

NSTA proposes the following guidelines for the development and implementation of such programs:

- The science education curriculum should include information about the effects of substance use and abuse.
- The thrust of such programs should be to promote healthful living.
- The programs should include information to help students make rational judgments regarding the consumption of commonly accepted over-the-counter drugs such as nicotine, alcohol, caffeine, and aspirin.
- The fact that the use of tobacco or tobacco products in any form is harmful to good health should be clearly documented.

- Student should be informed of the research which demonstrates clearly that marijuana, cocaine, and other illegal substances does cause physiological harm.
- Facts concerning the effects of the use of substances that may be abused should be presented, rather than counter-productive detailed discussion and explanation of the substances themselves.
- The programs should make available to students medical evidence that will help them to understand the inherent dangers of substance use and abuse.
- The ultimate goal of substance use/abuse awareness programs should be to eliminate substance abuse by giving students the up-to-date scientific knowledge they must have in order to make informed decisions.

—Adopted by the NSTA Board of Directors, January 2000

Science Competitions

The NSTA recognizes that many kinds of learning experiences, including science competitions, can contribute significantly to the education of students of science. With respect to science competitions such as science fairs, science leagues, symposia, Olympiads, and talent searches, the Association takes the position that participation should be guided by the following principles:

I. Student and staff participation in science competition should be voluntary.
II. Emphasis should be placed on the learning experience rather than on the competition.
III. Science competitions should supplement and enhance other educational experiences.
IV. The emphasis should be on scientific process, content, and/or application.
V. Projects and presentations must be the work of the student with proper credit to others for their contributions.

—Adopted by the NSTA Board of Directors, July 1986

Keeping Living Things . . . Alive

Living Materials in the Classroom*

Animals

Before introducing animals into the classroom, check the policy of your local school district. When animals are in the classroom, care should be taken to ensure that neither the students nor the animals are harmed. Mammals protect themselves and their young by biting, scratching, and kicking. Pets such as cats, dogs, rabbits, and guinea pigs should be handled properly and should not be disturbed when eating. Consider the following guidelines for possible adoption in your science classroom.

1. Do not allow students to bring live or deceased wild animals, snapping turtles, snakes, insects, or arachnids (ticks, mites) into the classroom, as they are capable of carrying disease.

2. Provide proper living quarters. Animals are to be kept clean and free from contamination. They must remain in a securely closed cage. Provision for their care during weekends and holidays must be made.

3. Obtain all animals from a reputable supply house. Fish should be purchased from tanks in which all fish appear healthy.

4. Discourage students from bringing personal pets into school. If pets are brought into the classroom, they should be handled only by their owners. Provision should be made for their care during the day—give them plenty of fresh water and a place to rest.

5. When observing unfamiliar animals, students should avoid picking them up or touching them.

6. Caution students never to tease animals or insert fingers, pens, or pencils into wire mesh cages. Report animal bites and scratches to the school's medical authority immediately. Provide basic first aid.

7. Rats, rabbits, hamsters, and mice are best picked up by the scruff of the neck, with a hand placed under the body for support. If young are to be handled, the mother should be removed to another cage—by nature she will be fiercely protective.

8. Use heavy gloves for handling animals; have students wash their hands before and after they handle animals.

9. Personnel at the local humane society or zoo can help teachers create a wholesome animal environment in the classroom.

Plants

Create a classroom environment where there are plants for students to observe, compare, and possibly classify as a part of their understanding of the plant world. Plants that are used for such purposes should be well-known to you. Plants that produce harmful substances should not be used.

*From "Living Materials in the Classroom," *Science Scope* 13, no. 3 (November/December 1989): p. 517. Used with permission of the National Science Teachers Association.

Because many plants have not been thoroughly researched for their toxicity, it is important for students and teachers to keep in mind some common-sense rules:

1. Never place any part of a plant in your mouth. (*Note:* Emphasize the distinction between nonedible plants and edible plants, fruits, and vegetables.)
2. Never allow any sap or fruit juice to set into your skin.
3. Never inhale or expose your skin or eyes to the smoke of any burning plant.
4. Never pick any unfamiliar wildflowers, seeds, berries, or cultivated plants.
5. Never eat food after handling plants without first scrubbing your hands.

The reason for these precautions is that any part of a plant can be relatively toxic, even to the point of fatality. Following is a list of some specific examples of toxic plants. This list is only partial; include additional poisonous (toxic) plants for your specific geographical area.

A. Plants that are poisonous to the touch due to exuded oils are:

Poison ivy (often found on school grounds)   Poison oak
Poison sumac   (other)

B. Plants that are poisonous when eaten include:

Many fungi	Belladonna	Pokeweed	Indian tobacco
(mushrooms)	Wake robin	Tansy	Jimson weed
Aconite	Henbane	Foxglove	(other)

C. The saps of the following plants are toxic:

Oleander	Trumpet vine	Poinsettia	(other)

Note: Also be aware that many common houseplants are toxic.

The Plant Picker

Plants That Will Survive with Little Sunlight

African Violet	Corn Plant	Peperomia	Spider Plant
Asparagus Fern	English Ivy	Philodendron	Spiderwort
Begonia	Ficus	Piggyback (Tolmeia)	(Tradescantia)
Boston Fern	Hen and Chickens	Snake Plant	Staghorn Fern
Chinese Evergreen	Parlor Palm		

Plants That Need a Great Deal of Sunlight

Agave	Echeveria	Mimosa (Acacia)	Spirea
Aloe	Geranium	Oxalis	Swedish Ivy
Blood Leaf	Hibiscus	Sedum	(filtered sunlight)
Cactus	Jade Plant		Yucca
Coleus	(filtered sunlight)		

Safety Management Helper

Safety Checklist*

The following general safety practices should be followed in your science teaching situation:

_____ Obtain a copy of the federal, state, and local regulations which relate to school safety, as well as a copy of your school district's policies and procedures. Pay special attention to guidelines for overcrowding, goggle legislation, and "right to know" legislation.

_____ Know your school's policy and procedure in case of accidents.

_____ Check your classroom on a regular basis to ensure that all possible safety precautions are being taken. Equipment and materials should be properly stored; hazardous materials should not be left exposed in the classroom.

_____ Before handling equipment and materials, familiarize yourself with their possible hazards.

_____ Be extra cautious when dealing with fire, and instruct your students to take appropriate precautions. Be certain fire extinguishers and fire blankets are nearby.

_____ Be familiar with your school's fire regulations, evacuation procedures, and the location and use of fire-fighting equipment.

_____ At the start of each science activity, instruct students regarding potential hazards and the precautions to be taken.

_____ The group size of students working on an experiment should be limited to a number that can safely perform the experiment without confusion and accidents.

_____ Plan enough time for students to perform the experiments, then clean up and properly store the equipment and materials.

_____ Students should be instructed never to taste or touch substances in the science classroom without first obtaining specific instructions from the teacher.

_____ Instruct students that all accidents or injuries—no matter how small—should be reported to you immediately.

_____ Instruct students that it is unsafe to touch their faces, mouths, eyes, and other parts of their bodies while they are working with plants, animals, or chemical substances and afterwards, until they have washed their hands and cleaned their nails.

When working with chemicals:

_____ Teach students that chemicals must not be mixed just to see what happens.

_____ Students should be instructed never to taste chemicals and to wash their hands after using chemicals.

_____ Elementary school students should not be allowed to mix acid and water.

_____ Keep combustible materials in a metal cabinet equipped with a lock.

_____ Chemicals should be stored under separate lock in a cool, dry place, but not in a refrigerator.

_____ Only minimum amounts of chemicals should be stored in the classroom. Any materials not used in a given period should be carefully discarded, particularly if they could become unstable.

*Reprinted with permission from *Safety in the Elementary Science Classroom.* Copyright © 1978, 1993 by the National Science Teachers Association, 1840 Wilson Boulevard, Arlington, VA 22201-3000.

Safety Management Helper

Glassware is dangerous. Whenever possible, plastic should be substituted. However, when glassware is used, follow these precautions:

_____ Hard glass test tubes should not be heated from the bottom. They should be tipped slightly, but not in the direction of another student.

_____ Sharp edges on mirrors or glassware should be reported to the teacher. A whisk broom and dustpan should be available for sweeping up pieces of broken glass.

_____ Warn students not to drink from glassware used for science experiments.

_____ Thermometers for use in the elementary classroom should be filled with alcohol, not mercury.

Teachers and students should be constantly alert to the following safety precautions while working with electricity:

_____ Students should be taught to use electricity safely in everyday situations.

_____ At the start of any unit on electricity, students should be told not to experiment with the electric current of home circuits.

_____ Check your school building code about temporary wiring for devices to be used continuously in one location.

_____ Electrical cords should be short, in good condition, and plugged in at the nearest outlet.

_____ Tap water is a conductor of electricity. Students' hands should be dry when touching electrical cords, switches, or appliances.

Materials to Keep in Your Science Closet

Primary Grades

Depending on the maturity of your students, you may wish to keep some or most of these items in a secure location in the room:

aluminum foil
aluminum foil pie plates
aquarium
baking soda
balance and standard
    masses
basic rock and mineral
    collection
beans, lima
camera and supplies
cardboard tubes from
    paper towel rolls
clipboard
cooking oil
corks
dishes, paper

dishes, plastic
egg cartons
feathers
first aid kit
flashlight
food coloring
globe
hand lenses
hot plate
iron filings
latex gloves
lemon juice
lunch bags, paper
magnets, various sizes
    and shapes
masking tape

measuring cups
measuring spoons
meterstick
microscope
mirrors
modeling clay
peas, dried
plastic bucket
plastic jugs
plastic spoons
plastic wrap
potholder
potting soil
rain gauge
rubber balls of various
    sizes

salt
sandwich bags, plastic
scales and masses
seeds, assorted
shell collection
shoe boxes
small plastic animals
small plastic trays
sponges
string
sugar
tape measure
terrarium
vinegar
yeast, dry

Middle Grades

Depending on the maturity of your students, you may wish to keep some or most of these items in a secure location in the room:

aluminum foil
assorted nuts and bolts
balance and standard
    masses
balloons
barometer
batteries
beakers
binoculars
cafeteria trays
calculator
candles
cans, clean, assorted,
    empty
cellophane, various
    colors
chart of regional birds
chart of regional rocks
    and minerals
clothespins, spring-
    variety

compass, directional
compass, drawing
desk lamp
extensive rock and
    mineral collection
eyedroppers
first aid kit
flashlight
flashlight bulbs
forceps or tweezers
glass jars
graduated cylinders
graph paper
hammer
hand lenses
hot glue gun*
hot plate*
hydrogen peroxide (3%)*
incubator
iron filings
isopropyl alcohol*

latex gloves
lenses
litmus paper
map of region, with
    contour lines
map of country, with
    climate regions
map of world
marbles
microscope slides and
    coverslips
mirrors
net for scooping material
    from streams and/or
    ponds
petroleum jelly
plastic bucket
plastic containers,
    wide-mouth, 1- and 2-L
plastic straws
plastic tubing

plastic wrap
pliers
prisms
pulleys
safety goggles
screwdriver
seeds, assorted vegetable
sponge, natural
steel wool
stop watch
sugar cubes
switches for circuits
tape, electrical
telescope
test tubes (Pyrex or
    equivalent)
thermometers
toothpicks
washers, assorted
wire for making circuits
wood scraps

*Keep these items in a locked closet.

The Metric Helper

Length

1 centimeter (cm) = 10 millimeters (mm)

1 decimeter (dm) = 10 centimeters

1 meter (m) = 10 decimeters

1 kilometer (km) = 1,000 meters

Liquid Volume

1,000 (mL) = 1 liter (L)

Dry Volume

1,000 cubic millimeters (mm³) = 1 cubic centimeter (cm³)

Mass

1,000 milligrams (mg) = 1 gram (g)

1,000 grams (g) = 1 kilogram (kg)

Some Important Metric Prefixes

kilo = one thousand

deci = one-tenth

centi = one-hundredth

milli = one-thousandth

micro = one-millionth

Temperature

Water freezes at 0° Celsius

Normal body temperature is 37° Celsius

Water boils at 100° Celsius

Approximate Sizes

millimeter = diameter of the wire in a paper clip

centimeter = slightly more than the width of a paper clip at its narrowest point

meter = slightly more than 1 yard

kilometer = slightly more than ½ mile

gram = slightly more than the mass of a paper clip

kilogram = slightly more than 2 pounds

milliliter = 5 milliters equal 1 teaspoon

liter = slightly more than 1 quart

Content Coverage Checklists

The following content checklists can be used to evaluate various elementary science textbooks, curriculum materials, audiovisual materials, software packages, and other resource materials for use in your classroom. Obviously, these lists do not include every concept, but they will provide a framework for analysis.

The Earth/Space Sciences

_____ The universe is 8 to 20 billion years old.

_____ The earth is about 5 billion years old.

_____ The earth is composed of rocks and minerals.

_____ Evidence of the many physical changes that have occurred over the earth's history is found in rocks and rock layers.

_____ The study of fossils can tell us a great deal about the life forms that have existed on the earth.

_____ Many species of animals and plants have become extinct.

_____ Our knowledge of earlier life forms comes from the study of fossils.

_____ Such forces as weathering, erosion, volcanic upheavals, and the shifting of crustal plates, as well as human activity, change the earth's surface.

_____ Natural phenomena and human activity also affect the earth's atmosphere and oceans.

_____ The climate of the earth has changed many times over its history.

_____ *Weather* is a description of the conditions of our atmosphere at any given time.

_____ The energy we receive from the sun affects our weather and is the primary source of energy for life on earth.

_____ The water cycle, a continuous change in the form and location of water, affects the weather and life on our planet.

_____ Weather instruments are used to assess and predict the weather.

_____ The natural resources of our planet are limited.

_____ The quality of the earth's water, air, and soil is affected by human activity.

_____ Water, air, and soil must be conserved, or life as we know it will not be able to continue on the earth.

_____ The responsibility for preserving the environment rests with individuals, governments, and industries.

_____ Our solar system includes the sun, the moon, and eight planets.

_____ The sun is one of many billions of stars in the Milky Way galaxy.

_____ Rockets, artificial satellites, and space shuttles are devices that enable humans to explore the characteristics of planets in our solar system.

_____ Data gathered about the earth, oceans, atmosphere, solar system, and universe may be expressed in the form of words, numbers, charts, or graphs.

The Life Sciences

_____ Living things are different from nonliving things.

_____ Plants and animals are living things.

_____ Living things can be classified according to their unique characteristics.

_____ The basic structural unit of all living things is the cell.

_____ All living things proceed through stages of development and maturation.

_____ Living things reproduce in a number of different ways.

_____ Animals and plants inherit and transmit the characteristics of their ancestors.

_____ Species of living things adapt and change over long periods of time or become extinct.

_____ Living things depend upon the earth, its atmosphere, and the sun for their existence.

_____ Living things affect their environment, and their environment affects living things.

_____ Different areas of the earth support different life forms, which are adapted to the unique characteristics of the area in which they live.

_____ Animals and plants affect one another.

_____ Plants are food producers.

_____ Animals are food consumers.

_____ Animals get their food by eating plants or other animals that eat plants.

_____ The human body consists of groups of organs (systems) that work together to perform a particular function.

_____ The human body can be affected by a variety of diseases, including sexually transmitted diseases.

_____ Human life processes are affected by food, exercise, drugs, air quality, and water quality.

_____ Medical technologies can be used to enhance the functioning of the human body and to diagnose, monitor, and treat diseases.

The Physical Sciences

_____ _Matter_ is anything that takes up space and has weight.

_____ Matter is found in three forms: solid, liquid, and gas.

_____ All matter in the universe attracts all other matter in the universe with a force that depends on the mass of the objects and the distance between them.

_____ Matter can be classified on the basis of readily observable characteristics, such as color, odor, taste, and solubility. These characteristics are known as _physical properties of matter._

_____ Matter can undergo chemical change to form new substances.

_____ Substances consist of small particles known as _molecules._

_____ Molecules are made of smaller particles known as _atoms._

_____ Atoms are composed of three smaller particles called _protons, neutrons,_ and _electrons._ (Protons and neutrons are composed of yet smaller particles known as _quarks._)

_____ Atoms differ from one another in the number of protons, neutrons, and electrons they have.

_____ Some substances are composed of only one type of atom. These substances are known as *elements*.

_____ In chemical reactions between substances, matter is neither created nor destroyed but only changed in form. This is the law of conservation of matter.

_____ An object at rest or moving at a constant speed will remain in that state unless acted upon by an unbalanced external force.

_____ *Acceleration* is the rate at which an object's velocity changes.

_____ The amount of acceleration that an object displays varies with the force acting on the object and its mass.

_____ Whenever a force acts on an object, an equal and opposite reacting force occurs.

_____ The flight of an airplane results from the interaction of four forces: weight, lift, thrust, and drag.

_____ *Energy*—the capacity to do work—manifests itself in a variety of forms, including light, heat, sound, electricity, motion, and nuclear energy.

_____ Energy may be stored in matter by virtue of an object's position or condition. Such energy is known as *potential energy.*

_____ Under ordinary circumstances, energy can neither be created nor destroyed. This is the law of conservation of energy.

_____ The law of conservation of matter and the law of conservation of energy have been combined to form the law of conservation of matter plus energy, which states that under certain conditions, matter can be changed into energy and energy can be changed into matter.

_____ The basic concepts of matter, energy, force, and motion can be used to explain natural phenomena in the life, earth/space, and physical sciences.

_____ The diminishing supply of fossil fuels may be compensated for by the increased utilization of alternate energy sources, including wind, water, and synthetic fuels, and by energy-conservation measures.

Your Science Survival Bookshelf

The Bookshelf

Abruscato, Joseph. *Whizbangers and Wonderments: Science Activities for Young People.* Boston: Allyn and Bacon, 2000.

Abruscato, Joseph, and Jack Hassard. *The Whole Cosmos Catalog of Science Activities.* Glenview, IL: Scott Foresman/Goodyear Publishers, 1991.

Adelman, Benjamin. *The Space Science.* Teaching Hand book, Silver Springs, MD: 1962.

American Chemical Society. *The Best of Wonder Science.* Florence, KY: Wordsworth, 2000.

Blough, Glenn, and Julius Schwartz. *Elementary School Science and How to Teach It.* Fort Worth, TX: Holt Rinehart & Winston, 1990.

Carin, Arthur A. *Teaching Science through Discovery.* Columbus, OH: Merrill, 1996.

Esler, William K., and Esler, Mary K. *Teaching Elementary School Science.* Belmont, CA: Wadsworth, 1996.

Friedl, Alfred E. *Teaching Science to Children.* New York: Random House, 1991.

Hassard, Jack. *Science Experiences: Cooperative Learning and the Teaching of Science.* Menlo Park, CA: Addison-Wesley, 1990.

Jacobson, Willard J., and Bergman, Abby B. *Science for Children.* Englewood Cliffs, NJ: Prentice-Hall, 1991.

Lorbeer, George C., and Nelson, Leslie W. *Science Activities for Children.* Dubuque, IA: W. C. Brown,1996.

Martin, Ralph, and Sexton, Colleen, and Franklin, Teresa. *Teaching Science for All Children: an Inquiry Approach. Boston:* Allyn and Bacon, 2008.

Mitchell, John, and Morrison, Gordon. *The Curious Naturalist.* Amherst, MA: University of Massachusetts Press, 1996.

Neuman, Donald B. *Experiencing Elementary Science.* Belmont, CA: Wadsworth, 1993.

Tolman, Marvin H., and Hardy, Gary R. *Discovering Elementary Science.* Boston: Allyn and Bacon, 1999.

Van Cleave, Janice Pratt. *Chemistry for Every Kid.* New York: Wiley, 1989.

Victor, Edward, and Kellough, Richard E. *Science for the Elementary School.* New York: Macmillan, 1997.

The Magazine Rack

For Teachers

Audubon Magazine
National Audubon Society
225 Varick St.
New York, NY 10014

Natural History
The American Museum of Natural History
Central Park West at Seventy-Ninth Street
New York, NY 10024

Science Activities
Heldref Publications
1319 Eighteenth Street, NW
Washington, DC 20036

Science and Children
National Science Teachers Association
1840 Wilson Boulevard
Arlington, VA 22201-3000

Science Scope
National Science Teachers Association
1840 Wilson Boulevard
Arlington, VA 22201-3000

Science Teacher
National Science Teachers Association
National Education Association
1840 Wilson Blvd.
Arlington, VA 22201-3000

For Children

Chickadee
Young Naturalist Foundation
P.O. Box 11314
Des Moines, IA 50340

Current Science
Xerox Education Publications
5555 Parkcenter Circle Suite 300
Dublin, OH 43017

Junior Astronomer
Benjamin Adelman
4211 Colie Drive
Silver Springs, MD 20906

Ladybug
Cricket Country Lane
Box 50284
Boulder, CO 80321-0284

National Geographic Kids Magazine
National Geographic Society
Seventeenth and M Streets, NW
Washington, DC 20036

Owl Kids
Maple Tree Press
10 Lower Spadina Avenue
Toronto Ontario
MSV 22 Canada

Ranger Rick
National Wildlife Federation
1412 Sixteenth Street, NW
Washington, DC 20036-2266

Science Weekly
CAM Publishing Group
Subscription Department
P.O. Box 70638
Chevy Chase, MD 208B-0638

Science World
Scholastic Magazines, Inc.
557 Broadway
New York, NY 10012

SuperScience
Scholastic Magazines, Inc.
557 Broadway
New York, NY 10012

Your Science Source Address Book

Free and Inexpensive Materials

American Solar Energy Society
2400 Central Avenue, Suite G–1
Boulder, CO 80301

American Wind Energy Association
777 North Capitol Street, NE, Suite 805
Washington, DC 20002

Environmental Protection Agency Public Information
  Center and Library
401 M Street, SW
Washington, DC 20460

Environmental Sciences Services Administration
Office of Public Information
Washington Science Center, Building 5
Rockville, MD 20852

Fish and Wildlife Service
U.S. Department of the Interior
1849 C Street, NW
Mail Stop 304 Web Building
Washington, DC 20240

Jet Propulsion Laboratory (JPL)
Teacher Resource Center
4900 Oak Grove Drive
Mail Stop CS–530
Pasadena, CA 91109

National Aeronautics and Space Administration (NASA)
NASA Education Division
NASA Headquarters
300 E Street, SW
Washington, DC 20546

National Institutes of Health
Office of Science Education
6100 Executive Blud.,
Suite 3E01
MSC 7520
Bethesda, MD 20892-7520

National Park Service
U.S. Department of the Interior
1849 C Street, NW
Washington, DC 20240

National Science Foundation
Division of Pre-College Education
1800 G Street, NW
Washington, DC 20550

National Wildlife Federation
8925 Leesburg Pike
Vienna, VA 22184-0001

Superintendent of Documents
U.S. Government Printing Office
732 North Capital Street, NW
Washington, D.C. 20401

U.S. Bureau of Mines
Office of Mineral Information
U.S. Department of the Interior
1849 C Street, NW
Washington, DC 20240

U.S. Department of Education
555 New Jersey Avenue, NW
Washington, DC 20208

U.S. Department of Energy
Conservation and Renewable Energy Inquiry
  and Referral Service
P.O. Box 8900
Silver Spring, MD 20907

U.S. Department of the Interior
Earth Science Information Center
1849 C Street, NW, Room 2650
Washington, DC 20240

U.S. Forest Service
Division of Information and Education
Fourteenth Street and Independence Avenue, SW
Washington, DC 20250

U.S. Geological Survey
Public Inquiries Office
U.S. Department of the Interior
Eighteenth and F Streets, NW
Washington, DC 20240

U.S. Public Health Service
Department of Health and Human Services
66 Canal Center Plaza, Suite 200
Alexandria, VA 22314

The "Wish Book" Companies

AIMS Education Foundation
P.O. Box 7766
Fresno, CA 93747

Carolina Biological Supply Co.
2700 York Road
Burlington, NC 27215

Central Scientific Company (CENCO)
3300 CENCO Parkway
Franklin, Park, IL 60131

Connecticut Valley Biological Supply Co., Inc.
82 Valley Road
Southhampton, MA 01073

Delta Education, Inc.
P.O. Box 915
Hudson, NH 03051-0915

Exploratorium Store
3601 Lyon Street
San Francisco, CA 94123

Flinn Scientific, Inc.
131 Flinn Street
P.O. Box 291
Batavia, IL 60510

Frey Scientific
905 Hickory Lane
Mansfield, OH 44905

Hubbard Scientific
3101 Iris Avenue, Suite 215
Boulder, CO 80301

Learning Things, Inc.
68A Broadway
P.O. Box 436
Arlington, MA 02174

LEGO Systems, Inc.
555 Taylor Road
Enfield, CT 06802

NASCO West, Inc.
P.O. Box 3837
Modesto, CA 95352

Ohaus Scale Corp.
29 Hanover Road
Florham Park, NJ 07932

Science Kit and Boreal Labs
777 East Park Drive
Tonawanda, NY 14150

Ward's Natural Science Establishment, Inc.
5100 West Henrietta Road
P.O. Box 92912
Rochester, NY 14692

Wind and Weather
P.O. Box 2320-ST
Mendocino, CA 95460

Young Naturalist Co.
614 East Fifth Street
Newton, KN 67114

Bilingual Child Resources

Alabama, Florida, Georgia, Kentucky, Mississippi, South Carolina, Tennessee

Bilingual Education South Eastern Support Center [BESES]
Florida International University
Tamiami Campus, TRM03
Miami, FL 33199

Alaska, Idaho, Montana, Oregon, Washington, Wyoming

Interface Education Network
7080 SW Fir Loop, Suite 200
Portland, OR 97223

American Samoa, Hawaii

Hawaii/American Samoa Multifunctional Support Center
1150 South King Street, #203
Honolulu, HI 97814

Arizona, California (Imperial, Orange, Riverside, San Bernardino, San Diego Counties)

SDSU-Multifunctional Support Center
6363 Alvarado Court, Suite 200
San Diego, CA 92120

Arkansas, Louisiana, Oklahoma, Texas Education Service Regions V–XIX

Bilingual Education Training and Technical Assistance Network [BETTA]
University of Texas at El Paso
College of Education
El Paso, TX 79968

California (all counties north of and including San Luis Obispo, Kern, and Inyo), Nevada

Bilingual Education Multifunctional Support Center
National Hispanic University
255 East Fourteenth Street
Oakland, CA 94606

California (Los Angeles, Santa Barbara, Ventura Counties), Nevada

Bilingual Education Multifunctional Support Center
California State University at Los Angeles School of Education
5151 State University Drive
Los Angeles, CA 90032

Colorado, Kansas, Nebraska, New Mexico, Utah

BUENO Bilingual Education Multifunctional Support Center
University of Colorado
Bueno Center of Multicultural Education
Campus Box 249
Boulder, CO 80309

Commonwealth of Northern Mariana Islands, Guam, Trust Territory of the Pacific Islands

Project BEAM [Bilingual Education Assistance in Micronesia]
University of Guam
College of Education
UOG Station,
Mangilao, GU 96923

Commonwealth of Puerto Rico, Virgin Islands

Bilingual Education Multifunctional Support Center
Colegio Universitario Metropolitano
P.O. Box CUM
Rio Piedras, PR 00928

Connecticut, Maine, Massachusetts, New Hampshire, Rhode Island, Vermont

New England Bilingual Education Multifunctional Center
Brown University, Weld Building
345 Blackstone Boulevard
Providence, RI 02906

Delaware, District of Columbia, Maryland, New Jersey, North Carolina, Ohio, Pennsylvania, Virginia, West Virginia

Georgetown University Bilingual Education Service Center
Georgetown University
2139 Wisconsin Avenue, NW, Suite 100
Washington, DC 20007

Illinois, Indiana, Iowa, Michigan, Minnesota, Missouri, North Dakota, South Dakota, Wisconsin

Midwest Bilingual Educational Multifunctional Resource Center
2360 East Devon Avenue, Suite 3011
Campus Box 136
Des Plaines, IL 60018

New York

New York State Bilingual Education Multifunctional Support Center
Hunter College of CUNY
695 Park Avenue, Box 367
New York, NY 10021

Texas Education Service Center, Regions I through IV, XX

Region Multifunctional Support Center
Texas A&I University
Kingsville, TX 78363
Native American Programs

Alaska, Arizona, California, Michigan, Minnesota, Montana, New Mexico, North Carolina, Oklahoma, South Dakota, Utah, Washington, Wyoming

National Indian Bilingual Center
Arizona State University
Community Services Building
Tempe, AZ 85287

Special-Needs Resources

Alexander Graham Bell Association for the Deaf
3417 Volta Place, NW
Washington, D.C. 20007

American Foundation for the Blind
15 West Sixteenth Street
New York, NY 10011

American Printing House for the Blind
1839 Frankforth Avenue, Box A
Louisville, KY 40206

American Speech, Language, and Hearing Association
10801 Rockville Pike
Rockville, MD 20852

Center for Multisensory Learning
University of California at Berkeley
Lawrence Hall of Science
Berkeley, CA 94720

Council for Exceptional Children
1920 Association Drive
Reston, VA 22091

ERIC Clearinghouse on Handicapped and Gifted Children
1920 Association Drive
Reston, VA 22091

The Lighthouse for the Blind and Visually Impaired
1155 Mission Street
San Francisco, CA 94103

National Technical Institute for the Deaf
One Lomb Memorial Drive
Rochester, NY 14623

The Project on the Handicapped in Science
American Association for the Advancement of Science
1776 Massachusetts Avenue, NW
Washington, DC 20036

Recording for the Blind
20 Roszel Road
Princeton, NJ 08540

Sensory Aids Foundation
399 Sherman Avenue
Palo Alto, CA 94304

Science Teachers Associations

The major association for teachers with an interest in science is the National Science Teachers Association (NSTA). For information on membership, write to this address:

National Science Teachers Association
1840 Wilson Boulevard
Arlington, VA 22201-3000

This affiliated organization may also be reached through the NSTA address:

Council for Elementary Science International

Other science-related associations that may be of interest include the following:

American Association of Physics Teachers
c/o American Institute of Physics
335 E. 45th Street
New York, NY 10017

American Chemical Society
1155 Sixteenth Street, NW
Washington, DC 20006

National Association of Biology Teachers
1420 N. Street, NW
Washington, DC 20005

National Earth Science Teachers Association
P.O. Box 2194
Liverpool, NY 13089-2194

School Science and Mathematics Association
16734 Hamilton Court
Strongsville, OH 44149-5701

NASA Teacher Resource Centers

NASA Teacher Resource Centers provide teachers with NASA-related materials for use in classrooms. Contact the center that serves your state for materials or additional information.

Alabama, Arkansas, Iowa, Louisiana, Missouri, Tennessee

NASA Marshall Space Flight Center
Teacher Resource Center at the U.S. Space
   and Rocket Center
P.O. Box 070015
Huntsville, AL 35807

Alaska, Arizona, California, Hawaii, Idaho, Montana, Nevada, Oregon, Utah, Washington, Wyoming

NASA Ames Research Center
Teacher Resource Center
Mail Stop 253-2
Moffett Field, CA 94035

California (cities near Dryden Flight Research Facility)

NASA Dryden Flight Research Facility
Teacher Resource Center
Lancaster, CA 93535

Colorado, Kansas, Nebraska, New Mexico, North Dakota, Oklahoma, South Dakota, Texas

NASA Johnson Space Center
Education Resource Center
1601 NASA Road #1
Houston, TX 77058

Connecticut, Delaware, District of Columbia, Maine, Maryland, Massachusetts, New Hampshire, New Jersey, New York, Pennsylvania, Rhode Island, Vermont

NASA Goddard Space Flight Center
Teacher Resource Laboratory
Mail Code 130.3
Greenbelt, MD 20771

Florida, Georgia, Puerto Rico, Virgin Islands

NASA Kennedy Space Center
Educators Resource Laboratory
Mail Code ERL
Kennedy Space Center, FL 32899

Kentucky, North Carolina, South Carolina, Virginia, West Virginia

NASA Langley Research Center
Teacher Resource Center at the Virginia Air
   and Space Center
600 Settlers Landing Road
Hampton, VA 23669

Illinois, Indiana, Michigan, Minnesota, Ohio, Wisconsin

NASA Lewis Research Center
Teacher Resource Center
21000 Brookpark Road
Mail Stop 8-1
Cleveland, OH 44135

Mississippi

NASA Stennis Space Center
Teacher Resource Center
Building 1200
Stennis Space Center, MS 39529-6000

Virginia and Maryland Eastern Shore

NASA Wallops Flight Facility
Education Complex-Visitor Center
Building J-17
Wallops Island, VA 23337

General inquiries related to space science and planetary exploration may be addressed to:

Jet Propulsion Laboratory
NASA Teacher Resource Center
Attn: JPL Educational Outreach
Mail Stop CS-530
Pasadena, CA 91109

For catalogue and order forms for audiovisual material, send request on school letterhead to:

NASA CORE
Lorain County Joint Vocational School
15181 Route 58 South
Oberlin, OH 44074

Your Science Source Address Book

Index

Photo, Figure, and Text Credits